MINNESOTA'S GOLDEN AGE OF WRESTLING

Minnesota Historical
Society Press

GEORGE SCHIRE

MINNESOTA'S GOLDEN AGE

of WRESTLING

from VERNE GAGNE to the ROAD WARRIORS

www.mhspress.org

The Minnesota Historical Society Press is a member
of the Association of American University Presses.

Manufactured in the United States of America

10 9 8 7 6 5 4 3 2 1

∞ The paper used in this publication meets the minimum requirements of the
American National Standard for Information Sciences—Permanence for Printed
Library Materials, ANSI Z39.48-1984.

International Standard Book Number
ISBN: 978-0-87351-620-4 (paper)

Library of Congress Cataloging-in-Publication Data
Schire, George, 1951–
Minnesota's golden age of wrestling : from Verne Gagne to the Road Warriors /
George Schire.
p. cm.
ISBN 978-0-87351-620-4 (pbk. : alk. paper)
1. Wrestling—Minnesota—History—20th century. I. Title.

GV1198.13.M6S35 2010
796.81209776—dc22

2009050017

Images on pages 23, 24, and 55: MHS collections
Image on page 189 by Tom Arndt, from *Home: Tom Arndt's Minnesota,*
courtesy the University of Minnesota Press

Front cover: Moose Evans prepares to body slam the Crusher;
bottom, left to right, Stan Mayslack wrestles an unknown man (MHS collections);
Hans Schmidt with arm-lock on Doug Gilbert; the Crusher; Kinji Shibuya and
Mitsu Arakawa with tag team trophy

Back cover: Doctor X strikes a menacing pose

Unless otherwise indicated, all images from author's collection

★ ★ ★

Minnesota's Golden Age of Wrestling was designed and set in type at
Cathy Spengler Design, Minneapolis. The typefaces are Malaga, Franklin Gothic,
and Juanita. Printed by Thomson-Shore, Incorporated, Dexter, Michigan.

To my daughter Kari, for always telling me to "just do it!"
And for forever having faith in me that I can.

CONTENTS

ACKNOWLEDGMENTS AND SOURCES

All of the written content and photographs herein are from my own research and personal collection, but this book would not have been possible without a good many talented and creative individuals. Just as in a match two wrestlers work together to tell a story, I've been blessed with some fine partners in creating the book you now hold in your hands.

To Pam McClanahan, director of the Minnesota Historical Society Press, who had faith that a book on Minnesota wrestling was a good idea. Her support and wisdom along the way have been invaluable. A simple thank-you to the press's devoted staff of editors and freelancers—Ted Anderson, Shannon Pennefeather, Mary Russell, and Marilyn Ziebarth—is hardly enough: what a sheer joy to work with each of you. To the team of Cathy Spengler, who designed the book, and Daniel Leary and Judy Gilats, who oversaw production: you are all masters of your craft. The hardworking marketing group of Alison Aten, Mary Poggione, and Leslie Rask made certain word of my book reached fans of wrestling's Golden Age. Former production manager Will Powers sadly passed away before our project was completed: I will always appreciate the genius of Will's work.

Most importantly, I thank Dick Beyer, Nick Bockwinkel, Tom Andrews, Greg Gagne, and Jim Raschke, who call me their friend. You all have been most kind to me through the years. And to the dozens of wrestlers and promoters who have supported my efforts to keep what they did in the ring factual and accurate: thanks guys; you're great! And to my friends Karl Lauer, Doug Fratallone, Brian Hoops, Mick Karch, and the late Jim Melby, who have all shared my addiction to wrestling.

To my buddy Stew Thornley, who encouraged me to write this book: I hope you enjoy it. A special thanks to Karen Henningsen for her support and confidence, and last but not least to my daughters, Amy and Kari, and my wife, Lorraine, for putting up with "my world" your whole lives. I love you.

Assembling this book has been a wild journey and truly a labor of love. I hope you enjoy reading it as much as I enjoyed writing it.

INTRODUCTION

MY CHILDHOOD was hardly something you would have seen on *Leave It to Beaver,* and my parents were nothing like Ward and June Cleaver. I came from a broken home, and in 1960 my parents divorced. I went to live with my dad and had few chances to play with kids my own age. I was eight years old, and I resented having to become an adult at such an early age.

I needed an escape and found it in professional wrestling. I would glue myself to the TV set when wrestling was on, eagerly anticipate buying a new wrestling magazine at the drugstore, and once or twice a year go to the matches at the Twin Cities auditoriums.

After I was old enough to get my driver's license, I never missed another live "card," or night of matches, in the Twin Cities, and I began driving to cities like Omaha, St. Louis, Kansas City, and small towns in Minnesota and Wisconsin to see wrestling. I made friends with fellow fans and got to know many of the wrestlers. I began collecting programs from each city I visited and set up trade arrangements with fans, wrestlers, and promoters from other cities so I could collect wrestling programs from all over the country.

What started out as a hobby became my life. I wrote stories for various wrestling magazines, and I ran a fan club for Ramon Torres. I became committed to preserving pro wrestling history—not an easy task when working with a business that has a deceptive foundation and little sense of its own past.

I've worked as an announcer for wrestling matches, hosted a TV wrestling program, cohosted radio wrestling programs, and even worked as a wrestling manager for a small independent promotion. I've served as an executive board member of the Cauliflower Alley Club, and I cohost a weekly Internet wrestling podcast with Brian Hoops, a nostalgic venture that remembers wrestling's Golden Age.

It isn't often that one can meet their childhood idols, much less become their friends. But I've enjoyed the honor of having wrestlers like Nick Bockwinkel, Mad Dog Vachon, Baron Von Raschke, Doctor X, Greg Gagne, and countless others call me friend.

My years of collecting have paid off. My personal collection of photos, programs, posters, and magazines has assisted me over the years in keeping the wacky, wild world of wrestling's facts and statistics in order—and also shows how much wrestling has changed since the 1980s. Gone are the "territories," and local cards are no longer presented regularly in huge auditoriums. Even the definition of what professional wrestling *is* has changed.

In the mid-1980s, Vince McMahon, Jr., owner of the World Wrestling Federation, went public with the statement that professional wrestling was a "prearranged exhibition." McMahon was essentially saying that professional wrestling was not "real." In making this revelation, he broke a decades-old code of honor, known as "kayfabe" among wrestlers and promoters, who would rather have been executed by a firing squad than admit that their matches were not real. Former pro wrestler Eddie Sharkey says, "My parents went to their graves believing that what I did for a living was real. We were programmed from the minute we entered the business that we were to honor the business and always live it as if it were 100 percent on the up and up."

Is professional wrestling real? Is it fake? If you had asked these questions in the Golden Age, you would have been told that of course it was real! But if you ask these same questions today, your answer would be: it's entertainment!

Professional wrestling in the Golden Age was a live performance by men who were actors and entertainers—but they were athletes first. A good majority of wrestlers from the 1940s through the 1970s started as great amateur wrestlers and football players: Verne Gagne, Leo Nomellini, Bronko Nagurski, Wahoo McDaniel, Wilbur Snyder, Joe Blanchard, Gene Kiniski, and Dr. Bill Miller, to name just a very few. These men were physical marvels who knew how to train to get into shape and how to stay that way. On average a wrestler would compete anywhere between five to seven nights a week for three hundred or more days a year. They were expected to work their match from thirty to ninety minutes per night, and to endure that kind of work, they had to be in shape. If they weren't, they didn't last long.

The outcome of the matches was predetermined. Promoters, bookers, matchmakers, and the wrestlers themselves would determine in advance who would win, when it would happen, and how it would happen. But the matches were true athletic contests that required the wrestlers to be in excellent physical condition. Just because the results of the matches were planned in advance didn't mean that the wrestlers wouldn't be hurt. Wrestlers had to learn how to fall when slammed to the mat or floor by an opponent. They had to know how to hit an opponent with a steel chair in such a way that he wouldn't be seriously hurt. In fact, if a wrestler did suffer an injury in the ring—a sprained ankle, a pulled muscle, or even a broken bone—he still had to finish the match and give the fans their money's worth.

Of course, not all the injuries were real. One way of being injured was "blading" in order to produce blood during a match. This was done usually by the wrestler himself. Before entering the ring, he would take a small piece of razor blade and attach it to a finger with tape or hide it in his wrestling tights. At a certain time during a match, the wrestler would very lightly cut his forehead with the blade. The result: copious amounts of blood. They usually used the forehead because even a tiny cut would produce the horrific effect of bleeding profusely.

Often an injury would be an "angle," a way of building a story in the ring. If one wrestler was "injured" by another, it was a reason for the two of them to start a feud. Or a grappler could be "injured" so badly he couldn't wrestle for months at a time—thus explaining his absence from local rings while he went to tour other wrestling promoters' territories.

Wrestling was an athletic contest, but it was more than that: it had to have a story. Verne Gagne once told me, "Once we've gotten the fans in their seats for a particular card, we have to give them a reason to want to come back. We have to be thinking of the next week or the next month, and the weeks and months after that."

During those early years, the "heels," or bad guys, and the "babyfaces," or good guys, would enter auditoriums through separate doors, never ride or drive in the same car, and use different locker rooms at the auditoriums. If wrestlers broke these rules, they could be, and in some instances were, black-balled from the business. The premise was that if two guys hated each other in the ring, they must also hate each other outside the ring. In fact, some of the bitterest feuds in wrestling were waged between men who were good friends in reality. And sometimes friends and allies in the ring couldn't stand each other outside it.

Was the Golden Age of professional wrestling real? Was it fake? Former wrestler Nick Kozak explained it best when he said, "For those who don't believe, there is no explanation that will do. For those who do believe, there is no need to explain." Professional wrestling is a lot like Santa Claus: it's more fun when you believe!

So was wrestling real? Yes! The great athletes and performers who entered rings all over the world, night after night, made it their goal to make it real for all of us who can remember the Golden Age. Believing in professional wrestling enhanced the matches, feuds, and characters. Suspending disbelief was part of the fun.

If you were privileged to witness professional wrestling during its Golden Age, you know that today's "wrestling" is much different than it once was. There's still a ring, but the lights above the ring have been replaced by brightly lit auditoriums, with pyrotechnic machines spraying fireworks and monster-size speakers blasting high-decibel music. Gone, too, are the intense contests that once took place in those rings. Gone are the one-fall-to-a-finish death matches, the one-hour "broadways," or draws, between two outstanding performers who had the stamina and endurance to go an hour. Matches are no longer expected to be anything close to an athletic contest. They barely last more than a few minutes. Wrestling today is all about the fireworks, the music, and some really, really outlandish and unbelievable characters. Today's wrestlers don't enter the ring wearing the Golden Age boots, tights or trunks, and ring jackets. There is no difference between a good guy and a bad guy, as their roles seem to change almost daily.

This is the story of wrestling before it became a spectacle. Do you remember Verne Gagne and the Crusher? Or maybe you preferred the bad guys like Killer Kowalski and Hans Schmidt. Or do you simply want to learn about what the sport once was? Well, pull up a ringside seat, settle back, and return with me to a time when wrestling was real—as real as you wanted it to be.

MINNESOTA'S GOLDEN AGE OF WRESTLING

★ ONE ★

THE EARLY DAYS

Professional wrestling got its start in the United States in the early 1900s, when matches were held in small venues like bingo halls or, more often than not, smoke-filled taverns and bars. During the Great Depression of the 1930s and both world wars, professional wrestling matches were among the few sporting activities that suffered no noticeable drop in attendance in big cities like New York and Chicago. In a time when money was hard to come by, people were eager to release a few tensions and enjoy themselves at noisy wrestling matches.

Wrestling in the United States began to grow in popularity after World War II, but many up-and-coming wrestlers were still in the armed forces, while the older grapplers were long past their primes and many of the most talented had already retired.

In St. Paul and Minneapolis, the main venues for wrestling were the civic auditoriums and the National Guard armories. Wrestling matches were sometimes staged in small towns, but it was the big cities to which fans flocked.

Wrestling in Minnesota began its most exciting era in the Twin Cities when Tony Stecher presented his first professional card at the Minneapolis Auditorium on February 21, 1933. A "card" is a list of the night's wrestling matches, generally three to five total. The first few bouts were preliminaries, leading up to the night's main event, which was the match the fans were really there to see. Usually the main event pitted a local favorite against a roughneck, or "heel." The February 21 card, presented in front of 3,000 fans, featured Tony's brother, Joe, and concluded this way: "In 19 minutes 32 seconds, John Richtoff won over Bill Davis; Joe Stecher went to a 30 minute draw with Joe Cox; Bronko Nagurski got the edge over Al Tagerson in just a little over 2 minutes; Ray Richards beat Jack Edwards; and in the opening event, Charles Lepannen defeated Joe Hubka."

Tony set out to create what would become one of the most successful professional wrestling franchises of all time. No promoters in the Twin Cities ran professional wrestling on any regular schedule. Tony Stecher believed that fans would flock to see the big names of the era at local auditoriums on certain nights, as they did in cities like Chicago and New York.

Trains were the main mode of travel for long distances, and the Twin Cities was a primary stop for the railways, so it seemed a natural place to start up a wrestling company. Top wrestling talent performed in Kansas City, Des Moines, Omaha, and beyond. The Twin Cities, with Tony Stecher at the helm, was added to the circuit.

At the time, the Chicago Bears boasted a huge football star by the name of Bronko Nagurski. He'd gotten his start playing for the University of Minnesota's Gophers, and he was already a local hero. Tony got his brother Joe Stecher (a three-time wrestling champion in his own right), along with wrestlers Pete Sauer and Harry Sampson, to provide wrestling training for Nagurski. Tony, a wrestler in his early years, also decided to work a little with Bronko.

They ended up with a hometown hero that Tony Stecher could tout as someone the fans had to see. As time passed, Stecher brought in names like Stan Mayslack, Milo Steinborn, and Dick Shikat, and Minneapolis became a territory wrestlers wanted to visit.

Fans attending matches in Minneapolis first received an invaluable souvenir on December 28, 1943, when Stecher began publishing *Sports Facts*, a four-page program that included facts and stats about the cards for the event they were attending and featured pictures and stories of the fans' favorite grapplers. The cost was ten cents—going all the way up to a quarter as the years went by. St. Paul fans had their own program, *Wrestling Facts*, which also featured facts, stats, photos, and stories, with the lineup of matches included. *Sports Facts* and *Wrestling Facts* remained fan staples for the next twenty-eight years.

After World War II the United States was divided into dozens of wrestling territories, each boasting their own big-name wrestlers, and even their own champions. In those early days, television was just becoming available to many people, and professional wrestling became one of the most popular things to watch. Because not everyone could afford a television, folks in a neighborhood would gather at the house on the block that did have a TV to watch the heroes and villains of the squared circle. Television gave wrestlers a huge new audience.

It was a time when the world more clearly defined good and bad, right and wrong. And in wrestling's early postwar years, it was easy to tell the babyfaces (the good guys) from the heels (the bad guys). The babyfaces tended to be tall, well-mannered, and movie-star-handsome, embodiments of the ideal American male.

The heels, on the other hand, were dastardly devils who often resembled schoolyard bullies. Heels would kick dirt in your face, brag that they were the best, and cheat to prove it. When challenged, though, the heels always backed down, denying their evil deeds and ways. The two together in a ring created a classic scenario that pulled in the fans.

Television changed the wrestling business. It encouraged colorful characters with a tinge of violence, fancy robes, wild storylines, and (sometimes weird) gimmicks. People from many backgrounds could relate to them—or take offense with them. The wrestlers learned that to get over with the fans, they had to project not only their ability, but also an image. Less talented wrestlers fell back on a gimmick to distract from their often minimal talent.

George Wagner was one such gimmick wrestler, and even today many consider him the showman supreme. Wagner was born in Nebraska in 1915. He was raised in Texas, and started wrestling while still in his teens in Los Angeles. He was just an average-looking guy: not too tall, a little pudgy, not a man who would stand out in a crowd. But George had an idea that—as it turned out—would transform the business forever. Up until this time, heels always appeared in the ring as unshaven, scowling brutes. Wagner let his hair grow, bleached it yellow, and got a permanent wave. His gimmick infuriated fans,

As plain George Wagner, he went nowhere. But when he dyed his long hair blonde and put on fancy robes, Gorgeous George was the heel every fan wanted to see defeated.

who expected their wrestlers to be traditional he-man types. He billed himself as Gorgeous George, the Human Orchid.

Suddenly, Wagner's newfound (un)popularity had fans lining up to see the Gorgeous one, and to see him get beat. Entering the ring with a valet to hold the ropes, George would fastidiously insist that the ring be sprayed by the valet to eliminate all germs and dirt. He infuriated the fans by strutting around the ring in his colorful robes and taking what seemed like an eternity to remove them before the match could get under way.

And the topper? He tossed gold-colored bobby pins (he called them Georgie Pins) to the fans as they booed and jeered him. He turned those boos into cash, and became one of the most sought-after and highly paid wrestling performers in the business throughout the 1950s. When he appeared in a town, local newspapers would chronicle his every move. It was reported that he owned more than eighty satin robes, each costing several hundred dollars. In the 1940s, which was still a conservative time, George's actions and behavior were seen as outrageous.

In the early days of televised professional wrestling, Gorgeous George became one of television's hottest properties. Viewers demanded more, and promoters were quick to oblige. Wagner became one of the most hated—and richest—wrestlers on the West Coast. His income zoomed to $70,000 a year, and eventually increased to over $100,000. Before long, California wasn't big enough for George, and he began traveling to other territories around the United States. Some hardcore wrestling enthusiasts loathed what George was doing to their sport, but fans, some of whom had never dreamed of attending a wrestling match before, flocked in droves to see Gorgeous George.

Beneath George's colorful persona was a competent wrestler. He reigned supreme in the wrestling world, often putting genuine grapplers in the shadows. This certainly didn't set well with his fellow wrestlers, who felt that Wagner's actions were disrespectful and, in the long haul, would hurt wrestling. Their fears, as history reflects, were without foundation. George's flamboyant and arrogant manner proved immensely popular with the fans, and encouraged them to come to his matches—if only to see him lose.

George worked hard at preserving his image. When he arrived in a city he was working, he would walk the streets to be seen, and often show up at a local beauty salon, where he would have his hair set and waved. He also made it a practice to grant interviews to local newspapers, in which he would commend the great work of his hairdresser, thus adding to his effeminate image.

In actual fact, Wagner was twice married and had three children. He was intelligent, an extrovert, and an opportunist. He worked through most of the 1950s, drawing huge crowds wherever he appeared, until his death at age forty-eight in 1963.

The arrogant bleached-blonde look started by Gorgeous George became one of the most duplicated gimmicks in wrestling. It was used with tremendous success by such notable ring villains as "Nature Boy" Buddy Rogers, "Classy" Freddie Blassie, Ray "the Crippler" Stevens, and Johnny Valentine, to name just a few. Another thing that worked well with long blonde hair was blood. When a blonde wrestler was cut, the blood streaming through his golden locks was money in the bank. A bleeding wrestler could tear at the fans' hearts if he was the babyface, and bring cries for more if he was a heel.

Another money-maker for wrestling was the champion wrestler—or at least the wrestler who was promoted as a champion. Having a champion on the cards always meant more fans buying tickets. The perception was that the champion was the best—or, if a heel, the worst—wrestler the sport had to offer, and everyone wanted to see him either successfully defend his laurels or be relieved of them by a top challenger.

Was there one legitimate world champion? No. However, some promoters

As six-time world champion, no wrestler is respected more than Lou Thesz, a "wrestlers' wrestler" who consistently brought credibility to the profession.

billed certain grapplers as champions, which caused some confusion—when fans read about their favorite grapplers in magazines, they often saw multiple champions.

Around 1947 several midwestern promoters started thinking about forming a union to recognize a champion. From these meetings came the formation of the National Wrestling Alliance (NWA). Local promoters from the various wrestling territories in the United States and Canada paid membership dues, and in return the NWA sent the nationally recognized champion to meet the local top challengers. Fans hoped to see their favorite hometown hero wrest the title from the defending champion, who often played the heel role in the matches.

When the NWA was formed, the first question was who the new champion would be. Local favorites were proposed, but ultimately the promoters agreed that Lou Thesz and Orville Brown should compete for the honor. The match was arranged, but fate stepped in. Brown was injured in an automobile accident that ended his wrestling career. Thus Lou Thesz was awarded the first NWA World Championship in late 1949.

Lou Thesz was a natural choice to be the first "unified" world champion. He had an almost magical charm that drew fans to him, and he was ruggedly handsome. He moved like a cat in the ring, actually knew how to wrestle, and went on to hold the NWA world title a then-record six times. In the 1950s, Thesz defended the title dozens of times against Minnesota wrestlers.

Among them was a natural for the television era: Minnesota's own hometown hero Verne Gagne. He was handsome and talented, and he came to the professional ranks with an amateur wrestling background.

VERNE GAGNE EARNED THE FOLLOWING HONORS AS AN AMATEUR WRESTLER:

★ Northwest AAU Champion, 1942

★ Minnesota State High School Champion, 1943

★ Big Nine Champion, 1944, 1947, 1948, and 1949

★ National AAU Champion, 1948

★ Place on the U.S. Olympic team, 1948

★ AAU and NCAA Champion, 1949

Verne Gagne graduated from Robbinsdale High School at seventeen, and had no thoughts of going to college. His plans changed, though, when football coach Walter "Red" Sochacki arranged for him to talk with the University of Minnesota's Dal Ward and George Hauser. They had taken over the Gopher football team while Bernie Bierman served in the army. Verne was granted a scholarship and a starting position on the Gopher football team, the youngest man to start as an end for the Gophers. He interrupted his college career to join the Marines in 1944, where he taught hand-to-hand combat and played football for the famous El Toro Marines. When he returned to the U of M, he picked up right where he left off, and was named to the College All-Star team.

Verne Gagne was drafted by the Chicago Bears in 1948 but didn't accept the offer. He was still playing football for the University of Minnesota Gopher squad. The Green Bay Packers tried to lure him away from Minnesota, but George Halas of the university would not release him. Instead of football, Gagne wanted to give professional wrestling a try. He trained under the great Joe Pazandak and Canadian legend George Gordienko.

Verne made his professional wrestling debut in Minneapolis on May 10, 1949, for Twin City promoter Tony Stecher. His opponent for the match was a mean and experienced ring bully by the name of Abe "King Kong" Kashey. To the fans' delight, Verne won the match when referee Wally Karbo disqualified Kashey for fighting with Gagne outside the ring.

Ironically, Verne Gagne was considered too small to be taken seriously in the heavyweight division of professional wrestling. Verne decided to do a little traveling and carve out a reputation for himself by meeting the best of the best in other territories. He and his wife, Mary, packed up their personal belongings and lived in a travel trailer for the next three years, as the talented grappler played one-night stands from Texas to Oklahoma. Gagne believed that if he combined his scientific wrestling fundamentals with a little showmanship, he could overcome his size disadvantage.

While wrestling in Texas, Verne captured his first professional title. He won the coveted Texas State Wrestling Championship from Texas favorite Blackie Guzman on September 8, 1950, in Houston, Texas. The Texas state title was highly regarded as a major championship, as Texas was always one of the top-drawing territories in pro wrestling. Because of its size, at times Texas had several different territories running completely independent of each other. Many cities in Texas had their own—Dallas, Fort Worth, and Houston were all independent territories at one time. Promoters in each town would often share and exchange talent.

Gagne dropped the Texas state title in Houston on October 27, 1950, to Rito Romero, after successfully defending it fifteen times in less than two months. Later that year, Verne won an even more important title in Tulsa, Oklahoma, when he captured the vacant NWA World Junior Heavyweight Championship. When he defeated popular Sonny Myers in the final match of the tournament on November 13, 1950, Verne was presented with the title belt by former champion LeRoy McGuirk, who was forced to forfeit the championship when he lost his eyesight in an automobile accident earlier that year. With Verne vowing to defend the title with the same honor that McGuirk had, and against all worthy contenders, he became a tremendous gate attraction throughout the Southwest.

Gagne went on to defend the NWA World Junior Heavyweight belt until November 19, 1951, in Memphis, Tennessee, when he lost it to the villainous "Irish" Danny McShane.

Professional football tried once again to steal Verne Gagne away from wrestling. The San Francisco 49ers offered him a contract that would start at $5,000 a year. Gagne turned it down. He was already reportedly bringing in $30,000 annually for tossing foes around the ring. It was then that he decided to forego football for professional wrestling for good. It was a decision he never regretted.

★ TWO ★

THE 1950s

THE BIRTH OF THE TAG TEAM

Professional wrestling came into its own in Minnesota in the 1950s. Engaging young wrestlers provided the star power, and a crowd-pleasing spin-off known as tag team wrestling locked down the hearts of fans loyal to the growing new spectator sport.

Verne Gagne met NWA World Champion Lou Thesz in the ring on three occasions, but he couldn't capture Thesz's title. Gagne was unable to get any more shots at the title after April 1951—the NWA considered him too small to fight in the coveted heavyweight division.

Gagne was determined to be recognized as world champion, and added the pounds he needed to become a heavyweight contender. He got a big break when the old Dumont Network started to telecast wrestling nationwide out of Chicago. Gagne became the leading attraction, and after a September 5, 1953, victory in Chicago over veteran grappler Joe Christie, he was awarded the NWA U.S. Heavyweight Championship. Gagne adopted a move that would become his trademark over the years: a devastating dropkick followed by a sleeper hold. The result was a hand raised in victory, in city after city around the country.

While he was U.S. Heavyweight Champion, Verne defended the belt to superstars of the day including Bob Orton, Sr. (grandfather to modern-day WWE star Randy Orton), Pat O'Connor, Sky Hi Lee, the Mighty Atlas, Chest Bernard, and Hans Schmidt (who Verne often stated in interviews was his toughest opponent in the ring).

Other popular wrestlers included Art Neilson, Yukon Eric, Hans Hermann, Dick "the Bruiser" Afflis, Wilbur Snyder, and Killer Kowalski. Kowalski was famous for a 1953 match that saw him jump off the top rope onto foe Yukon Eric,

Left to right:

The granddaddy of today's WWE star Randy Orton, Bob Orton, Sr. forged a villainous career along with his son Bob Jr. during the 1950s, 1960s, and 1970s.

The goose-stepping German, Hans Schmidt, displaying a painful arm-lock on speedy and popular Doug Gilbert

taking off one of Eric's ears. After this incident, promoters had a gold mine main event whenever they were able to sign Kowalski to face Eric.

Hard Boiled Haggerty, the self-proclaimed "king of the wrestlers," was one of the big stars of the 1950s and a longtime rival of Gagne's. A champion out in California, Haggerty made his debut in Minnesota in a match against the huge Yukon Eric on July 14, 1953. Their contrasting ring styles made it one of the most anticipated matches of the year, and Haggerty became an infamous heel Twin Cities fans loved to hate, facing off against such brawlers as "Dirty" Dick Raines, Lu Kim the Sailor, and Karl Karlsson.

It was announced in late November that NWA World Champion Lou Thesz would be coming to Minneapolis, so promoter Stecher signed a rematch between Haggerty and Lu Kim, with the winner promised the shot at Thesz. Hard Boiled Haggerty won the honor. The match was held November 30, 1954, and Haggerty lost to the champ by disqualification. (Disqualification results from using illegal holds or maneuvers, outside interference, or loss of control by the referees.)

Haggerty always claimed to be a gentleman, though fans thought otherwise. So when Sir Alan Garfield claimed that he could "out-gentleman" the Hard Boiled one, Haggerty became furious. The two met in a wild no-contest ruling on December 14, 1954, and again on December 21, which saw Haggerty come out on top.

The really big event of 1954 came on December 28. That night Verne Gagne was joined by Pat O'Connor in the ring, and the duo triumphed over Haggerty and Hans Hermann—four superstars in one ring. This event marked a first for tag team wrestling in Minnesota. Tag team wrestling paired two or more wrestlers who touched or tagged each other in and out of the ring because they were not allowed in the ring at the same time. Specific rules varied, and rules were often broken in the actual matches, especially by heel teams or the heel members of a team.

★ 1955 ★

On January 4, 1955, *Sports Facts* magazine stated that New Zealand's Pat O'Connor was willing to put up any amount of money to get his hands on Hard Boiled Haggerty. Pat had been pinned in the tag match that saw him teamed with Verne Gagne against Haggerty and Hans Hermann.

Fellow New Zealander Fred Atkins debuted in the Twin Cities on the January 4 card. Upon his arrival, Atkins was touted as "the world's toughest wrestler," a billing that he lived up to with a hard-fought victory over roughneck Karl Karlsson. Atkins remained undefeated when he triumphed over Sir Alan Garfield in the January 11 main event.

January 18 was a huge night for wrestling fans in Minneapolis. NWA World Champion Lou Thesz was in town again for another outing with Hard Boiled Haggerty, but he had to settle for a time-limit one-hour draw. That same night, Fred Atkins made it three wins in a row with a victory over Nick Roberts. Atkins was gaining raves and living up to his "toughest wrestler" reputation. On January 25 he got the best of popular Johnny Kostas in a Minneapolis main event.

Promoter Tony Stecher brought in his big gun, Bronko Nagurski, to meet Atkins on February 1 and it was Atkins who walked away the victor. This match, however, was merely a setup for Minnesota's favorite son, Verne Gagne, to return on February 15 and take his shot at the undefeated Atkins. Verne won the match by disqualification.

Even though they were tag team partners earlier in the year for an elimination match against Leo Nomellini and Bronko Nagurski, Hard Boiled Haggerty

"BRUISER" TURNS TO WRESTLING

He has bigger arms than the legendary Yukon Eric. He is a former professional football player who will make his local wrestling debut at the Minneapolis Auditorium tonight. The burly fellow in question is Dick "Bruiser" Afflis, 249 pounds of grappling fury.

The Bruiser played pro ball a few years ago for the Green Bay Packers, captained the team one year, and was the highest paid lineman in the game.

Afflis says he turned to wrestling for the simple reason that he has a weakness for money. After watching gridders like Verne Gagne and Leo Nomellini pile up fortunes on the mat, the Bruiser decided to follow suit.

— *Sports Facts,* January 11, 1955

"If I can't beat Hard Boiled Haggerty," growled Bronko Nagurski, "I should quit!"

Big Bronk takes that belligerent mood with him into the ring for his FIGHT TO A FINISH with Haggerty Tuesday night, March 1, at the Minneapolis Armory.

Although he's never been one to pop off about his opponents, Nagurski was a different man this time.

"Haggerty is the big crybaby type," the Bronk exploded.

"I've never heard him do anything but complain. If a bigger showoff ever lived, it's news to me."

The Nag had his reasons for blasting Haggerty. It was H.B. who came to town four years ago and sprang a huge surprise by pinning Nagurski. It was this win that rocketed Haggerty into the local and national spotlight and paved the way for his great success.

Tonight it's the showdown! And on top of everything else, who should be the special referee but "Dirty" Dick Raines.

— *Sports Facts,* March 1, 1955

and Big Fred Atkins were forced to face off against each other by Minneapolis matchmaker Wally Karbo on March 8, lured by the prospect of being named the number-one challenger for the NWA World Championship. Atkins won the bout when the Hard Boiled one was disqualified.

Haggerty was the hottest draw in the Twin Cities. Next up for him, on March 15, was Japanese ace Kinji Shibuya, with popular Minneapolis native Butch Levy signed as the special referee. Shibuya got the nod when he blinded Haggerty with his own blood and dazed him with judo chops, leaving him a helpless hulk at the end of the match. In a rematch between the two on March 22, another special referee was signed to try to keep law and order: Joe Louis, back again to referee Haggerty. Again, Shibuya came out with the decision in his favor when Haggerty was disqualified. Haggerty drew a sixty-day suspension from the Twin Cities.

Shortly after the suspension, a teaser about Haggerty leaving town appeared in *Sports Facts,* the kind of story whose "facts" became a staple in the wrestling programs. The fans weren't the wiser, because they lacked the resources to know when wrestlers were really injured, injured as part of an "angle," or just plain done in the Twin Cities.

On April 5, wrestling's hometown favorite Verne Gagne was back for a main event against the equally popular Ilio DiPaolo. Their battle promised fans a match between two outstanding ring stars of "scientific" wrestling, meaning no-holds-barred matches won usually only by pins or submissions. It was Gagne, though, who got the edge in the one-fall bout, which had to produce a winner by pin fall, submission, countout, draw, or disqualification.

Fans were treated to another stellar scientific battle on April 12, when Gagne wrestled New Zealand's Pat O'Connor. They battled to a one-hour broadway (draw) in a match that had fans on the edges of their seats. On May 3, NWA World Heavyweight Champion Lou Thesz made an appearance in Minneapolis in a successful defense against Fred Atkins.

By spring 1955, Tony Stecher had turned the promoting reins over to his son Dennis Stecher and Wally Karbo, who were now co-promoters in the Twin Cities. Karbo also refereed for some of the weekly cards.

The summer of 1955 continued with torrid matches on June 7 and June 14, with Verne Gagne battling Ike Eakins. In the first encounter, "Big Ike" was disqualified for hitting Verne over the head with a chair, and in the second contest, Gagne pulled out a victory.

In the early years of Minneapolis wrestling, cards were regularly held in conjunction with the Minneapolis Aquatennial. July 1955 featured one of the most spectacular main events ever held in the Twin Cities: the return of Hard Boiled Haggerty. But that wasn't the only shocker. The July 19 card had H.B. in a team match with none other than longtime foe Verne Gagne as his partner. Their opponents were Haggerty's hated nemesis "Big Ike" Eakins and Kinji Shibuya.

Fans were the winners in this one. Everyone wondered if—or maybe just when—Haggerty and Gagne would turn against each other, since they were by no means the best of friends. The premise of the match, though, was that Haggerty wanted longtime rival Eakins, which was the only reason he agreed to team with Gagne, who wanted to get his hands on Shibuya. Few were surprised when Haggerty deserted Gagne during the match, causing him to fall prey to the double-teaming efforts of Eakins and Shibuya.

Verne Gagne, at this time, was recognized as the U.S. champion, and he successfully defended his claim to that title on July 26 against Ike Eakins. The program for this card splashed a story that Hard Boiled Haggerty had once again left Minneapolis in a huff and returned to Texas.

August 9 saw the Minneapolis debut of a very young Stan Kowalski, who lost an opening match to prelim grappler Oni Wiki Wiki from Hawaii. The main event on this card featured partners Ilio DiPaolo and Farmer Marlin winning by disqualification from Ike Eakins and Kinji Shibuya. Also making his local debut on this card was Shibuya's "cousin" Mitsu Arakawa.

On September 13 Eakins and Shibuya were being billed as "Hatchet Men," but this time it was against each other. They met in the main event after a reported falling out, with a possible title shot promised to the winner. Their match ended in a bloody "no-contest," meaning no winner could be declared. A rematch on September 20 saw Shibuya come out on top over Eakins.

CAN YUKON ERIC PIN VERNE GAGNE?

Yukon Eric, 280 pound Fairbanks, Alaska giant, will be shooting at big stakes tonight, September 27, at the Minneapolis Auditorium when he attempts to become the first wrestler in more than 500 to pin Verne Gagne's shoulders to the mat.

The big stakes are a potential $250,000 in wrestling purses which the experts estimate are waiting to be plucked by the grappler able to subdue Gagne. In addition to the quarter million dollars in profits, Gagne's $10,000 United States Championship belt will be on the line, and also an all important probable match with NWA World Champion, Lou Thesz.

— *Sports Facts,* September 27, 1955

Just a week later Gagne got the nod for another challenge to his run of five hundred failed pins when the big Alaskan Yukon Eric was disqualified. After the bout, Gagne was asked how it felt to be in the ring with Yukon Eric. His answer was short and sweet: "Like wrestling a Kodiak bear while riding the Excelsior Park roller coaster."

Meanwhile, a pair of bearded Russians named Ivan and Karol Kalmikoff had been racking up ring victories in other territories. When October 1955 rolled along, fans were teased with the possibility of seeing the hated "brothers" come to the Twin Cities. To add further sugar to the pudding, promoter Dennis Stecher stated that Mitsu Arakawa and Kinji Shibuya were boasting of teaming together to stop the Russian invasion.

The Kalmikoffs made their debut in Minneapolis on October 25, 1955, and their first test—and victory—came at the hands of another pair of brothers, Adrian and Paul Baillargeon. The Kalmikoffs were wrestling's most hated tag team, only in part because of Cold War anti-Russian sentiments. They took out favorites Butch Levy and Herbie Freeman on November 1, and also racked up wins against the Baillargeon brothers on November 22 and the team of Bronko Nagurski and Butch Levy on the twenty-ninth.

Then the stage was set. The promised match between the Russians and the Japanese took place in the Minneapolis Auditorium on December 6. Ivan and Karol Kalmikoff got by with a disqualification, and then eked out a victory in a rematch on December 13. After this match, Shibuya said he would consider rejoining Ike Eakins in an attempt to defeat the Russians. Fans were expected to have forgotten that Shibuya and Eakins had been partners in the past, but had had a falling out a few months earlier.

The year 1955 ended with the Kalmikoffs posting a win over Timothy Geohagen and Roy McClarty on December 20. On December 27, Shibuya really did team with Ike Eakins, only to be on the losing end of a decision to Verne Gagne and Butch Levy.

★ 1956 ★

The year 1956 started off with Ivan and Karol Kalmikoff, the hated Russians, still running roughshod on the tag team front. On January 3 at the Minneapolis National Guard Armory they battled to a one hour time-limit draw against Verne Gagne and Butch Levy. Of special note on a January 17 card was the appearance of a young star named Gene Dubuque, who defeated Ray Villmer. Later in his career, Dubuque was better known as "Magnificent" Maurice. He and tag partner Johnny Barend formed a heel combination that won them many victories.

All through January, the Kalmikoffs remained undefeated—and of course they were the team that fans most wanted to see beaten. They had two especially brutal showdowns with a couple of equally unpopular wrestlers, Texans by the names of Lou Plummer and "Dirty" Dick Raines. Ivan and Karol threw the cowboys out of Minneapolis after a pier-six match.

Then–NWA World Champion Lou Thesz defended his belt against popular Butch Levy on the February 14 card at the Minneapolis Armory. The match ended in a draw. A young Larry Hamilton appeared on this card in a losing bid against Bobby Managoff. Hamilton would return in the 1960s as "the Missouri Mauler," one of the toughest wrestlers on the local scene.

One of Verne Gagne's closest friends both in wrestling and outside the ring was Wilbur Snyder, often billed as "the world's most scientific wrestler." The two regularly joined together for tag team matches, but they also faced each other in a couple of now-legendary battles for the U.S. Heavyweight Championship. One of the matches took place in Milwaukee on August 4 and saw Verne win by disqualification in front of over 16,000 fans. Special referee for the match was former boxing champion Jack Dempsey.

Snyder was disqualified when he wouldn't let Verne get back into the ring

When especially brutal wrestlers meet, the result is often a "pier-six" brawl. In these matches, the grapplers throw out the rule book and fight like a couple of out-of-control dock workers. The term is generally used to describe matches between two heels or teams of heels.

Ladies' wrestling matches weren't often staged in the Twin Cities. One reason was that there were only a handful of women wrestlers. In February 1956, though, two of the better-known and -respected women wrestlers in the business appeared. The recognized women's champion, June Byers, got the edge of Pretty Penny Banner in a one-fall bout.

In the 1950s and early 1960s, when Americans were still fighting World War II in their minds, the hated Russians, Boris and Nicoli Volkoff, played off fans' emotions to become one of the most hated tag teams of their era.

during the third fall of the match. This sort of tactic was out of the ordinary for Snyder, as he, like Gagne, played a good guy and was loved worldwide by fans. Verne eked out another win over Snyder on September 22 in Milwaukee, and they battled to a draw in Buffalo, New York, on November 21.

The following year, on May 17, 1957, Gagne and Snyder teamed up and won a version of the World Tag Team Title from Nicoli and Boris Volkoff in Chicago. They later lost the belts back to the Volkoffs in a Chicago rematch on December 4.

★ 1957 ★

The year 1957 roared onto the scene with a wild battle between the hated Russians, the Kalmikoffs, and a pair of equally hated Germans, Karl Von Schober and Fritz Von Erich. Adding interest to their January 8 showdown was the addition of a special referee: none other than legendary wrestler Edward "Bearcat" Wright. When the smoke cleared, Ivan and Karol Kalmikoff got the nod over the Germans.

It was always big news in any city when a world champion was coming to town, and Minneapolis was no exception. Lou Thesz, the reigning NWA World Champion in 1957, was signed to defend his belt on January 15 against a most formidable challenger—Hard Boiled Haggerty. The Hard Boiled one fell short

A long smoldering feud between Hard Boiled Haggerty and the Kalmikoff Brothers reaches the explosive pitch tonight when the belligerents tangle in the feature of a tag team bout at the Minneapolis Auditorium.

Unlike most athletes who battle every inch of the way in the ring or on the field and are friends when it is over, the Russians hate Haggerty, 24 hours a day. And the feeling is mutual. Haggerty's hate for the Russians is just as deep.

For that reason, there'll be plenty of fireworks tonight when Haggerty teams with slick Johnny Rougeau in the Minneapolis Wrestling Club's headliner. It's the first defense the Russians have made of their newly-won title rights.

The mutual dis-admiration society is obviously a matter of professional jealousy, according to Wally Karbo.

"When the Russians first came to Minneapolis, all they heard was 'Haggerty, Haggerty, Haggerty,'" explained Karbo.

"Now when Haggerty comes back to town, all he hears is, 'Kalmikoffs, Kalmikoffs, Kalmikoffs' and he's jealous."

That's not unusual in sports of course. Strangler Lewis and Ray Steele had a running feud. It was the same with Pollard and Mikan in basketball, with football players, track men and all athletes.

But here is a professional rivalry that's really hot . . . and it'll probably show up tonight.

— *Sports Facts,* January 22, 1957

of claiming the title, though, when he got himself disqualified. A standing-room-only crowd at the Minneapolis National Guard Armory witnessed the contest, cheering on the popular Thesz.

As unpopular as Haggerty was, though, the fans came to his side when he was engaged in a war with the Kalmikoff Brothers. On January 22, Hard Boiled was joined by fan favorite Johnny Rougeau to meet the Russians at the Minneapolis Auditorium that saw H.B. and Johnny lose by disqualification.

Another event of the month, according to *Sports Facts,* was Lou Thesz's refusal to fight Gagne for a huge purse. This offer, of course, might only have been a fan teaser, although wrestlers were beginning to make good money by the late 1950s.

At the end of January the wrestling and boxing world came together as

Lou Thesz turned down $10,000 when he was here last week. The World's Champion Wrestler was offered $10,000 by Wally Karbo to accept a title bout with Verne Gagne.

"He just laughed at me," Karbo said. "That shows you how much the championship is worth."

World's championship bouts cost money, Karbo pointed out, and the big-time promoters are bidding among themselves for the services of wrestlers like Thesz.

"Minneapolis has to match dollars with promoters in St. Louis, Chicago, Montreal, Winnipeg, and so on," Karbo said, "and it's expensive. But you can't blame wrestlers for going where the money is."

— *Sports Facts,* January 22, 1957

boxing legend "Jersey" Joe Walcott was brought in to officiate a showdown between Johnny Rougeau and Ivan Kalmikoff. Walcott got rave advance billings for his emergence as the third man in the ring, as the referee was known to have to maintain order. Both Pat O'Connor and World Champion Lou Thesz applauded his efforts as a referee.

February started off with something big: the first appearance of the renowned Lisowski Brothers, Reggie and Stan. This was the first of hundreds of appearances by Reggie Lisowski over the coming years. He'd had only one singles match in the Twin Cities to his credit prior to returning with "brother" Stan. Reggie and Stan fought a knock-down pier-six brawl with Ivan and Karol, but in the end the match was ruled a draw after each team had taken a fall.

The appearance of the Lisowskis on the Twin Cities scene was just the beginning, as many other top tag teams wanted to show their stuff here. Next in were the extremely popular and talented Brunetti Brothers, Joe and Guy. They were movie-star good-looking and regarded as one of the best babyface combinations in wrestling at the time. Fans will fondly remember their introduction by ring announcer Marty O'Neill: "And in this corner, weighing in at a combined weight of 461 pounds, from Salt Lake City, Utah . . . a good Joe and a great Guy . . . the Brunetti Brothers!" Resounding cheers would erupt from the crowd.

The Brunettis not only captured the hearts of fans, but also gave the Kalmikoffs one of their first losses in Minneapolis in the February 26, 1957, main event. The special referee for the bout was all-time great Bronko Nagurski. A rematch was immediately signed for March 5 but the result was the same: the Brunettis again turned the trick and defeated the Russians. This card also marked the return to the Twin Cities of the villainous "Killer" Kowalski. The March 12 edition of *Sports Facts* featured the headline, "It's Win or Get Out for the Russians!" To the fans' delight, the Brunettis scored a third straight win over the hated Russian brothers.

LISOWSKIS BATTLE RUSSIANS FOR TITLE!

Stan and Reggie Lisowski, a tag team combination that Chicago and Milwaukee claims as the best in the world, will challenge for the world's tag team championship here tonight.

The Poles from Milwaukee will tangle with Ivan and Karol Kalmikoff, the Russians, who are recognized through most of the Midwest as the best in the business, in a best two-out-of-three falls bout at the Minneapolis Auditorium.

To all practical purposes, it's a title bout. "It's a cham-

pionship bout as far as we're concerned," declared Wally Karbo of the Minneapolis Wrestling Club.

"The National Wrestling Alliance won't tell us whether they'll recognize the winner as champions or not, but we'll go ahead on that assumption."

The bout marks the first local appearance of the Lisowskis as a tag team, although Reggie made a "scouting" appearance in an individual bout here last year.

— *Sports Facts,* February 5, 1957

This third loss allowed the Kalmikoffs to leave the Twin Cities for a short time and made the Brunettis the number-one team on the local scene. The Russians being off local cards was explained by their being "suspended" due to their unruly ring tactics. Ivan and Karol blamed the referee, Butch Levy, for their suspension.

On March 19 they defended their honor in a winning effort against "Big Ike" Eakins and Fritz Von Erich. Next in to challenge Joe and Guy's supremacy were the Lisowski Brothers on March 26 in Minneapolis. The contest ended in a draw.

Just as quickly as they were supposedly suspended, Ivan and Karol Kalmikoff were back in the Twin Cities on April 2 against what the promoters billed as a "French" team: Verne Gagne and Johnny Rougeau. The nod went to Gagne and Rougeau when the Kalmikoffs were disqualified. In a rematch on April 9 in Minneapolis, though, the Russians were back in the winners' circle.

Of special note on the April 9 card was a wrestler who gained fame later in his career in other parts of the country: Lou Klein. In the early 1960s, Lou became famous as Lou Bastien, the "brother" of popular Minneapolis native Red Bastien. The Bastien Brothers were extremely successful on the East Coast and headlined many cards at Madison Square Garden. The Bastiens are fondly remembered for their colorful toga ring outfits, and for carrying a treasure chest of silver dollars into the ring with them. They had a long and successful money-making feud with the Golden Grahams, Eddie and Jerry. After his days as Red's brother, Lou resumed the name Klein and become a major star and later wrestling trainer in Detroit and other territories.

On April 26 in Minneapolis, another main event pitted the Brunettis against the Kalmikoffs, with boxing great "Jersey" Joe Walcott as the special referee. The match was ruled a draw. Wrestler Clyde Steeves made his debut on this same program. Although he was listed on the lineup page of *Sports Facts* as Clyde Steeves, he was introduced as Karl Steif, the name he worked under in the Twin Cities.

The Brunettis continued their ride to the top of the heap, defeating the villainous heel team of Al and John Smith. Next up, on April 30 in Minneapolis, was the Japanese duo of Kinji Shibuya and Mister Moto. In their first encoun-

PAGING CEDRIC ADAMS!

Cedric Adams, as you know, is always talking about the best method of losing weight. Far and away the best method discovered to date is to take part in a sixty minute wrestling match.

Here are the weight losses of individual wrestlers last week: Stan Lisowski lost 10 pounds, Reggie Lisowski lost 8 pounds, Joe Brunetti lost 6 pounds, and Guy Brunetti lost 6 pounds. Total lost . . . 30 pounds!

— *Sports Facts*, April 2, 1957

The late, great Cedric Adams was a trusted and beloved voice for radio listeners and television viewers.

ter, fans were shocked when Kinji and Moto beat the Brunettis. A rematch on May 7 saw the Brunettis prevail, and again in a third match on May 28.

Joe and Guy Brunetti had now proven their superiority over first the Kalmikoffs, then John and Al Smith, and finally Shibuya and Moto. It was hard to find a more popular duo in all of wrestling. They had gained recognition as NWA World Tag Team Champions and proudly carried the huge trophy acknowledging their accomplishment. But just as quickly as they rose, they came tumbling down on June 4, when they lost their honors to a ruthless Ivan and Karol Kalmikoff.

A rare event, heel versus heel, took place on the next Minneapolis card on June 11, when the Russians were forced to defend their newly won claim to the championship in a match against the team of Kinji Shibuya and his new partner for the match, Karl Steif. The Kalmikoffs were disqualified in a battle that saw all four wrestlers in the ring, with the referee often unable to maintain control of the action.

On forthcoming cards in the Twin Cities, fans were treated to more battles between the Russians and the Brunettis, in both tag and singles matches. Their matches were among the best attended by fans throughout the year.

On Saturday nights, even over-the-road truckers took time out of their busy schedules to catch All-Star Wrestling *at the Landfall truck stop in St. Paul.*

Mitsu Arakawa returned to the Twin Cities in June 1957. He was originally billed as "the Great Mitsu," and rumored to be a "cousin" of Kinji Shibuya. Promoters began talking of a possible paring of the two. It finally happened on July 2 when the Japanese duo, who were also experts in karate, then a largely unknown martial arts technique in the United States, signed to face a formidable team of two former Minnesota Gophers, Verne Gagne and Leo Nomellini. After all hell broke out in the ring, fans left the auditorium happy when Verne and Leo won.

In July, Minneapolis wrestling fans looked forward to a great All-Star Wrestling card, a Minneapolis Aquatennial-sponsored event held in the air-cooled Minneapolis Auditorium. Fans purchased advance tickets at the Northwestern Bank Building or club headquarters in the Dyckman Hotel. Promoter Dennis Stecher and matchmaker Wally Karbo pledged the best card of the year in the July 16 *Sports Facts.* The main event was a spectacular six-man tag team contest that featured Verne Gagne, Leo Nomellini, and Bronko Nagurski up against Ivan and Karol Kalmikoff and their third mate, Nicoli Zolotoff.

Minnesota mat fans loved tag team wrestling and the wild action it always

"The third best wrestler in the world will be in the ring with us tonight," stated Ivan Kalmikoff.

"His name is Nicoli Zolotoff."

"Zolotoff hails from Windsor, Canada, but originally came from Russia. He's young, he's strong and he's great and we're a cinch to take local favorites Gagne, Nomellini and Nagurski."

When asked who he rated ahead of young Mr. Zolotoff, Ivan replied, "My brother and I . . . of course!"

— *Sports Facts*, July 23, 1957

provided. The Minneapolis Wrestling Club continued to feed fans' appetites by providing top-flight tag teams—from around the world and closer to home. On July 30, 1957, *Sports Facts* ran the headline "Gopher Civil War!" The main event featured Verne Gagne and Leo Nomellini going head to head with Joe Pazandak and Butch Levy. The popular Gagne and Nomellini won the match when Pazandak and Levy were disqualified in the third fall. And, not to disappoint their audience, promoters had the Kalmikoffs in singles matches on the card against a couple of fellow heels. Karol was tested by Stan "Krusher" Kowalski, but defeated the Fridley, Minnesota, native, and Ivan battled to a wild no-contest with Kinji Shibuya. Young and popular Red Bastien won over veteran Carl Engstrom in the opening match.

After his battle with Kinji, Ivan got his brother Karol to agree to once again go into war against the Japanese team of Shibuya and "cousin" Mitsu Arakawa. The August 5 showdown was one of the bloodiest tag team bouts ever staged in Minneapolis. It was eventually won by the Russians, but with everyone covered in blood it was hard to distinguish the winners.

After the donnybrook between the Japanese and the Russians, a rematch was set for the following week to try to settle the score. Wally Karbo returned as special referee, assisted by Butch Levy. Ivan Kalmikoff went into the match with nine stitches over his left eye, a result of the previous week's war. The rematch was a war too. This time Shibuya and Arakawa won out, but not before the ring looked like the back room of a butcher shop.

Everyone continued to gun for the Russians. Besides Shibuya and Arakawa, the Scott Brothers, George and Sandy, wanted them, and so did Tiny and Al Mills. The Twin Cities was touted as the tag team capital of the world on TV's *All-Star Wrestling*. And for the first time, the Twin Cities had bragging rights to the first-ever father-and-son tag team, when veteran ring bully Abe "King Kong" Kashey returned with his son Al Kashey. Their styles were completely different: Abe, true to his nickname, preferred the roughhouse style, while Al took the scientific approach. And Al was good-looking to boot, which drew some of the lady fans to his corner.

In October 1957, Hard Boiled Haggerty made his way back to Minnesota,

What fans didn't know about Nicoli Zolotoff was that Zolotoff was not his real name. He was actually Paul Vachon. Later in his career, Paul would become famous as "the Butcher," wrestling along with his real-life older brother, Maurice "Mad Dog" Vachon. They gained tag team fame in many territories and in the late 1960s captured the American Wrestling Association's (AWA) World Tag Team Title.

On June 14, 1957, the NWA title situation was muddled when then-champion Lou Thesz faced challenger Edouard Carpentier in Chicago. The referee, Ed Whalen, stopped the match when Thesz was unable to defend himself after the third fall. This unusual circumstance put NWA members at odds over whether Thesz should retain the title or not. ★ Joe Dusek, a promoter in Omaha, began recognizing Carpentier as the NWA World Champion based on this match. On August 9, 1957, Carpentier was soundly defeated by Verne Gagne, who was then billed (in Omaha) as the world champion. Gagne also held the U.S. Heavyweight Belt, and the two titles were often used interchangeably. Sound confusing?

★ Well, it was, but in the days before cable TV and the Internet, fans were less aware of matches outside their respective cities. Verne Gagne went on to defend his title until November 15, 1958, when (again in Omaha) he lost the belt to his friend and rival Wilbur Snyder. Some promoters were billing it as a U.S. Heavyweight Championship title change, not an NWA World Championship title change.

★ It didn't seem to matter that Thesz later defeated Carpentier in a rematch. The fact remained that Thesz and subsequent NWA

Wearing his long ring robe, Verne Gagne proudly displays his U.S. championship belt.

and immediately engaged in a main event grudge battle with Tiny Mills, besting him in a wild no-contest that saw both grapplers out of control; the referee stopped the match.

In November two new teams were formed. On November 5, Hard Boiled Haggerty took Kinji Shibuya as his partner, and they faced the popular Al Kashey and Buddy "Nature Boy" Rogers, making one of his rare Twin Cities appearances. The latter duo won the match by disqualification.

The big singles match showdown of 1957 took place November 26, when the feud between Verne Gagne and rival Hard Boiled Haggerty was renewed. As in past battles, they fought each other hard, Verne honorably wrestling by the rules, and H.B. pulling every cheap trick in the book to win. For his efforts,

Haggerty was disqualified. The tag bout on this card saw the return to Minneapolis of Joe and Guy Brunetti, in a wild melee against Shibuya and Arakawa. The Brunettis won. One final high point of this card was Johnny Valentine making a Twin Cities appearance to win over popular Jack Pesek.

A rematch between Gagne and Haggerty was held on December 3. The two battled in and out of the ring until the referee disqualified them both and ruled the match a no-contest.

Some big news in wrestling took place on November 14 in Toronto, when Dick Hutton, out of Tulsa, Oklahoma, defeated longtime NWA World Champion Lou Thesz to win the coveted title.

Twin Cities promoters were quick to sign the new champion, and pitted him against Haggerty on December 10 at the Minneapolis Auditorium. The new champ only managed to come away with a draw against H.B., but he retained the championship, as a title could not change hands with a draw.

Yet another tag team debuted on this same card: "the Atomic Blondes," a duo made up of blonde bombers Johnny Valentine and Chet Wallich. Clad in long pink tights, pink boots, pink boas, and of course bleached-blonde hair, Valentine and Wallich were easy for fans to hate. To their disappointment, the new duo defeated the popular Joe and Guy Brunetti.

This victory for the Atomic Blondes not only earned them recognition as World Tag Team Champions, but also gave them momentum to win a few other local matches, to fans' further dismay. Their winning streak was stopped on the final card of 1957, when on December 26 they were defeated by Verne Gagne and Bronko Nagurski, who with the win became the new World Tag Team Champions. Gagne and Nagurski would make multiple defenses of the title in early 1958 until finally dropping it to a couple of Bronx brawlers, Mike and Doc Gallagher, on March 22 in St. Paul.

★ 1958 ★

Another tag team of brothers found their way to the Twin Cities in January 1958: the famous Baillargeon Brothers, Lionel and Paul, from Canada. Their first match on January 21 with Haggerty and Chet Wallich resulted in a wild no-contest decision. On the same card was the popular Farmer Marlin, thrilling fans with his unorthodox mule kick and cut-off blue jeans.

Hard Boiled Haggerty, not unexpectedly, took exception to the fans' appreciation of the Baillargeon Brothers, and aggressively sought to run them out of Minnesota. He got a disqualification win over Paul on January 28, but lost to him in a rematch on February 4.

As a reward for his victory over Haggerty, Paul Baillargeon was granted a title match with NWA World Champion Dick Hutton on February 18 in Minneapolis, but was unable to take the champion down. He made a credible effort,

World Champions ducked a match with Verne Gagne at every turn. ★ Gagne was recognized as world champion and U.S. champion by most midwestern promoters. His schedule in those days took him all over the country, but he often found time to return to Minneapolis and St. Paul to headline cards for his hometown followers.

though, demonstrating why he was considered one of the best in the game. Bearcat Wright also returned to local action on this card in a feature match against Karl Von Brawner (Jack Wilson). The program also announced that Nicoli Zolotoff (Butcher Vachon) was set to return to the Twin Cities.

At the top of the lineup page of every wrestling program in the country was this statement:

PROGRAM SUBJECT TO CHANGE. THE PROMOTER IS NOT RESPONSIBLE IF CONTESTANTS FAIL TO APPEAR IN THE RING BECAUSE OF CONDITIONS BEYOND OUR CONTROL. WHENEVER POSSIBLE, SUBSTITUTE BOUTS WILL BE ARRANGED.

Those conditions arose on February 25 in Minneapolis. The main event was supposed to be Haggerty and Pazandak against Bearcat Wright and Paul Baillargeon. The latter had to cancel because of an infected head injury. Fans got good value, though, when Verne Gagne and Bronko Nagurski substituted for Wright and Baillargeon.

In March, Doc and Mike Gallagher from the Bronx made their way to Minnesota. They boasted that they were in town to prove they were the number-one tag team in the business. On March 18, they made quick work of the team of Red Bastien and Thor Hagen. It was the first of many victories. On March 22 in St. Paul, they took the World Tag Team Title from Gagne and Nagurski in a hard-fought match.

On the March 25 card in Minneapolis, the popular Frenchman Edouard Carpentier returned with a main-event win over Chet Wallich, and in a feature match on the card, Nicoli Zolotoff defeated Thor Hagen. April 8 saw the Gallaghers put their newly won championship on the line with a victory over Haggerty and Wallich.

Fans got something different for a main event on the April 15 card. Hard Boiled Haggerty boasted that he could defeat both of the Gallagher Brothers on his own, and promoters gave him the chance to prove it. He won, to the delight of the fans. After this victory, H.B. claimed the World Tag Team Title, but promoters did not recognize his claim.

On the April 22 card in Minneapolis, Haggerty took Kinji Shibuya as his partner for another try at wresting the championship from the Gallaghers. Haggerty and Shibuya won this match, too, and claimed the championship, but their declaration apparently wasn't honored because of questions over the referee for the match, Ilio DiPaolo. On the April 29 card, the Gallaghers again were introduced as champions.

On May 6, Verne Gagne hooked up with his old college friend Leo "the Lion" Nomellini, and together they finally thrashed the Kalmikoffs, who until then had been undefeated. Nomellini had carved out a professional career with the San Francisco 49ers before he started wrestling on a full-time basis. He made several main-event appearances in the Twin Cities and held tag team championships multiple times with different partners, including Gagne, Butch Levy, and Wilbur Snyder.

An exciting newcomer to the Twin Cities scene appeared on the April 8 card: the heel known as Ivan the Terrible. Ivan gained his greatest success in the 1960s when he returned to Minnesota under the name Pampero Firpo. Billed as an Argentinean, he became known as "the Wild Bull of Pampas." He fought legendary battles against the Crusher, and in 1966 served out an infamous three-year suspension from the AWA. During this time he was active in southern rings, where he often formed a tag team with another noted AWA star, Rocky Hamilton. ★ Upon his return to Minnesota in 1969, Firpo was as ruthless as ever. Despite his bad-guy image, fans began to like his wild style, and he was partnered with the Crusher for tag matches against then–World Tag Team Champions Mad Dog and Butcher Vachon. ★ Firpo conducted a long-running feud with Baron Von Raschke in local rings that lasted into the 1970s. Fans remember his raspy voice and exuberant howling during TV interviews.

Singles competition was still Verne's passion, and he continued to issue challenges to the NWA for an official shot at the world champion. But Lou Thesz refused to meet Gagne again, and "Whipper" Billy Watson, Dick Hutton, and Pat O'Connor, who held the championship after Thesz, also all refused to defend the title to him. Verne's frustration was mounting.

May 15 in Minneapolis saw the end of Doc and Mike Gallagher's reign as World Tag Team Champions. They were defeated by Verne Gagne and Leo Nomellini. Hard Boiled Haggerty lost a close contest to Ilio DiPaolo on the same card.

Minneapolis presented a world title match on July 29. Champion Dick Hutton managed to save his belt by going to a sixty-minute broadway with Ilio DiPaolo. This card also saw future all-time great Joe Scarpa in a match against local star "Farmer" Floyd Ude.

A wrestler from Fairbanks, Alaska, named Yukon Eric was on the April 29 card, billed as 273 pounds and with a tremendous advance reputation. His famous bear-hug hold often subdued his ring foes. Who better to test him against than Hard Boiled Haggerty? ★ Yukon Eric's real name was Eric Holmbeck. He was one of the most popular and sought-after wrestlers in the business, and he made many appearances in the Twin Cities during the late 1950s and early 1960s. He was especially popular in Florida and Atlanta. Yukon Eric died in 1963, beloved by not only the fans, but by wrestlers and promoters as well.

For about eight years running, Verne Gagne's old mentor Joe Pazandak had a standing challenge open to anyone, professional or amateur: $1,000 to any man who could defeat him in thirty minutes or less. Many tried. Pazandak was a master defensive wrestler, and very good at stalling and working the clock. Gagne took up the challenge in a TV studio bout on May 10, 1958, and proved that the student was now better than the teacher. Verne reportedly donated Joe's $1,000 to a local charity.

"The Wild Bull of the Pampas . . . It is I; it is me . . . it is Pampero Firpo . . . Oooohhhh, Yeaaah!" His battle cry struck fear into opponents' hearts and sold tickets to fans who wanted to see him tamed.

Reggie and Stan Lisowski, former International Tag Team champions, were recognized as World Tag Team Champions based on a supposed tournament win in November 1958, although their claim to the title was questionable. The World Tag Team Title—known as both the NWA World Tag Team Title and the Upper Midwest Tag Team Title at this time—had been vacated earlier in 1958 by Fritz Von Erich and Hans Hermann. The Lisowskis' claim quickly faded, and by January 15 of the next year, the Lisowskis lost their honors to Herb and Seymour Freeman. The rugged Poles regained their title in a January 22 rematch.

★ 1959 ★

January 9 in St. Louis saw a new NWA World Champion when Dick Hutton was unseated by New Zealand's Pat O'Connor. Pat made his first Minneapolis defense of his new title and defeated the Mighty Ursus on February 5 at the National Guard Armory.

At the Minneapolis Auditorium on February 10, a double main event featured Verne Gagne defeating Japanese ace Mitsu Arakawa. In a tag team contest Ivan and Karol Kalmikoff had to settle for a draw against Herb and Seymour Freeman.

In a rematch on February 17, the bearded Russians again defeated the Freemans to earn a crack at the champion Lisowski Brothers on February 24. Though Ivan and Karol lost this match, a return bout with the Lisowskis granted them the title on March 5. In the same month champion Pat O'Connor was back in town again, this time to take the measure of hated German Hans Schmidt.

Ivan and Karol Kalmikoff as World Tag Team Champions were hogging the headlines in the Twin Cities, and the search began for a team who could stop their bragging. Minnesota favorites Verne Gagne and Butch Levy stepped up in a March 24 match billed as the "Match of the Year" by *Sports Facts,* the official program for wrestling fans in Minneapolis. This card also saw a very young Larry Hennig make one of his early appearances in a Twin Cities ring.

Another tag team had gained national prominence. Veterans Al Costello and Roy Heffernan, known as the Fabulous Kangaroos, wanted a shot at the Russians, and were signed to a match on April 2 at the Minneapolis Armory. Ivan Kalmikoff injured his back before the match, and was forced to curtail his ring work for a time. He was replaced by huge 275-pound Baron Gattoni, who, with the blessing of the Minneapolis Wrestling Club, was allowed to defend the tag team title with Karl Kalmikoff.

April 28 brought an end to Kalmikoff and Gattoni's reign as champions, when they were defeated by Verne Gagne and Butch Levy for the title. Of note, too, on this card was an appearance by a young Mike Valentino. He was better known later in his career as Baron Michel Scicluna in the World Wide Wrestling Federation (WWWF).

Billed as "cousins," Japanese aces Kinji Shibuya and Mitsu Arakawa were always high on fans' hate lists. They used illegal karate and judo holds on their opponents, but always behind the referee's back. Here they pose with the tag team trophy presented to them by Schmidt Brewing of Minneapolis.

A masked menace made his first local appearance on the April 2 card. He was simply called "the Mask," and disappeared from the Twin Cities after only a couple of matches. It is believed that it was Len Montana under the mask. ★ This was the second time a wrestler called himself "the Mask" in the Twin Cities. Jim "Bull" Wright donned a hood in 1955, and was eventually unmasked by Pat O'Connor in a Winnipeg match. He moved to the Buffalo territory in 1958, this time as "the Masked Marvel," and was defrocked on December 12, 1958, by Ilio Di-Paolo. ★ Another local masked wrestler, Joe Christie, was known as "the Masked Mauler." He was unmasked by Hard Boiled Haggerty on November 23, 1957, in St. Paul.

After winning the tag team championship, Leo Nomellini resumed his professional football career. The title was declared vacant, and this version of the championship was no longer recognized in the Twin Cities. Later in the year, it was replaced with the NWA International Tag Team Title. The first champions were Tiny Mills and Stan "Krusher" Kowalski, who called themselves "Murder Inc." It was reported on *All-Star Wrestling* that they had won the championship while on tour of Japan and Australia.

One of wrestling's great ring technicians, Otto Von Krupp relied on rule-breaking tactics to win his matches over the fans' favorites. In the early 1960s he shared the AWA World Tag Team Title with "Texas" Bob Geigel and also challenged Verne Gagne for the world title.

A six-man tag team match headlined a card in St. Paul on May 9, with Japanese greats Kinji Shibuya and Mitsu Arakawa uniting with Tosh Togo (Harold Sakata) to win over Thor Hagen, Timothy Geohagen, and Butch Levy.

In what was billed as Wrestling's Greatest Rivalry, Verne Gagne faced old nemesis Kinji Shibuya in the main event of the June 11 card at the Minneapolis Armory. The Japanese star was back in a main event on June 30 when he met NWA World Champion Pat O'Connor.

Scheduling problems kept Gagne from making a date to defend the tag team title, and he and Butch Levy were relieved of their championship, which the Minneapolis Wrestling Club announced would be awarded once again to Ivan and Karol Kalmikoff. The Russians' first test as champions came on July 4 when they met Levy and new partner Leo Nomellini. Though the Kalmikoffs barely scraped out a win, they weren't as lucky in a July 14 rematch. Levy and Nomellini wrestled the title away, and then proved their worth in still another rematch on July 21.

Fans witnessed a monumental event on August 18, 1959—though they weren't aware of it at the time. This night marked the first time that Verne Gagne met Reggie Lisowski in a singles match in Minnesota. The winner of the match was promised a possible future title match with champion Pat O'Connor. With a title shot on the line, Gagne got the best of Lisowski that night.

When popular Irish champ Pat O'Connor showed up on August 25, though, it was neither Gagne nor Lisowski that he faced, but rather his old rival Kinji Shibuya. Fans were treated to a successful defense of the championship as Pat defeated the wily Japanese star.

September and the fall season ushered in a new star to the area. He was Otto Von Krupp, reported to be from Germany. In his first match on September 10, he eked out a win over popular Arman Hussien. Next up for him was Bill Wright on September 17. Also on this card, Joe and Guy Brunetti returned and faced off with the Minnesota combination of Bob Rasmussen and Butch Levy. Another newcomer entered the Twin Cities fray that night, as Frank Townsend made his local debut.

One of Frank Townsend's favorite tag team partners was Butch Levy. On October 8 they paired up and tangled with the duo of former world champion Dick Hutton and German ace Hans Schmidt, in a match that saw all four disqualified by the referee. The meeting was ruled a no-contest.

Townsend faced current world champion Pat O'Connor on October 15, but despite the fans pulling for him, he was unable to upset the equally popular champion.

Aside from Verne Gagne himself, Townsend was the most adored wrestler in the Twin Cities. He locked horns with rugged Tiny Mills in a hard-fought no-contest on November 12 in Minneapolis, and defeated him by disqualification in St. Paul on December 26. He teamed with Gagne in a tag match on November 26, and they won over Mills and Kowalski when the latter team was disqualified. The Mills and Kowalski combo was the hottest ticket go-

In the 1960s Reggie returned to the Twin Cities as "the Crusher," and had many battles with the well-liked Gagne. After Crusher turned over a new leaf and became a fan favorite, he and Gagne were frequent tag team partners, and even held the AWA World Tag Team Title together.

Von Krupp was a ring name used by Larry Simon, who gained tremendous fame in Florida and the southern states in the 1960s and early 1970s under the name Boris Malenko. He gained notoriety in Minnesota as Von Krupp, and he and "Texas" Bob Geigel captured the AWA World Tag Team Title from Dale Lewis and Bobby Graham on November 23, 1961, in Rochester, Minnesota. In January 1962, it was reported that Von Krupp had been injured and the championship was declared vacant. Otto's reported "injury" was a way to explain his departure from the territory.

Frank Townsend began his wrestling career in 1956 in Baltimore. He was a favorite of the ladies, with his matinee-idol good looks and classy ring style. He wrestled in Minnesota until June 1960. After leaving the Twin Cities and Upper Midwest territory, Frank headlined in Canada and in Texas, Kansas, and Missouri before a few return dates in Minneapolis and St. Paul in 1962. In Tacoma, Washington, Townsend changed his ring style, donned a mask, and became a heel called "Mister X." His last recorded match was March 12, 1963, in Tacoma.

ing on the tag team front, so this match was a big one for Twin Cities fans. Townsend faced Mills and Kowalski again on December 3, and this time had crowd-pleaser Roy McClarty at his side for the victory.

As 1959 was winding to a close, Verne Gagne was back in town to settle old scores with longtime enemy Tiny Mills. He defeated the big lumberjack on December 10. For the final Minneapolis card of the year, on Christmas Day, Gagne was again teamed with Townsend. Gagne claimed another disqualification win over Mills and Kowalski that night.

★ **THREE** ★

THE 1960s

NEW ALLIANCES

With the continuing stronghold of the NWA and new AWA and WWA, wrestling fans were assured of seeing the biggest and best wrestlers on a nightly basis all over the United States. Each organization could tout their own champions and feature the best challengers for them. The fans were the winners!

Minnesota's top-name wrestler, Verne Gagne, who was gaining a national reputation for his skill and persona, decided he would no longer tolerate being overlooked and ignored for title shots by the NWA, which still favored physically larger wrestlers. The group of midwestern promoters based in the Twin Cities who recognized him as "their" world champion, Wally Karbo, Joe Dusek, and Verne Gagne himself, decided to give the NWA's president Sam Munchnick an ultimatum about putting Gagne in the ring for the NWA Heavyweight World Championship.

★ 1960 ★

The Minneapolis Auditorium was the site of the year's first card in the Mill City. On January 19, old rivals Verne Gagne and Stan Kowalski faced off. Stan had knocked Verne out cold at a previous tag team match and this was Verne's chance to even the score. Unfortunately he lost his French temper and was counted out of the ring while chasing Stan's second for the evening, Tiny Mills.

For the February 4 main event, fans were treated to what was breathlessly billed as a Death Match! The Minneapolis Armory was crammed to the rafters

THE NEWS

GAGNE MEETS KOWALSKI IN . . . THE DEATH MATCH

What promises to be the top wrestling attraction of 1960 is in store for fans tonight at the Minneapolis Armory when Verne Gagne and Stan "Krusher" Kowalski tangle in the most dreaded combat of them all . . . the Death Match.

Gagne requested the death match following his questionable defeat on January 19 at the Auditorium. In that match, referee Larry Hennig declared Kowalski the winner over Gagne when the latter failed to return to the ring within the allotted 20 seconds. Gagne left the ring to chase Tiny Mills, who interfered with earlier Gagne-Kowalski action as a spectator.

Verne said, "This thing has gone far enough. Few fans figure Kowalski earned the victory, although I realize under the conditions which existed, it had to be entered into the books as a loss for me. I want the guy in a battle to the end."

In a death match, there is no time limit and pin falls do not count. The winner is declared when his opponent is rendered helpless and cannot continue the bout. The "anything goes" style usually is followed with the exception of strangleholds, punching, etc.

Kowalski considers the death match with Gagne as just another step on his way to the top. He said, "I beat the guy once, now I have to repeat to get a shot at some of the other top men. Don't forget . . . I'm claiming the uncrowned title Gagne held. He left the ring as the loser January 19 and you can look for the same tonight."

— *Sports Facts,* February 4, 1960

with fans hoping to see Verne Gagne silence Stan Kowalski. This kind of bout was a way to settle the score when two wrestlers' feuding was raging out of control.

The result of the showdown, though promising to settle things between Gagne and Kowalski, did nothing of the sort. Though Verne did come out with his hand raised in victory, Stan screamed long and loud about Gagne's win.

Sports Facts, February 16, 1960, featured the following quote from Kowalski: "The match at the Armory on February 4 was an example of how I'm legislated against by everyone. I earned a pin fall against Gagne with a legitimate knee drop, and Gagne was supposed to have a one minute rest period. Instead, I get tossed out of the ring and they allow me 20 seconds to return . . . imagine that? Gagne should have been the one who was clocked, after all, it was my pin fall . . . And furthermore," Kowalski continued, "How do you explain this: They bar Tiny Mills from the building because everyone figures he'll come to my aid. What happens? Gagne has Frank Townsend working for him, and Townsend in street clothes grabs a chair and cracks me over the head. That's justice?" Tiny Mills added, "Tell anyone I'll take on that Gagne guy anyplace, anytime, and to make it a better match, we'll save money by eliminating the referee."

The year was off to a torrid start with Gagne feuding with the Mills and Kowalski duo, and Hans Schmidt trying to eliminate popular Frank Townsend from the scene. But the real shocker for mat fans came when promoters signed a Heel Versus Heel main event for March 8 at the Minneapolis Auditorium. Tiny Mills faced the rugged Hans Schmidt in what was billed as the Roughest Wrestler Showdown. In a second match that night, Kowalski squared off against Townsend.

Mills beat Schmidt, but fans saw him hit the big German with something that knocked him out. Schmidt's manager, sometime partner, and fellow German Hans Hermann was quick to point out that Tiny had obviously cheated. A rematch took place at the Minneapolis Armory on March 17, and this time Schmidt was victorious.

All this was just a prelude to the real main event. On March 22, Mills and Kowalski put their International Tag Team Title on the line against Schmidt and Herman, in a heel showdown between the Germans and Murder Inc.

The tag team showdown was followed with another donnybrook. This time it was Mills meeting huge Hans Herman in a singles main event on March 29, followed by another tag match between the two teams on April 5.

Meanwhile, another tag team was beginning to get raves: Frank Townsend and Man Mountain Campbell, a pair with the potential to knock Mills and Kowalski off their title roost.

Campbell was one of the most popular grapplers on the Twin Cities mat scene, so it was natural to promote him to main events against the top heels. First up for him was Schmidt on April 12 in Minneapolis. Their match was

In 1960 TV's *All-Star Wrestling* started to promote vitamin products endorsed by Verne Gagne: Gera-Speed and Protein Power Pack. Gagne touted Gera-Speed for many years. After interviewing Verne, announcer Marty O'Neill concluded the commercial like this: ★ "Fans, refuse all substitutes. It's not genuine if Verne Gagne's picture and signature are not on the label. Gera-Speed by Verne Gagne . . . get yours today at all better stores."

In between matches on All-Star Wrestling, fans viewed commercials delivered by show host Marty O'Neill and champion Verne Gagne. At the end of the commercial for Gera-Speed, Marty would say, "Gera-Speed, with Verne Gagne's picture and signature on the label."

ruled a no-contest when both wrestlers were declared out of control. In St. Paul on April 23, Campbell was pitted against Stan Kowalski, with the winner promised a bout with Verne Gagne.

Fans were told that Gagne's absence from local matches was partly due to St. Paul promoter Eddie Williams's unwillingness to use Verne on his cards until he agreed to prove that his famous sleeper hold was not a choke hold, as some wrestlers (including Kowalski) claimed. On the April 26 segment of the TV show *Sports Hot Seat,* Gagne finally agreed to demonstrate the hold before a panel made up of Marty O'Neill (TV announcer), Reidar Lund and Mark Tierney (local sports writers/columnists), and newspaper columnist Don Riley.

The demonstration took place as scheduled, and promoter Eddie Williams was put to sleep by Gagne. After he was rudely awakened, Williams announced that Gagne's sleeper hold was NOT a choke hold. Eddie said he was glad the issue had been settled and he was eager to have Gagne on future cards in St. Paul.

The sleeper hold controversy was an issue in St. Paul, but not in Minneapolis. St. Paul, which was promoted by Eddie Williams, and Minneapolis, promoted by Wally Karbo, considered themselves rival territories, at least as far as the fans were concerned. The two promoters actually did work together, shared the same talent, and even worked out of the same office. Williams and Karbo were both employees of the Minnesota Wrestling Club, but Williams had the promoter's license in St. Paul.

Verne Gagne came back to Minneapolis for a main event bout on April 26, with his U.S. championship on the line against Hans Schmidt. In St. Paul on April 30, Williams brought back Ivan and Karol Kalmikoff to face Townsend and Campbell.

Kowalski and Mills had laid a strong foundation for their claim to be the territory's top tag team, but the April 30 issue of *Wrestling Facts* disputed their claim. Ivan and Karol Kalmikoff boasted that they, not Mills and Kowalski, were wrestling's best combination, and clamored that if Murder Inc. really wanted to see a top-rated team, they should get in the ring with them. *Wrestling Facts* fanned the flames by hinting at a Gagne versus Kowalski match.

In the heel department, the goose-stepping German Hans Schmidt was the fan favorite. The babyface charge was headed up by Don "Man Mountain" Campbell, who had debuted in the Twin Cities in March, and Frank Townsend. With Campbell's power and Townsend's smooth moves and good looks, fans were confident Schmidt could be toppled. Campbell had already put Schmidt's fellow German Hans Hermann out of action, and Schmidt was seeking revenge.

The May 5 Minneapolis lineup stood out as one of best cards of the 1960s. The main event featured champion Verne Gagne once again defending his heavyweight title against Hans Schmidt, and the semi-windup match pitted Mills and Kowalski, aka Murder Inc., against Campbell and Townsend.

The *Sports Facts* program for this card featured another article about Gagne's sleeper hold. Loudest among the detractors were, of course, Tiny Mills and Stan Kowalski. They claimed that referees and promoters looked the other way whenever the popular Gagne applied the hold. In the May 14 edition of St. Paul's *Wrestling Facts,* Stan Kowalski promised to quit professional wrestling if Gagne could defeat him without using his signature hold. The heels' opposition to Gagne's sleeper hold would provide entertaining conflict for most of his career.

On June 28, another brutal showdown took place between the heel teams Murder Inc., Mills and Kowalski, and the Germans, Schmidt and Hermann. The card also featured the Twin Cities debut of George "Catalina" Drake from Los Angeles. Drake would be a regular feature on local cards for the remainder of the decade.

In July, fans were treated to the return of Leo Nomellini, who returned to

George "Catalina" Drake once played a wrestler on the old *Superman* TV show, in an episode about mob-run wrestling.

"SPORTS FACTS"

Published by

MINNEAPOLIS BOXING & WRESTLING CLUB

605 DYCKMAN HOTEL   MINNEAPOLIS 2, MINNESOTA

VOL. 16—No. 35   MINNEAPOLIS, MINNESOTA, TUESDAY, JULY 19, 1960   15c PER COPY

WORLD TAG-TEAM TROPHY AT STAKE

MILLS and KOWALSKI vs. NOMELLINI and SCARPELLO

Stan Kowalski, Tiny Mills and the world tag-team championship held by the two will

◄ FACTS ►

ON TONIGHT'S PRO WRESTLING BOUT

PLACE: MINNEAPOLIS AUDITORIUM

WHEN: TUESDAY, JULY 19

TIME: STARTS 9:00 P. M.

WORLD TAG TEAM CHAMPIONSHIP BOUT

WHO: TINY MILLS and STAN KOWALSKI
vs.
LEO NOMELLINI and JOE SCARPELLO

TICKETS:
TICKETS ON SALE AT NEW TICKET OFFICE—9 So. 8th St. GROUND FLOOR

CALL FEderal 5-8826

PRICES: $3.00 — $2.25 — $1.50

be back on the firing line at the auditorium tonight (Tuesday, July 19), but the Mills-Kowalski team isn't too happy about a re-match with Leo Nomellini and Joe Scarpello.

"What's there to prove?" asked Kowalski. "We tipped those guys last week in a fair and square match and now we have to meet them again. As far as Tiny and I are concerned, it's just another payday—we want some tougher competition."

The thousands of fans who attended last week's match—plus Nomellini and Scarpello, have other ideas, however. They point out that each team traded pin falls, and the third

fall came about because Kowalski used his knee to stun Scarpello before registering the fall.

"Mills and Kowalski are the world champs, and we were within a whisper of beating them last week," Nomellini said. "I think that proves what Joe and I said before last week's bout: We have trained hard to win the world title and we have the ability to defeat the top team."

Actually, Mills and Kowalski didn't have a choice on tonight's match. They were a bit concerned about the abilities of Scarpello and Nomellini before the July 12 card, so when the contract was signed, a re-match clause was included.

Scarpello was ready to give himself the proverbial "boot" after the match. He said, "I guess I lost my temper and hurt our chances of a win. The tactics those guys use is enough to make anyone boil, but I'll change all that tonight."

Heaps of praise were tossed at the Scarpello-Nomellini team after last week's match, because both proved their statements of a week earlier when they said, in effect, "watch out, we're ready." Nomellini's shoulder blocks and Scarpello's over-all aggressiveness had the fans buzzing all during the bout.

Also on tonight's card will be Big George McArthur, 205-pounds against 311-pound Man Mountain Campbell in the semi-windup; George Grant against Jack Pesek in a special bout and Roy McClarty against an opponent yet to be named in the 8:30 p.m. opener.

TINY MILLS

LEO NOMELLINI

STAN KOWALSKI

Minneapolis fans always looked forward to purchasing their souvenir Sports Facts *program: each edition listed the matches on tap and offered pictures of favorite wrestlers.*

the grappling game during the football off-season. He immediately picked up where he had left off, feuding with Mills and Kowalski, backed by fellow baby-faces Joe Scarpello, Butch Levy, and Verne Gagne.

The Twin Cities wrestling scene during this time was still under the jurisdiction of the NWA. However, change was on the horizon. Ever since Verne Gagne's 1957 victory over Edouard Carpentier, Gagne had declared the NWA championship title his, but the NWA did not recognize his claim. Gagne often complained in the wrestling programs and on *All-Star Wrestling* of being ignored by the NWA and their designated champion, Pat O'Connor, who refused to give Gagne a shot at the championship. Backed by promoter Wally Karbo, Gagne gave O'Connor ninety days to fight him, or else forfeit the title.

There was never a serious chance of Pat O'Connor coming to Minneapolis to defend his championship because the NWA had agreed to give up the Minneapolis territory, but it made a great storyline, and the thought of such a showdown cemented Gagne's supremacy in most fans' minds. The August 9 edition of *Sports Facts* reported that the August 1 deadline had passed, and on August 16 *Sports Facts* declared that Verne Gagne was world champion because Pat O'Connor had failed to meet his challenge. This was the official beginning of the American Wrestling Alliance, or AWA, and Gagne was named its official world champion wrestler.

THE NEWS

CONGRATS OVERWHELM VERNE AS NEW TITLEHOLDER

The congratulatory telegrams and messages began pouring into the Minneapolis Wrestling Club office a few days ago and Verne Gagne was the recipient of them all.

Promoters and well wishers across the country were wishing Gagne good luck and congratulations in his new role as World Heavyweight Wrestling Champ.

Readers of *Sports Facts* will remember that Gagne issued a challenge to Pat O'Connor some two months ago. Champ O'Connor was given until August 1 to either meet Gagne or agree to a match on a definite date. O'Connor failed to reply, so Gagne, who has met the best in the world, automatically took the title. Efforts are still being made to book a match with O'Connor to settle the issue inside the ring.

Minneapolis promoter Wally Karbo pretty well summed up the feeling and attitude of other promoters on the matter when he said, "Verne made a legitimate effort to meet O'Connor and Pat refused to answer. Gagne deserved the title shot more than any other wrestler in the game today, but O'Connor didn't even have the common courtesy to send a reply. Other promoters all over the nation are now regarding Verne as the Champion of the World."

There is some speculation amongst close wrestling fans that O'Connor's hand has now been forced. When he wrestles without the world title under various promoters, he'll almost be forced to meet Gagne mighty soon, in an effort to restore some of his prestige.

Gagne said, "I now consider myself the world champ. I don't plan to take the title and duck away like many have in the past. I'll continue to meet the top wrestlers anyplace . . . but preferably in my home town of Minneapolis. You can be sure of one thing: the new title will be put on the line to all aspirants more than any other in the history of wrestling."

— *Sports Facts*, August 16, 1960

With the AWA off and running, the Minneapolis Wrestling Club was no longer affiliated with the NWA office out of St. Louis, Missouri. The NWA now had a rival, and their monopoly on the championship market was broken. For the first time since 1949, wrestling had two different organizations laying claim to the one true world title. Certainly with his strong amateur and professional background, Gagne was an intimidating champion. The Twin Cities, and the wrestling business in general, had a hero they could count on to (fans hoped) ward off all challengers.

Gagne set out to make the AWA one of the best wrestling territories in the country. In those days, he had only the NWA to contend with. Gagne was backed in his efforts by a solid base of core cities and towns that recognized the AWA and by promoters willing to recognize him as the champion. The AWA primarily held jurisdiction in the Midwest, and the NWA held on to their monopoly in the rest of the United States.

With a new alliance also came the opportunity for many wrestlers who for one reason or another chafed under the NWA to move into the limelight of the AWA. Over the next thirty years, the AWA at times ranked as an equal of the NWA. The fact that there were now at least two powerhouse companies essentially controlling most of U.S. wrestling meant that claims to the championship became even more confusing.

Meanwhile in California, Los Angeles promoters Jules Strongbow, Cal Eaton, and Gene LeBell also got tired of the NWA stronghold on the world title. Taking matters into their own hands, as Gagne had done, they formed the World Wrestling Alliance (WWA) as a result of the same June 14, 1957, match in Chicago where Edouard Carpentier faced then-NWA world champion Lou Thesz. Carpentier was thus indirectly responsible for creating two new wrestling organizations to compete with the NWA. Technically Carpentier is the only wrestler to be unofficially recognized as NWA world champion and also hold the WWA title.

As the fall season of 1960 continued, new wrestlers made their AWA debuts and many former stars returned. Among the newcomers were Gene Kiniski, Len Montana, and Bob Geigel, and among the returning greats were Wilbur Snyder and Hard Boiled Haggerty. Haggerty and Montana were forged into a team and quickly upset champions Mills and Kowalski for the AWA World Tag Team Championship. Haggerty revived his old feud with Gagne, and they had many contests in the months that followed.

Wilber Snyder, Gagne's old friend and rival, was often either chasing or teaming with Gagne. They formed one of the most popular combinations of the time and were often challengers to Haggerty and Montana for the tag team title.

As 1960 ended, fans were treated to Gagne defending his honors against the likes of Gene Kiniski and Hard Boiled Haggerty, as Haggerty and Montana battled to keep their crown against former champs Mills and Kowalski. Kiniski also fought Wilbur Snyder to be AWA U.S. Champion—one rank below world

From 1949 to 1957, the NWA was the most widely recognized promotion in wrestling. In August 1960, Verne Gagne succeeded in creating his AWA, and in June 1957 California promoters created the WWA. This was followed by the World Wide Wrestling Federation, or WWWF, in 1963. The WWWF is the ancestor of today's dominant Wrestling Entertainment promotion, the WWE.

During the 1960s, wrestling's primary fan magazines were *Wrestling Revue* and *Wrestling World*, followed later by others such as *Inside Wrestling* and *The Wrestler*. These magazines often printed "Official World Ratings." ★ No major wrestling organizations ever ranked their wrestlers. The "Official World Ratings" presented in the magazines, most published in New York, were nothing more than the personal opinions of the editors and writers. The only thing "official" about their ratings was that they listed the current champions at the date of the issue's publication.

champion. The Snyder-Kiniski wars continued over the years, in the AWA and in the NWA as well. Their conflicting ring styles offered fans an exciting match any time they faced off.

The last card of 1960 was held on December 27 in Minneapolis. The main event was a rare six-man tag team contest. On one side was the popular trio of Verne Gagne, Wilbur Snyder, and Joe Scarpello, and their opponents were Hard Boiled Haggerty, Len Montana, and Gene Kiniski. The hard-fought battle was eventually won by the good guys.

★ 1961 ★

The new year started off strong for AWA fans. Veteran names like Nick Roberts (who would later become a promoter in Lubbock, Texas), Jim Hady, and Roy McClarty were among those to hit the scene in January of 1961.

The January 17 main event picked up where the December six-man battle left off. It featured Haggerty and Montana defending their title belts against Gagne and Snyder. The results, however, were controversial, because Snyder didn't arrive for the bout until the third fall. Gagne explained to fans that his partner was delayed due to travel, and that he would take Bob Rasmussen as his mate. With the falls even at a fall apiece, Snyder finally arrived at the arena. When Gagne and Snyder won the third fall, Haggerty and Montana lost their titles—or at least that's what fans went home thinking.

The next week on *All-Star Wrestling,* it was announced that due to the substitution of Rasmussen for Snyder in the match, the title could not change hands. It was returned to a jubilant Haggerty and Montana, with the stipulation that a rematch be set for January 24. In that encounter, the champs were at their ruthless best, and they got by the popular Gagne-Snyder duo.

A January 21 card in St. Paul featured another chapter in the rivalry between Wilbur Snyder and Gene Kiniski. For this encounter, they each took on partners and battled it out in the main event. Snyder was joined by Jim Hady, while Kiniski paired up with Bob Geigel. The outcome was a win for Snyder's team

January ended on a high note when Gagne put his world title on the line against Kiniski, the first of many clashes between them. Like Kiniski's foe Wilbur Snyder, Gagne offered the right contrast to Gene's bruising roughhouse style, and fans always anticipated their matches.

Other wrestlers in the spotlight in early 1961 were Haggerty, Montana, Mills, Kowalski, Hady, and Geigel. When Gagne wasn't busy with Kiniski, he had his old nemesis Haggerty to contend with. They met on several 1961 cards in both singles and tag team matches. After Haggerty had his nose accidentally broken in a match with Gagne on March 21 in Minneapolis—which Haggerty won by disqualification—he was given approval to wear a special face mask similar to a hockey goalie's mask to protect himself in a March 28 death match with Gagne. Haggerty lost.

In July 1961, Kiniski got the nod over Gagne and left the ring as world champion. Though he only held the belt for about a month, Kiniski had the distinction of being the only wrestler to ever hold both the AWA and NWA world titles. His AWA reign began on July 11 and ended on August 8, when he lost the belt back to Gagne. Kiniski gained his greatest fame as NWA World Champion when he won the NWA belt from the legendary Lou Thesz on January 7, 1966. He held the honor for three years, until February 11, 1969, when he dropped the title to Dory Funk, Jr.

Billed as Canada's greatest athlete, big Gene Kiniski is the only wrestler to hold three of pro wrestling's major titles: AWA World Champion, NWA World Champion, and WWA World Champion. He also shared many tag team titles, among them the AWA World Tag Team belt with Hard Boiled Haggerty.

Meanwhile Snyder dropped his U.S. belt to Gene Kiniski, who added the AWA World Tag Team Title to his credentials on March 18, when he was picked by Haggerty to replace Len Montana on the championship team. Len Montana's leg was reported to have been broken by Verne Gagne in a match, so the AWA allowed Haggerty to name a replacement for him and retain the title.

★ ★ ★

The Haggerty-Kiniski partnership lost the tag team title on May 23 in Minneapolis to Wilbur Snyder and Leo Nomellini and then won it back on July 19, again in Minneapolis. But their championship was short-lived. On August 8 at Metropolitan Stadium, Kiniski faced Verne Gagne in a cage match fought in a ring with mesh sides and no ropes. During the match, Haggerty, who was Kiniski's second, picked up some dirt to throw in Gagne's face. He missed, hitting his own partner. Blinded by the dirt, Kiniski became an easy victim for Gagne.

Kiniski, angered by his partner's actions, dissolved the team, but they still held the AWA World Tag Team Title. The AWA resolved the problem by having Haggerty face Kiniski in a singles match, with the winner of the match allowed to choose a new partner and retain the championship. The first battle between the former friends took place on August 29 in Minneapolis and ended in a wild no-contest decision. Each clamored for a rematch. On September 26 in St. Paul, the Hard Boiled one came out on top. His choice for a new partner was rugged "Texas" Bob Geigel.

Haggerty and Geigel kept their hold on the AWA World Tag Team Championship until November 16, when they were upended by the newly formed and very youthful team of Dale Lewis and Bobby Graham in Rochester, Minnesota. Immediately after winning the title, Graham's name was changed to "Irish" Pat Kennedy on all AWA cards. No reason was given, but there was speculation that he took the name because of the popularity of the nation's young president, John F. Kennedy.

Another outstanding addition to AWA cards during the latter half of 1961 was the great Karl Gotch. He too got a name change, and became Karl Krauser upon his arrival in the Twin Cities. He and Dr. Bill Miller were close friends, though they were often ring foes. Gotch was one of several wrestlers—including Gagne, Thesz, and Danny Hodge—known as "shooters." Although the outcomes of matches were determined in advance, occasionally wrestlers in the ring didn't want to follow the script and wouldn't cooperate with their opponent. Gotch and other shooters had the skill and strength to do real harm to any opponents who tried to change the outcome of the match, sometimes breaking a finger or snapping a wrist to get them to stick to the script. As a result, Gotch and others occasionally had trouble getting matches with other wrestlers.

The October 31 main event featured a Battle of Unbeatens, and Karl Krauser faced the mysterious Mister M. Fans figured that one of them would have to lose, and anticipated that if it was M, they might finally see who was under the mask. They left the auditorium disappointed. Bill Miller preserved his identity one more time when he defeated Krauser. A rematch on November 7 saw the same result. The matches staged by these two veterans were talked about for months. On November 4, Mister M was pitted against huge Tex McKenzie, who had come to the Twin Cities to reveal who was under the M mask. He too failed.

On the annual Christmas card held in Minneapolis on December 26, Verne

Gagne successfully defended his title against Otto Von Krupp, who returned as the heel counterpart to babyface Gotch. In the other main event, Mister M downed yet another superstar, Bobo Brazil.

★ 1962 ★

In debates over the AWA's greatest year, 1962 gets a high ranking. The year started off with Mister M making good on his boast to defeat Verne Gagne. The masked man took the champ's belt on January 9 in Minneapolis. And in a January 23 rematch he scraped by Gagne again to retain the title.

As champion, Mister M didn't have to look far for challengers. The Alaskan giant Yukon Eric was quick to throw his name in the hat. In a January 30 match, M got himself disqualified, and left the ring the loser, but still champion.

A new young tag team took the Twin Cities and the AWA by storm early in the year. Duke Hoffman and Larry Hennig surprised many veterans and won the AWA World Tag Team Title in an eight-man tournament on January 15 at the St. Paul Auditorium. They played good guys, a refreshing change from the previous rule-breaking teams to hold the AWA belt.

Their reign as champions was short-lived, however. On February 13 in Minneapolis, the young lions ran into veterans Stan Kowalski and Bob Geigel, and lost their belts to them.

Hennig and Hoffman continued to team up for a short time in the Twin Cities. In the spring they ventured to Japan, where they picked up some much-needed experience that would serve them well in their later careers.

On the February 20 card in Minneapolis, Mister M put the AWA title on the line to former NWA champion Pat O'Connor in a match that ended in a one-hour time-limit draw. It was a homecoming of sorts for the popular O'Connor. He began his career in his native New Zealand, then got his big break when former Minneapolis promoter Tony Stecher brought him to the United States.

Pat O'Connor was extremely talented and in demand. He won the NWA world title from Dick Hutton on January 9, 1959. O'Connor held the NWA crown until June 30, 1961, when he dropped the belt to "Nature Boy" Buddy Rogers in Chicago's famed Comiskey Park. The match drew the largest crowd to date, when 38,622 fans packed the stadium and paid a record $141,345 to see Rogers take the championship.

WRESTLING'S TV AUDIENCE

How many people watch professional wrestling on WTCN-TV (Channel 11) every Saturday night? The exact figures naturally are not available, but the highly regarded Nielsen ratings have some interesting figures.

The ratings for December 1961 showed that TV sets in 73,000 homes were tuned to wrestling at 6:30 PM. Just fifteen minutes later, at 6:45 PM, the figure jumped to 79,000.

By 7:00 PM the report shows that 84,000 TV sets were tuned to wrestling, with the peak of almost 90,000 TV sets tuned in by 7:50 PM.

— *Sports Facts,* February 20, 1962

By March other great names were making their marks in Twin Cities wrestling rings. One of them was Russian Nikita Kalmikoff, who was reported to be the younger brother of Ivan and Karol Kalmikoff, the infamous heel tag team. In actuality he was Nikita Mulkovitch, who had been a solid performer in other territories before dropping in on Minnesota fans. He even got a title shot against Mister M on March 13, in Minneapolis.

Another newcomer to the Twin Cities was speedy Doug Gilbert. He had a ring style similar to Verne Gagne's, striking good looks, a punishing dropkick, and a high-flying style, and *All-Star Wrestling* claimed he was as good as Verne Gagne. High praise indeed, and it led to solid main events for the young Gilbert. He got a shot at the championship against Mister M on March 27. Gilbert actually held the edge going into his showdown with M, due to winning the only fall in an earlier TV match between the two, but this encounter ended in a time-limit draw, thus M retained his championship.

On the tag team scene, Hoffman and Hennig had left for Japan after losing to Kowalski and Giegel, who were then reported to have lost the championship to the Neilson Brothers, Art and Stan. The match was supposedly waged in Cincinnati in early April, but no record of the two teams actually meeting has ever surfaced. It is safe to assume it was a fake match, used as an excuse to drop the title to the Neilsons.

Doug Gilbert was the latest speedy young wrestler to steal fans' hearts, and it made sense to match him up with Verne Gagne. Together, they were the first to challenge the Neilson Brothers' claim to the AWA World Tag Team Championship. They had earned a shot at the champions by defeating the rugged combination of Mister M and Bob Geigel.

On May 1, 1962, Minneapolis fans saw the much-talked-about Neilson Brothers make their way to the Twin Cities. Fans figured their hold on the belts would be short-lived when they faced Gagne and Gilbert. It was not to be, though, as the Neilsons left town as they had come in: as champions.

With his highly touted tour of Japan finished, Larry Hennig was back on the scene in June 1962. Hennig immediately put out a challenge to Mister M, and boosted his stock when he dazed the champion with a new nerve hold that he had discovered on his tour. Mister M was so upset that he demanded a chance to shut the young Hennig down on June 12, in Minneapolis. The match was billed as experience versus youth. In the end, experience won out. Despite his loss, Larry Hennig had proved to the fans that he was a serious contender, and that he was around for good. He boasted that he would be the second native Minnesota wrestler to become a world champion.

Moose Evans was another big man who made his way to the Twin Cities in 1962. During his initial appearances, he teetered between the roles of heel and face. Moose became one of the most popular wrestlers to ever grace the local rings. He was billed out of Albany, New York, and reported to be 305 pounds and 6'4" tall. He adopted a lumberjack gimmick, and entered the ring wearing a flannel shirt and cut-off jeans. His claim to fame was his bear hug hold, which

Early in his career, the young Reggie Lisowski hooked up with the veteran Art Neilson to gain championship recognition from many midwestern wrestling promoters.

forced many an opponent to submit. Evan's debut match saw him down seasoned veteran Jack Daniels on July 17.

Doug Gilbert was back in the main event against Mister M on July 31, in Minneapolis, and then it was Verne Gagne against the masked man on August 21. Not only did Gagne defeat Mister M to once again become world champion, but M finally lost his mask.

One of Mister M's biggest supporters had been his partner Bob Geigel. Their friendship came to a bitter end after the Gagne bout on August 21. When Gagne won the title, Geigel jumped into the ring and raised Gagne's hand, earning the wrath of the now-unmasked Bill Miller. The two were signed to a grudge bout for August 28 in Minneapolis.

The *Sports Facts* program for this card also announced that "Crusher" Lisowski was reportedly headed to the Twin Cities. A picture from his Reggie Lisowski days was featured in the program.

During this time period, Larry Hennig was a popular babyface on the local scene. He was often billed as "the Viking," a handle he picked up because he had tried out for the Minnesota Vikings football team earlier in the year. The tag also referred to his short-lived alliance with Bob Morse in the Central States territory. Morse wrestled most of his career billed as "the Viking." ★ At the January 12 Minneapolis card that featured Hennig against Mister M, fans displayed a huge banner at ringside that read "Welcome Home Viking!"

The Crusher (spelled with a C) had a few words of advice for another Krusher (spelled with a K) this week. The few words are: "Get out of town or meet me to see who deserves carrying that kind of name."

Obviously Milwaukee's Crusher was aiming the verbal doubts at Stan (Krusher) Kowalski from Minneapolis, who has appeared here often over the last couple of years.
— *Sports Facts*, September 18, 1962

As the fall season started, the St. Paul program *Wrestling Facts* raised its price from fifteen cents to twenty-five cents. To justify the higher price, promoters added a special insert with pictures of all the stars currently on the local scene, along with a challenge to the reader to get all the pictures autographed. ★ Pictured in the program were the Crusher, Tiny Mills, Bill Miller, Doug Gilbert, Larry Hennig, Verne Gagne, Wilbur Snyder, Gene Kiniski, Pat O'Connor, Don Leo Jonathan, Dick the Bruiser, Moose Evans, Frank Townsend, Hard Boiled Haggerty, Kinji Shibuya, George "Cry Baby" Cannon, and Mitsu Arakawa.

The Geigel-Miller feud continued on the September 8 card, which also featured Verne Gagne making his first local defense of his title against fellow babyface Ilio DiPaolo from Buffalo, New York. The other card highlight was the debut of "the Crusher," with a quick win over veteran local favorite "Farmer" Floyd Ude.

After his series of grudge battles with former friend Bob Geigel, Bill Miller was thrust into a war with the Crusher. During this period, the Crusher carried out a brutal slaughterhouse attack on all the local fan favorites. Promoters figured, who better than Miller to try to stop him? They met for the first time on September 29, and the match ended when Dr. Bill Miller was disqualified. Also on this card was a team match that pitted the lumberjack combination of Moose Evans and Tiny Mills against the popular duo of Larry Hennig and "Cowboy" Jack Lanza. The match went to Evans and Mills. Finally, another roughneck added his name to the list of contenders to challenge Gagne, a bruiser by the name of "Rocky" Hamilton, who was billed as the "Missouri Mauler."

The Evans-Mills combination was a powerhouse, and Mills claimed that Evans was an even better partner than Stan Kowalski. Evans was still alternating between heel and babyface. He played the heel while teamed with Mills, and the fans booed him.

With the October 16 card in Minneapolis, *Sports Facts* also raised its price to twenty-five cents. Ticket prices for both St. Paul and Minneapolis events were $3 for ringside, $2.25 for reserved seating, and $1.50 for general admission, a bargain compared to other markets.

October also saw the debut of another speedy youngster who took the Twin Cities by storm. He was good-looking Dick Steinborn, and he was teamed with Doug Gilbert. Together, they were referred to as "Mr. High" (Gilbert) and "Mr. Low" (Steinborn) and given a mega push as the team who would dethrone the Neilson Brothers for the AWA World Tag Team Title.

Promoters announced in October that Moose Evans would challenge Verne Gagne—but first he had to get by the Crusher. Evans and the Crusher were both unbeaten in their local matches, and the winner was promised an eventual bout with the champion. On the October 30 Minneapolis card, the Crusher won over Evans when the latter was disqualified. In a second show-

From Albany, New York, and weighing in at 305 pounds, the 6'4" Moose Evans was one of Minnesota's most popular grapplers of the early 1960s. He co-held the AWA World Tag Team Title with Verne Gagne after they defeated the Crusher and the Bruiser.

down between the Crusher and Evans, the Milwaukee strongman came out on top, and he was quick to demand his match with Gagne.

The newly formed team of Gilbert and Steinborn continued their rapid rise on the October 30 card with a victory over "Cry Baby" Cannon and Kurt Von Brauner. Their outstanding ring work was the talk of the show on *All-Star Wrestling,* where they were called the greatest scientific tag team in history. A match with Art and Stan Neilson seemed inevitable.

The Crusher, in his continuing effort to be the premier "roughhouse" wrestler in town, was signed to meet up with fellow bad man Rocky Hamilton on the November 13 card at the Minneapolis Auditorium. When Hamilton didn't appear, Crusher found himself again facing big Moose Evans. Crusher won by disqualification in front of 4,085 fans.

Despite losing his battles with the Crusher, Moose Evans was granted a title match with champion Verne Gagne on November 22. Fan support was divided between the two babyfaces. The match drew a sold-out crowd of 8,650, with many turned away, proving that fans would support a babyface champion pitted against a babyface challenger. Gagne prevailed in the hard-fought, back-and-forth match, and retained his championship.

Because of the record crowd, a rematch took place on December 1, and Gagne was the clear-cut winner. Gilbert and Steinborn were also featured on this card, defeating the Germans Kurt Von Brauner and Karl Von Schober.

The Neilson Brothers announced that they were ready to defend their tag team championship, and fans clamored for their opponents to be Gilbert and Steinborn, aka Mr. High and Mr. Low. They got their wish on December 16, when the duo handily defeated Art and Stan Neilson for the tag team crown. The new title holders were reputed to be the youngest wrestlers in history to reign as champions.

★ 1963 ★

The New Year was ushered in with a tremendous main event for fans, pitting newly crowned AWA World Tag Team Champions Doug Gilbert and Dick Steinborn against the hated Russians, former champions Ivan and Karol Kalmikoff. It was the stiffest challenge yet for Mr. High and Mr. Low. They had gotten by the Kalmikoffs on December 22 in St. Paul, when the two teams battled to a wild no-contest decision. But to fans' dismay, the Russians proved superior on January 1 and took the championship. Gilbert and Steinborn vowed to regain it.

Every wrestler in the territory wanted a piece of the newly crowned Kalmikoffs. One in particular was big Moose Evans. For the January 8 Minneapolis card, fans were offered a rare treat when Evans was signed to meet both Ivan and Karol in a handicap match. Evans's size wasn't enough to counter the double-team attack of the Kalmikoffs, and the Russians pounded him into defeat. The same card featured a showdown between the Crusher and champion Verne Gagne. Their match ended in a draw after each had taken a fall.

Of course the Crusher wasn't satisfied with a draw, so a rematch was set for January 20 in the St. Paul Auditorium. When the smoke cleared, Gagne narrowly scraped by after twenty-three minutes of being pounded on by Crusher. Moose Evans also sought revenge on this card for the beating he had endured by the Russians, and was joined by Doug Gilbert for a title match against them. But even the unique combination of size and speed that Moose and Doug brought to the ring wasn't enough to grab the championship from the Russians.

The always-popular Battle Royale was the feature event on January 22 in Minneapolis. In this event, multiple wrestlers compete simultaneously in one ring and are disqualified only after being thrown out over the top rope. The winner was promised a title shot against Verne Gagne. Twelve wrestlers battled that night for the prize: Doug Gilbert, Bob Geigel, Rocky Hamilton, Dick Stienborn, Ivan Kalmikoff, Stan Kowalski, Gordon Nelson, Jack Pesek, Cowboy Jack Lanza, Johnny King (who was the behind-the-scenes manager for Moose Evans), Duke Hoffman, and Karol Kalmikoff. "Missouri Mauler" Rocky Hamilton survived the mayhem to earn the shot at Gagne.

Rocky Hamilton's promised title match with Gagne took place on January 29 in Minneapolis. The champion retained his belt, but only because the bout was ruled a no-contest by the referee. Fans left the auditorium not really sure that their hero Verne Gagne was going to be able to overcome the Mauler.

Gilbert and Steinborn were back together on this card as well, and scored an impressive victory over the makeshift combination of Duke Hoffman and Stan Kowalski. Fans were also treated to the debut of the popular 300-pound giant from Madrid, Spain: Hercules Cortez. His opponent for the night was veteran grappler Kurt Von Brauner, who was billed as hailing from Hamburg, Germany. Milwaukee wrestling fans would have recognized "Von Brauner" as Jack Wilson. Cortez lived up to his advance hype, and thrilled the fans with a quick victory over "the German."

In early 1963 a match between champion Verne Gagne and his pupil Larry Hennig was hinted at for the first time. After his tour of Japan the year before, Hennig had reportedly wrestled on the West Coast and gained some valuable experience. Twin Cities fans quickly noticed the big redhead's new bruising style. Announcer Marty O'Neill claimed that Hennig had become a brute. Hennig countered that he was better than the local wrestlers, and offered to prove it by beating them all—including Verne Gagne.

Meanwhile the Crusher ran roughshod in the Twin Cities, defying opponents' attempts to control him. He was pitted against Hercules Cortez in a series of battles of strength against strength. Crusher's name finally went into the record books as the winner of their feud. He won over Cortez by disqualification on the February 26 card in Minneapolis, and won a best-of-three-falls victory on March 9 in St. Paul, with Duke Hoffman as the special referee.

Cortez and Moose Evans teamed up to meet the Kalmikoffs on March 17. The Russians walked away with their belts after a disqualification when Cortez and Evans got tired of the Russians' rule-breaking tactics and lost their tempers. They still managed to soundly punish Ivan and Karol after the referee tried to restore order.

The impressive Cortez-Evans tag team was broken up only a week later, on March 26, when the big Moose faced Cortez in a singles match. Cortez emerged victorious after a hard-fought (but clean) battle. In the other main event on the card, the Crusher edged out a win over fellow bully Rocky Hamilton in just a little over six minutes of chaos.

Ivan and Karol Kalmikoff continued to boast of their Russian superiority, and proved it by eliminating any team that came up against them. Finally

The Hoffman-Kowalski team was a surprising pairing. Only a year earlier, Kowalski and Bob Geigel relieved Hoffman and his partner Larry Hennig of the AWA World Tag Team Championship. *Sports Facts* reported only that both Hoffman and Kowalski had previously held the tag crown, and therefore made a natural team. Promoters figured that fans wouldn't remember the clash between Kowalski and Hoffman, and for the most part, they were right.

Verne Gagne began to share his craft during the 1960s, training young hopefuls in the art of professional wrestling. Over the years, Verne trained some of the biggest names in the sport. Wrestlers including Lars Anderson, Larry Hennig, Bob Brown, Baron Von Raschke, Rock Rogowski, Gene Anderson, Ken Patera, Ricky Steamboat, Sgt. Slaughter, "Playboy" Buddy Rose, the Iron Sheik, Black Jack Lanza, Jim Brunzell, "Nature Boy" Ric Flair, and even Verne's own son Greg owe their introduction to the business to Verne Gagne. It is hard to imagine what the wrestling scene would have looked like had Verne not taken the time to train aspiring wrestlers.

"Teacher [Verne Gagne] versus Student [Larry Hennig]" was one of Minnesota's ongoing feuds. The burly and roughhouse Hennig resented the scientific wrestling style displayed by Gagne, and at every turn the Robbinsdale High School graduates took their shots at each other in the ring.

Fans who have watched Larry Hennig wrestle since his return from the West Coast have to agree that he is in the best shape of his career and has developed a mean streak.

"I have learned that you have to be tough to win. Look at the wrestlers who are on top. They're all rugged men and rely on their strength and power to win their matches."

So far, Hennig's plan has worked fine. Everybody he has met since coming back to Minneapolis has remarked on how improved Hennig is.

So the question remains: Will Hennig ever be the champ? Only time and a string of victories will answer the question.

— *Sports Facts*, April 9, 1963

Minneapolis promoter Wally Karbo talked the Crusher into teaming up with his rival Rocky Hamilton on April 30 to try to dismantle the Kalmikoffs, with the winner taking the World Tag Team Championship. But once again the rugged Kalmikoffs were able to retain their title.

TV's *All-Star Wrestling* often proclaimed the Twin Cities the hotbed of the wrestling world, and viewers only had to look at the local talent roster to bear this out. In addition to the Kalmikoffs, Cortez, Evans, Crusher, Hennig, Gilbert, Steinborn, and Hamilton, there was a constant invasion of wrestling's best coming to town. In the early months of 1963 the Twin Cities hosted Tiny Mills, Bob Orton, Butch Levy, Jack Daniels, Bearcat Wright, and the very popular Don McClarty.

The star of the show, though, was Verne Gagne. The champion made frequent appearances in defense of his coveted belt, and again teamed up with "Mr. High" Doug Gilbert for some torrid encounters with Ivan and Karol Kalmikoff. Gagne stated on *All-Star Wrestling* that he wanted to be the first wrestler to hold both the singles title and the tag team belt, and teamed with the speedy Gilbert, fans believed he could make it happen. The team got the best of the hated Russians on May 28 in Minneapolis, but ended up disqualified. Ivan and Karol retained their belts.

Former NWA World Champion Pat O'Connor made his way back to the Twin Cities for a handful of appearances. In St. Paul on June 1, he took the measure of Tiny Mills, but was bested by the Crusher on June 4 in Minneapolis.

The June 4 Minneapolis card also marked the reunion of Murder Inc., when Tiny Mills and Stan Kowalski got back together after several years of bad blood between them. They had parted company when they lost their tag title, with Mills claiming that Kowalski didn't hold up his end of the team and Kowalski charging that Mills was old and over the hill. Another shot at the tag team title—and also at the Russians—was enough for them to temporarily bury the hatchet. In their initial match they downed the team of veteran Jack Pesek and young Jerry Miller, who worked under the name Jerry Hannigan in the AWA.

One of the biggest shows of 1963 was delivered on July 9 at the Minneapo-

Two East Coast promoters named Toots Mondt and Vince McMahon, Sr., both members of the NWA, were frustrated with the NWA's control of its reigning world champion Buddy "Nature Boy" Rogers, claiming that they couldn't get the champion to defend his belt on their cards. Instead Mondt and McMahon put their support behind Italian-born Bruno Sammartino, figuring that if they could get Sammartino recognized as champion, it would mean record gates. ★ Rogers lost a one-fall match to Lou Thesz on January 24, 1963, in Toronto, Canada. Arguing that the title could not change hands in a one-fall match, promoters including Mondt and McMahon formed the new World Wide Wrestling Federation (WWWF) and recognized Rogers as their first champion. They immediately started to push for the match fans wanted: Rogers defending to number-one challenger Sammartino. When the match took place on May 17, Sammartino beat Rogers in record time with his trademark bear-hug hold.

As if having the Crusher beating everyone wasn't bad enough, the Milwaukee brute announced in June that he was thinking of bringing in his "cousin" Dick the Bruiser. As the Crusher stated in *Wrestling Facts*, "We'll eliminate all the bums and turkey-necks, and that goes for those goofy Russians too."

Next page: A typical line-up page appearing in all Twin Cities Sports Facts *and* Wrestling Facts *souvenir programs*

lis Auditorium, with an entire card of main event matches. The feature bout was for the AWA world title, with Gagne successfully defending against the Crusher. The other matches featured Dick "the Bruiser" Afflis, reputed to be the Crusher's cousin from Milwaukee. The Bruiser stopped Doug Gilbert, and the Kalmikoffs successfully defeated former champions Mills and Kowalski. Don McClarty gained a victory over a wrestler named Maurice Vachon, who was making his Twin Cities debut. Vachon went on to become one of the best-remembered grapplers ever to enter a Twin Cities ring.

With the summer season in full swing, more great wrestlers from around the country visited the Twin Cities. "Tiger" Joe Tomasso, Paul Christy, "Iron" Mike DiBiase, and veteran Billy Goelz were among the grapplers who made their presence felt. In a Battle Royale staged on August 3 in Minneapolis, the huge 605-pound Haystacks Calhoun left the ring with a $5,000 check for outlasting no fewer than fifteen other wrestlers.

In St. Paul's Midway Stadium Larry Hennig got his long-awaited first shot at Verne Gagne's title. The big redhead fell short in his attempt to defeat his former teacher, but with this match Hennig finally became a full-fledged heel, and rivaled the Crusher for "most hated" on the fans' lists.

In a year with so many spectacular fights, what has to be considered the biggest match of 1963 took place on August 20, when Minneapolis hosted the first meeting between Ivan and Karol Kalmikoff and the team of the Crusher and the Bruiser. The lookalike "cousins" proved too much for the Russians and took the best two of three falls to snatch away the Kalmikoffs' tag team belts. The match was a blood fest, as was the rematch between the teams on September 7, which was billed as a Battle of the Butchers. The Kalmikoffs' title loss would prove to be final—they never again held the AWA belts.

In October, Gagne feuded with Dick the Bruiser, and the Crusher attempted to stop Mitsu Arakawa, who hoped to be a challenger for the title.

The average attendance for Twin Cities cards was between 4,500 and 7,000 fans. Verne Gagne's *All-Star Wrestling* was said to be the most watched TV show in the Twin Cities on Saturday nights. After a year like 1963, no one doubted the claim.

★ 1964 ★

Early in January 1964 the news was leaked that Bill Miller was coming back—still wearing his famous Mister M mask. The month started off with Miller clashing with the Crusher. Moose Evans also returned to the Twin Cities, hinting that he wanted a chance to win the world title. Fans also got their second chance to see "Mad Dog" Vachon, who made quick work of Maurice LaPointe. South St. Paul's Gene Anderson became a regular on local cards, showing a more aggressive ring style and saying that he was tired of being taken advantage of by opponents.

THE CARD

TUESDAY, MARCH 24, 1964

MAIN EVENT
WORLD'S HEAVYWEIGHT CHAMPIONSHIP

| VERNE GAGNE | —vs.— | MITSU ARAKAWA |
| Excelsior (226) | | Hiroshima (230) |

2 out of 3 Falls—1 Hour Time Limit

MAIN EVENT

| THE CRUSHER | —vs.— | WILBUR SNYDER |
| Milwaukee (248) | | Van Nuys (245) |

1 Fall—1 Hour

SPECIAL TAG TEAM MATCH

DOUG GILBERT		STAN KOWALSKI
South Bend (228)		Minneapolis (256)
RENE GOULET	—vs.—	GENE ANDERSON
Nice (232)		So. St. Paul (240)

SECOND BOUT

| TINY MILLS | —vs.— | MOOSE EVANS |
| Camrose, Can. (274) | | Albany (328) |

OPENER

| KAY NOBLE | —vs.— | ANNETTE PALMER |
| St. Joseph (131) | | Esmond (130) |

KIDS' TICKET SPECIAL

All kids, 14 and under, now admitted at half price, REGARDLESS OF SEAT LOCATION, when accompanied by a comparable paid adult admission.

The first really big stand-out card of the year took place on February 9 in Minneapolis, when Verne Gagne took Moose Evans as a partner to win the AWA World Tag Team Title from the Crusher and Dick the Bruiser. Over 7,000 fans screamed with jubilation when their hands were raised by the referee, former world boxing champion "Jersey" Joe Walcott.

Gagne had finally gotten his wish; he'd won the tag team championship. But it wasn't his for long. In a February 23 rematch, the Crusher and the Bruiser got their belts back after they opened a huge gash over Moose Evans's right eye and injured Gagne's leg. The attendance for this rematch was close to 10,000. No two wrestlers were more hated in the Twin Cities at that time than Crusher and Bruiser.

Another bully to return to the Twin Cities was the hated German Hans Schmidt. As in the past, he blasted the competition, and claimed that he would take on anyone—including the champion.

Larry Hennig was missing from the local scene. He had left Minneapolis to try his hand at some of the greats in Texas. Wrestling programs kept the fans abreast of his progress and announced that he had defeated rugged Dory Funk, Jr., for the coveted Texas state title.

Fans who appreciated a scientific match were rewarded with a rare treat when Verne Gagne defended his title against his friend and sometime partner, Wilbur Snyder. The two stars put on a classic match. Each took a fall, and then Gagne got the three-fall. They shook hands and left the ring together.

What Twin Cities fans didn't know was that Verne Gagne had suffered a rare defeat at the hands of Mad Dog Vachon in Omaha on May 2. Joe Dusek, an Omaha promoter, began billing Vachon as AWA champion. At this time, Omaha

Next page: Small-town Minnesota wrestling cards called spot shows often featured posters like this one, displayed in store windows and on telephone poles to entice fans to come to the local armory or arena to see their favorite wrestlers in action.

THE NEWS

MAD DOG VACHON HERE!

Twin City fans get the opportunity tonight to see the wrestler that has caused more fan comment in ring circles coast-to-coast in the past month than any other mat star . . . namely Mad Dog Vachon.

Vachon had the wrestling world in quite a turmoil regarding Verne Gagne's world championship until two weeks ago when the champion returned to Omaha and settled the question, at least for the time being, that he is definitely the rightful owner of the "title belt."

Vachon, who gave Gagne one of the worst physical beatings of his long and glorious ring career, forgot momentarily that Gagne has held on to his title in rough scrapes before by reaching way back and calling on his full store of vast wrestling knowledge amassed from the experts over the years; which is exactly what it took to beat Vachon.

Born in the area of recent international conflict in Algeria, Mad Dog Vachon is known to use any method, trick, or facility in not only trying to defeat his opponents but beat them to physical submission. In the past opponents who have the misfortune to end up in the same ring with the French master of meanness have been very vocal in their accusations that Vachon has resorted to biting, nail-scratching, gouging, kicking, stomping, and an assortment of other illegal actions too numerous to mention.

— *Sports Facts,* May 30, 1964

WRESTLING

OWATONNA
NATIONAL GUARD ARMORY

3 ALL STAR MATCHES

SAT.
FEBRUARY
11 TH
8:45 p.m.

MAIN EVENT — 2 FALLS OUT OF 3 - 60 MINUTE LIMIT

WLADEK "KILLER" KOWALSKI

v s

REGGIE PARKS

SEMI FINAL — 2 FALLS OUT OF 3 - 45 MINUTE LIMIT

BILLY Red Cloud

v s

THE ALASKAN

OPENING EVENT — ONE FALL - 30 MINUTE LIMIT
Doug GILBERT -vs- Harley RACE

— POPULAR PRICES —

TICKETS ON SALE

RINGSIDE	$2.00
GENERAL ADMISSION	$1.50
STUDENTS	$1.00

WRESTLING

and Minneapolis didn't always recognize the same champions. Gagne regained recognition in Omaha on May 16 when he defeated the hated Mad Dog.

Two other major events took place in 1964. One was the arrival of the powerful and superbly built "Sailor" Art Thomas. The popular African American giant engaged in a heated battle with the Crusher as to who had the better body. Fans were asked to send in their votes to the Minneapolis Wrestling Club, and infuriated the Crusher when they voted Thomas's physique better than his.

The year's other big event played out on *All-Star Wrestling* when Bill Wright changed his ring name to Billy Red Cloud on the program. Billy's Ojibwe heritage was acknowledged and he became a full-fledged member of the White Earth band. He remained one of the most popular attractions on local cards for the balance of the 1960s, and thrilled fans in matches against Mad Dog Vachon.

July 1964 marked the end of the Crusher's reign in the Twin Cities—and the entire AWA. He lost his chance to win the AWA world title from Verne Gagne and was forced to leave town per the stipulations of the match. For the most part, no one seemed to miss him.

When the fall season got under way, newcomer Reggie Parks proved to be one of the most popular grapplers to hit the scene in years, and was a solid threat for a title shot. Verne Gagne, who had dropped the belt to Mad Dog Vachon on October 20 in Minneapolis, sang Parks's praises and asked him to be his tag team partner.

THE NEWS

CHENE KILLED!

The Minneapolis Wrestling Club was jolted Friday morning when word was received that Larry Chene was killed in a car accident in Ottawa, Illinois, Tuesday night.

Chene was returning to his home in Detroit after winning a match in Moline, Illinois. He was 35 years old.

One of the most popular and respected men in wres-

tling, Chene was scheduled to team with "Cowboy" Jack Lanza in a tag team bout against Larry Hennig and Harley Race tonight.

A crestfallen Wally Karbo said that a substitute would be found by match time but as *Sports Facts* went to press no announcement had been received.

— *Sports Facts*, October 6, 1964

Other big heel news in town was the return of Pampero Firpo, although no mention was made of Firpo's previous Twin City appearances as Ivan the Terrible in the late 1950s. The Wild Bull of the Pampas, as he was called, had forged a solid reputation in the southern states and Texas before returning under his new ring name.

AWA World Champion Mad Dog Vachon was reported to be avoiding an-

Veteran wrestler Ivan Kalmikoff took the young Polish star Igor Vodik under his wing, and together they became one of wrestling's most popular combinations, often battling Larry Hennig and Harley Race in brutal and bloody matches.

other match with Verne Gagne, so Gagne turned to tag team bouts with Reggie Parks. They were intent on stopping the undefeated team of Larry Hennig and Harley Race, and finished out the year feuding with the rugged duo.

Fans were surprised when a much mellower Ivan Kalmikoff returned to the Twin Cities, minus his brother Karol, who had passed away after a match in Salt Lake City. Ivan's new attitude was attributed to his mentorship of a young Polish rookie, Igor Vodik. Ivan taught Igor wrestling, and the two became tag team partners. The duo became one of the most popular teams in the Twin Cities.

★ 1965 ★

The year 1965 belonged to three wrestlers in Minnesota and the AWA: Larry Hennig, Harley Race, and Mad Dog Vachon. On January 30, 1965, the Hennig-Race duo captured the World Tag Team Championship from the Crusher and Dick the Bruiser in Minneapolis. Vachon had a stranglehold on the AWA world title, though he would briefly drop it twice that year: on May 15 to Igor Vodik for one week, then to the Crusher on August 21, regaining it on November 12.

Hennig and Race were the team everyone wanted to see beat. Wrestling's elite united in an effort to dethrone the hated champions, with the Crusher, Igor, and Verne Gagne leading the pack as challengers.

Verne Gagne chased Vachon for the entire year, trying to get a rematch for the AWA championship. The Dog wouldn't have any part of the former king-pin, although he defended his title against the Crusher, Igor, Billy Red Cloud, and Reggie Parks.

The war between the Crusher and "the Wild Bull of Pampas," Pampero Firpo, also entertained Minnesota fans. The feud climaxed on May 27 inside a steel cage, and saw the mighty Crusher emerge victorious. The Crusher also met Hennig and Race in numerous singles contests, and was a thorn in the side of champion Mad Dog Vachon.

Over sixty wrestling cards were presented in Minnesota cities including Minneapolis, St. Paul, Mankato, St. Cloud, and Rochester, with an average attendance of around 5,000 fans. Professional wrestling was a hot ticket. All in all, 1965 is remembered as one of the most exciting years in Minnesota wrestling history.

★ 1966 ★

Gagne and Vachon battled for the championship on January 30 in Minneapolis. Gagne won the battle, but he didn't get the belt.

A new wrestling manager by the name of Bobby Davis appeared on the scene early in 1966. He came with solid credentials, having handled the affairs of legendary former NWA World Champion Buddy "Nature Boy" Rogers. Davis proclaimed that he had a new monster who was going to be all the rage in Minnesota. His name was Jay York, but wrestling knew him as "the Alaskan." York made an impact on the local scene throughout the year.

Another big newcomer to the territory was Ernie "Big Cat" Ladd. He entered professional wrestling during the off-season from pro football, where he played for the Kansas City Chiefs. Big Ernie was billed as standing 6'8" tall and weighing close to 300 pounds, and there was little doubt that it was all real. Football fans knew him well, and he brought the same power to wrestling that he had to football. In either sport, Ernie Ladd was impressive.

Another newcomer by the name of Chris Tolos got under the skin of the Crusher, among others. Tolos was new to Minnesota fans, but not to wres-

Chris and John Tolos were billed as "the Canadian Wrecking Crew" from Ontario, Canada. John entered the pro ranks in 1951, just a couple of years after brother Chris laced up his boots for the first time. Opponents like Gene Kiniski and Eric Pomeroy recall them as tough, rugged men who fought like machines, no nonsense in their approach. They came dressed for every match in simple black trunks and boots, and were experts at quick tags, knee drops, stomping, and, most importantly, bellowing at opponents, referees, and the fans. ★ Chris explained their style on his first TV interview: "We didn't need no clips, no pens or robes. We had a natural gimmick. Nobody really needs that stuff, foreign objects and all. The gimmick is to reach the fans. Understand them. Look them in the eye." On interviews, Chris and John worked off of each other, and at the end of every interview, they would remind fans that there was only one way to spell wrestling: "T-O-L-O-S."

tling. He was best known for his long association with his real-life brother John. Wrestling buffs consider the Tolos Brothers one of the greatest tag teams ever to enter the ring.

Chris Tolos bragged during interviews that he could bring in his brother John and together they could defeat Hennig and Race, Crusher and Bruiser, or any of the other top teams in the area. Fans were enthusiastic, but it never happened. Chris worked mainly as a singles wrestler in the AWA. He had his most notable matches with the Crusher throughout 1966.

On the March 19 card in St. Paul, fans were treated to a double main event, as Vachon defended his belt to popular Wilbur Snyder, and Crusher and Bruiser faced Hennig and Race in a no-disqualification match.

A new venue for wrestling action opened in 1966: the Minneapolis Convention Hall. Many of the cards in the new facility drew record crowds, there to see stars like Larry Hennig, Harley Race, Verne Gagne, Chris Tolos, Ernie Ladd, Reggie Parks, and many others. Convention Hall became a popular place to hold the cards when the adjacent Minneapolis Auditorium was unavailable. It could easily hold 10,000 fans, and often did.

Verne Gagne and Larry Hennig continued their long-running series of battles throughout the year. Other names who saw local action were Moose Cholak, Bob Morgan (who later wrestled as "Tank" Morgan in other territories), and Danny Hodge. Chris Markoff and his manager, Professor Steve Druk, had a running feud with the Crusher.

Left to right:

From Nome came Jay "The Alaskan" York, who had a torrid feud with the Crusher, challenged Verne Gagne for the world title, and made a formidable tag team with Stan "Krusher" Kowalski.

In the 1960s, the giant Ernie Ladd wrestled only during professional football's off-season. He soon realized he could make more money busting up bodies in a ring full time, and he left football to become one of wrestling's biggest and most popular stars.

Jay York dominated the Twin Cities wrestling scene, and it didn't take long for veteran Tiny Mills to challenge his credentials. The fans were solidly behind the big lumberjack. York aligned himself with Mills's former partner Stan Kowalski, and the duo made a good run at the tag team championship. Kowalski, after several years as a minor player, was finally back in the limelight, where most fans believed he should be. He was still one of the best workers in the business and excelled in tag matches, as he had years before when teamed with Mills.

In one of the most interesting angles of the year, Chris Markoff, who had been one of the AWA's top heels, actually received cheers when he joined the good guys for a while. On the May 7 card in St. Paul, Markoff teamed with Gagne and the Crusher to meet Hennig, Race, and the Alaskan. The fans went away happy when the babyfaces won.

Another hot angle featured Gagne in his eternal quest for more belts. He declared that if he couldn't get a showdown with Vachon, he would relieve Hennig and Race of their tag team belts. He made good on this threat on May 21 in Minneapolis, when he was joined by Ernie Ladd against the champions. Though they didn't win the belts, their opponents left the ring battered.

May 28 in Minneapolis was a big day for wrestling fans, who finally saw their heroes Crusher and Bruiser win the tag team championship back from Larry Hennig and Harley Race. They successfully defended the belts in a rematch on June 4 at the Minneapolis Convention Hall.

Also on this card was an eight-man Battle Royale featuring wrestlers who were more often on the losing ends of matches. Eddie Sharkey won the Royale when he outlasted Steve Druk, Guy Taylor, Kenny Jay, Jose Quintero, Paul Caruso, Bob Hirsch, and the Great Dane. Other matches on the card saw the Alaskan defeat Billy Red Cloud and Wilbur Snyder win over Moose Cholak.

KARBO SHOWS NO PROGRESS TRYING TO SIGN MAD DOG

Minneapolis wrestling promoter Wally Karbo has been burning up the telephone lines trying to nail down Maurice "Mad Dog" Vachon for an upcoming bout in the Mill City, but the Frenchman has been mighty elusive.

"Vachon is like the vanishing wind," Karbo moaned. "I can't get him to commit himself. I've offered him an outstanding purse to appear in Minneapolis, but he doesn't give me a satisfactory answer."

For a number of weeks now, Vachon has, in effect, told Karbo: "I can't promise a thing."

"I'm tired of chasing this guy all over the country. When you are champ, it's your job to defend against the top men, and that's what Vachon will do or I'll bar him from Minneapolis for good," Karbo said.

Everyone wants a crack at Vachon. When Verne Gagne held the title the former Robbinsdale athlete met all challengers regularly, and emerged triumphant most of the time. That's the way a champ should respond, but with Vachon it's the fade-away act, and Karbo is boiling in the meantime.

— *Sports Facts*, May 28, 1966

New tag champs Crusher and Bruiser faced the Alaskan and Stan Kowalski on August 13 in Minneapolis. Another Twin Cities favorite was also on this card: Killer Kowalski. The two Kowalskis were not related, but promoters often got them mixed up. Killer Kowalski was the bigger draw of the two—much to Stan's dismay. Some promoters in California and Detroit billed Stan as "Killer" to bolster their cards. This blending of personalities often confused fans—and historians as well.

Killer Kowalski (of Yukon Eric fame) put his name on the list of contenders for the AWA world title in 1966. He was a welcome addition to local cards. Another old favorite also returned to the Twin Cities in 1966: none other than "Mr. High," Doug Gilbert. Gilbert picked right up where he left off and formed another successful tag team, this time with Reggie Parks. Though the two never gained the AWA tag belts, they made a good run at it in matches against former champions Hennig and Race and the Alaskan and Stan Kowalski. Gilbert and Parks were easily the most popular wrestlers on the local scene in 1966.

For the August 20 card in Minneapolis, Mad Dog Vachon was finally secured for a main event—but his title would not be on the line. His opponent was Indian great Billy Red Cloud, and they clashed in a "Battle to the Finish—Indian Chain Match!" The popular Red Cloud was the victor when he dragged a bloody Vachon around the ring by a chain and touched all four ring posts to win the match.

In other matches on the card, Verne Gagne kept his number-one-challenger status by besting Stan Kowalski in a brutal match that reminded fans of their previous battles against each other in the early 1960s. The Alaskan got by Tiny Mills, and Killer Kowalski came out on top of veteran Billy Wicks, who was making a rare Minneapolis appearance.

September 10 in Minneapolis saw Billy Red Cloud rewarded for his Chain Match victory over Mad Dog Vachon when the champion was forced to de-

In June 1966, after dropping the AWA World Tag Team Title back to the Crusher and the Bruiser, Larry Hennig and Harley Race did some traveling, including a successful stint in Australia, where they became the first recognized Australian International Tag Team Champions upon their arrival. They lost the belts to Mark Lewin and Domenic DeNucci in Sydney, Australia, on July 1, 1966.

GAGNE VS. BIG K: REVIVAL OF OLD SIMMERING FEUD

There are many fans who feel tonight's attractive card offers, in reality, a double main event, because close followers of the mat wars in the Twin Cities for years wouldn't miss a match between the Big K and Verne Gagne for anything.

The bitter battling between these two veterans started about six years ago, and fans can still recall packed houses for their main events. One such match was at the Minne-apolis Armory in February 1960, and there wasn't even standing room.

"Gagne hasn't changed over the years," mused Big K. "He's still crying to promoters about the conduct of his opponents, and hand-picking soft touches to attempt to get top billing."

Gagne's attitude? "You don't know how long I've waited to get that slob into the ring again."

— *Sports Facts,* August 20, 1966

fend his title to the popular Indian star. The Dog, though, was at his brutal best, and managed to save his title by being disqualified.

Doug Gilbert and Reggie Parks continued to wow fans with their tag team wizardry, and Billy Red Cloud was a crowd favorite in a match against rugged Killer Kowalski. Hennig and Race returned to the Twin Cities in the later half of 1966.

Verne Gagne kept his challenger status alive with victories over Killer Kowalski and the Alaskan. Two young rookies trained by Gagne were also featured on many 1966 cards: Larry Heiniemi and Jim Raschke. Both grapplers would go on to make their mark in the Twin Cities and all over the wrestling world.

Fans who liked heel versus heel matches were treated to a couple of classic battles between the teams of Hennig and Race and the Alaskan and Big K. The latter duo enjoyed slightly more popularity in these encounters.

★ 1967 ★

Nineteen sixty-seven saw the entry of some of wrestling's biggest names into the sport. The year started off with Mad Dog Vachon defending his title to Reggie Parks on January 1, in Minneapolis. Also on the card was the return of Cowboy Jack Lanza, who teamed with Billy Red Cloud to form a very popular "Cowboy and Indian" combination. Hennig and Race were back with a vengeance, and recaptured the AWA World Tag Team Championship in Chicago on January 6 from the Crusher and the Bruiser, although this would be the last successful year for the new champions.

After winning back the title, Hennig and Race stormed into battle against fellow heels the Alaskan and his new partner Killer Kowalski. Tiny Mills was the special guest referee, and when the smoke cleared the "Dolly Sisters"— Crusher's pet name for Hennig and Race—retained their belts.

Challenges to Hennig and Race came one after another. There were constant hints that the Crusher and the Bruiser were in line for a return match, and one such bout took place on March 19 in St. Paul. A new team, Ernie Ladd and Earl Maynard, were touted by fans as the team to finally topple the champions.

Chris Markoff and his former manager Professor Druk had several matches, with Markoff coming out on top in most of them.

The really big news came on February 26 in St. Paul, when Verne Gagne finally got up with Mad Dog Vachon and defeated him to reign again as AWA World Champion. They had many other encounters with the title at stake throughout the year, including bouts in St. Paul on April 8 and April 15. Gagne was able to retain the title in both matches.

A big feud in 1967 was between the Crusher and Killer Kowalski. They met in many battles, with each taking the winner's purse at different times. In the end, the Crusher proved superior.

Ernie Ladd wrestled during the off season from his professional football career with the Kansas City Chiefs, with previous runs with the San Diego Chargers and Houston Oilers. Standing 6'8" and weighing close to 300 pounds, Big Ernie was an awesome specimen at a time when a wrestler his size was not the norm. He eventually realized that he could make more money wrestling than he could playing football, and quit the gridiron to take on ring foes full time. From the late 1960s through the 1980s, Ladd was one of the top attractions in the game. He is remembered for his excellent mic skills and solid ring work. Behind the scenes, he was one of the most respected and well-liked grapplers in wrestling.

At the April 23 main event in Minneapolis, the winner of an eleven-man Battle Royale was promised a shot at Verne Gagne. In order of their elimination, the losers were Bob Boyer, the Alaskan, Rene Goulet, Danny Hodge, Harley Race, Mad Dog Vachon, Larry Hennig, Earl Maynard, Johnny Valentine, and Ernie Ladd—leaving the winner, Johnny Powers.

This battle marked the debuts of Johnny Powers and Johnny Valentine. Both grapplers came to the territory with tremendous reputations, but Powers got the bigger push of the two. No mention was made of the fact that Valentine had appeared in the Twin Cities back in the late 1950s with partner Chet Wallick as the Atomic Blondes.

Another big boost for Powers came when he defeated Killer Kowalski in a singles match. Kowalski was by this time moving on from the Twin Cities. A new wrestler in a territory would often be put up against a bully who was on his way out.

Powers was immediately thrust into a feud with the Crusher. This was a sure way to get hated in a big hurry, as by this point, the Twin Cities and the AWA were "Crusher Country." In a match on June 10 in Minneapolis, Powers walked away the victor when the Crusher was disqualified—but not before he mopped the ring with the arrogant Powers.

On this same card, fans were treated to a rare scientific hookup between champion Verne Gagne and challenger Danny Hodge, which Gagne won. For those in the know, this really was a classic match between two of the best in the business. Fellow wrestlers, promoters, and historians rank Gagne and Hodge among the top five all-time greats. Along with Lou Thesz, Karl Gotch, Jack Brisco, and Billy Robinson, they are considered among the best wrestlers to ever take to the ring.

June 24 in Minneapolis saw a cage match between Powers and the Crusher. Over the years he had defeated the likes of Vachon, Pampero Firpo, and many

The August 5 Minneapolis cards saw the first rise in ticket prices in many years. Prices went from $3.50 to $4 for front row ringside, from $3 to $3.50 for ringside reserved, from $2.25 to $2.75 for balcony reserved, and from $1.50 to $2 for general admission.

THE NEWS

THESZ HOPES GAGNE DOESN'T SNUB HIS REQUEST FOR SHOT AT JEWEL-STUDDED BELT

Mighty Lou Thesz, a name associated with pro wrestling like bread with butter, makes no bones about it . . . he's in Minneapolis with hopes of snaring his seventh world championship.

Thesz, who seems to go on and on with the moves of a panther, has been world champion six times. Along with Verne Gagne, he is probably recognized by more fans than any other grappler in action.

What does he think about the chances of meeting Gagne for the title? "I'm hoping, but you never know. When I was champ, I snubbed Gagne a few times, and I know it rubbed him the wrong way. Maybe he'll do the same to me."

Thesz, admittedly no newcomer to the ranks, displays exceptional physical condition, and a desire to be in action all the time. "I've been that way ever since I started in the sport, and see no reason to change now. All wrestlers owe it to the fans to be in good shape and hustle all the time," Lou concluded.

— *Sports Facts,* August 5, 1967

Lou Thesz's bid for his seventh championship marked one of the rare times in wrestling that promoters allowed a real-life storyline to be told. Thesz had dodged Gagne for many years when Thesz was NWA World Heavyweight Champion—the reason Gagne eventually founded the AWA. The August 5 *Sports Facts* program said Lou had been world champion six times. What they didn't say was that Thesz held the NWA world title, not Gagne's AWA title. ★ Although Twin Cities fans were teased with the possibility of a Gagne versus Thesz title match, it didn't happen. The two did, however, meet twice in Chicago during 1967. The first match, on July 28 at the Amphitheater, went to a no-contest decision, and the second bout, on August 2, was won by Gagne. This marked the end to Thesz's bid to win the AWA world title from Gagne, and also the end of his AWA stay. ★ Lou Thesz won the sixth of his NWA titles on January 24, 1963, in Toronto, Canada, from then-champion Buddy Rogers. He held onto the championship for three years, until he dropped the belt to Gene Kiniski on January 7, 1966, in St. Louis, Missouri. Lou's record of winning the NWA title on six separate occasions, the most of any wrestler, would hold until Harley Race became a seven-time champion on June 10, 1983, by defeating Ric Flair in St. Louis. Race would go on to become an eight-time NWA World Champion.

others in cage matches. It was often said that the Crusher never lost a cage match—but historians know he lost this one to Powers.

Also on this card was a special appearance by the great Lou Thesz, who was teamed with flashy Rene Goulet to meet Hennig and Race. The champs retained their titles when Thesz and Goulet were disqualified.

Johnny Powers, by virtue of his win over the Crusher, was granted a title shot against Gagne on July 15 in Minneapolis. He threatened to win the belt and take it to his native Canada, forcing wrestlers to come to him for title matches. He failed to make good on his boasts when he was counted out of the ring, and Gagne retained the title. In a July 22 rematch in Minneapolis, after a fall apiece, Gagne was disqualified and kept the title.

Fans in the Twin Cities in 1967 saw the return of the Mighty Igor and the debut of a second-generation grappler named Al Kashey. Longtime followers of wrestling in Minneapolis were familiar with Al's father, the great Abe "King Kong" Kashey, who was Verne Gagne's first opponent when he made his wrestling debut back in 1949.

Promoters didn't waste any time teaming the young Kashey with Igor, and pit them against champions Larry Hennig and Harley Race in a non-title tag match on August 19 in Minneapolis. The "Dolly Sisters" weren't happy when they came out on the losing end. Another big event on this card was the debut of Gagne trainee Al Rogowski. He was introduced as "Brute" Rogowski for his first match, a win over Jose Quintero.

In August 1967 a new masked man, Doctor X, made his AWA debut before Twin Cities fans, and became one of the hottest heels in the history of Twin Cities wrestling. Not since Bill Miller paraded around local rings as Mister M had fans wanted so badly to see someone get unmasked.

Doctor X was scheduled in main events with the Crusher after he attacked Verne Gagne during a TV match. Promoters said that if the masked guy wanted to be a wrestler, they would put him in against the toughest wrestler in the territory.

Larry Hennig and Harley Race won the AWA Tag Team Title at the start of the year, but the August 19 match in Minneapolis was the last time the Twin Cities saw the duo defend their belts as a team. The end came for Hennig and Race on November 1 in Winnipeg, as Larry Hennig suffered a broken leg in a match against champion Verne Gagne.

The injury was unplanned and accidental, but it was used to build further heat between Hennig and Gagne over the years. It also marked the end of the "Dolly Sisters," as the AWA declared that due to Hennig's injury, Harley Race would be allowed to choose another partner and defend the championship. Race chose Chris Markoff, but they lost the title to Wilbur Snyder and Pat O'Connor in Chicago on November 10.

Harley Race made it clear that he felt he and Hennig were robbed of their titles. He claimed that the AWA forced him to make a rash decision in partnering with Markoff, and that the AWA was to blame for their loss to Snyder and O'Connor. Race vowed revenge.

Race met Verne Gagne in singles matches on November 11 in Minneapolis and again on November 25 in St. Paul. Race came up empty-handed in both matches. He cried foul, and demanded that Gagne get a partner and he would do the same. Race chose Bobby Graham and Gagne picked huge Cowboy Bill Watts, who had debuted earlier that month. That in itself would have made for an awesome combination, but on the night of the match, December 9 in Minneapolis, Bobby Graham didn't appear. In his place was Gagne's longtime enemy, Hard Boiled Haggerty. Gagne and Watts were the recorded winners, but Race and Haggerty proved they were a team to contend with on the local scene.

Challengers lined up to face new AWA tag team champions Snyder and O'Connor. First on the list were Mitsu Arakawa and Doctor Moto, who had been wreaking havoc in Chicago and Indiana rings. The champs also battled former kingpins Crusher and Bruiser, as well as Race and Haggerty and Bill Watts and Rock Rogowski. The Japanese team of Arakawa and Moto finally got to Snyder and O'Connor and won the championship on December 2 in Chicago.

As 1967 came to a close, Twin City fans were treated to a Battle Royale on December 25 in Minneapolis and a December 29 main event in St. Paul that saw Race and Haggerty lose by disqualification to Watts and Rogowski.

★ 1968 ★

The year started out with Verne Gagne defending his title against his old nemesis Hard Boiled Haggerty on January 13 in Minneapolis. The champ retained his belt when Haggerty was disqualified.

"Big Luke" Brown was among the stars to return to the Twin Cities in 1968. Fans weren't told that he had appeared eight years earlier under the name Man Mountain Campbell. Now with a full head of somewhat messy hair and a beard, Brown became a key player on the local scene.

Mad Dog Vachon surprised fans by appearing with a new tag team partner— Doctor X. They lost their first match together when they were defeated by Igor and Bill Watts. Watts had asked to be Igor's partner in place of Luke Brown because Watts was engaged in a war of his own with the masked man.

Harley Race became a persistent thorn in champ Verne Gagne's side. Race vowed revenge for his partner's broken leg, and stated that he would love nothing more than to take the championship belt to boot. He got his chance on a big card held on February 10 in Minneapolis, but it was Gagne who came out the winner. On the same card, Big Luke tried his hand at unmasking Doctor X, but fell short, and in another feature bout Bill Watts battled to a no-contest against Mad Dog Vachon.

With Race chasing Verne Gagne, Hard Boiled Haggerty announced that he had a new partner, none other than Dutch Savage. The big Dutchman had never

Al Rogowski's nickname was changed from "Brute" to "Rock" to avoid confusion with Dick the Bruiser, who was often referred to as Brute by promoters and who supposedly took exception to Rogowski being given the name. In his initial AWA matches Rogowski was said to be related to the Crusher and the Bruiser. At different times over the next couple of years, Rogowski was also said to be the Bruiser's nephew. When Al Rogowski left the AWA and Minneapolis, he took on the name Ole Anderson and became a "brother" to Gene and Lars Anderson. After Lars left his "brothers" to return to the AWA, Gene and Ole reigned as the top tag team in the South for over a decade.

Cowboy Bill Watts was no stranger to Minnesota sports fans. In 1963, at the urging of Verne Gagne, Watts tried out for the Minnesota Vikings, though he turned down a spot on the team. As he said, "I went and worked with the Vikings. They wanted me to try out, but Jim Finks, their general manager, would not let me wrestle in the off-season. A Viking contract in those days for a lineman in the NFL was only $6,000 to $8,000 and I could make a lot more wrestling, so I told them to go to Hell."

Above: From late 1959 into 1960, the giant of a wrestler Man Mountain Campbell became one of fans' most popular favorites, undertaking classic battles with Hans Schmidt, Tiny Mills, and Stan Kowalski.

Right: After leaving the AWA in 1960, Man Mountain Campbell earned a solid reputation as "Big Luke" Brown. Before returning to Minnesota, Luke and partner Jake "Grizzly" Smith wrestled as the Kentuckians.

WOULD HAGGERTY STEP ASIDE FOR HENNIG'S RETURN?

What happens to the tag team partnership between Hard Boiled Haggerty and Harley Race when Larry Hennig returns?

Haggerty has already stated that he came to town to help out Race when the latter needed a partner, and that he'll step down if Race and Hennig want to continue their partnership when Hennig is fully mended, but there are some "ifs."

If Haggerty and Race regain the world tag title from Mitsu Arakawa and Doctor Moto, will the Hard Boiled one step out under championship circumstances?

"This proves a real problem," said matchmaker Bill Kuusisto. "Haggerty likes that title feeling, and from my past association with him, I would say he would NOT step aside."

— *Sports Facts,* January 13, 1968

worked the Twin Cities before. He was only on the local scene for a short time, but he is remembered as one of the most rugged grapplers to step into a ring.

February 24 in Minneapolis saw Haggerty again disqualified against Gagne, and the Igor-Luke duo edging out a win over Doctor X and Vachon. Igor and Luke had the tables turned on them in St. Paul on March 2.

March 30 in Bloomington at the old Metropolitan Sports Center saw the return of Larry Hennig to action after his broken leg had healed. He was joined by Haggerty and Savage in a six-man battle against Bill Watts, Rock Rogowski, and Rene Goulet. The main event on this card was the long-awaited showdown between champion Verne Gagne and the masked Doctor X. The champ retained his title when X was disqualified for refusing to break his leg-lock hold when Gagne was on the ropes. Also on the card was Pat O'Connor, losing a close match to Mad Dog Vachon, who kept his title hope alive with the win.

The year marked the end of the line for Haggerty in the Twin Cities. He claimed that he was returning to California to pursue his movie and TV career, and that he felt he had gotten the raw end of the deal in his matches with Gagne. Actually, Haggerty's ring career was nearing its end, and he did become a full-time movie star.

Larry Hennig and Harley Race were reunited in 1968, and were expected to pick up right where they left off. Sadly for Minnesota fans, though, they never regained the AWA World Tag Team Title. Their last appearance in Minnesota as a team took place on December 7 in St. Paul, in a six-man tag match. Hennig and Race took Lars Anderson as their third partner in a winning effort against Watts, Lyons, and rookie Frankie Laine. This match marked the end of the Hennig-Race partnership in the AWA, when Harley Race left to wrestle in the rival NWA territory.

In other big news on the tag team front, Mad Dog Vachon brought his little brother Paul—who was small only in age, not stature—to the AWA, and hit Minneapolis in July in a team match against former champions the Crusher and the Bruiser.

Popular redhead Billy "Red" Lyons appeared on the local scene in August and immediately took the measure of Doctor X in a TV match. War raged for the rest of the year between the two. Fans were solidly behind Lyons in his efforts to finally unmask the mystery man.

Pampero Firpo, banned from the AWA in 1965 for excessive rule violations, ended his three-year suspension with a return to the Twin Cities in December 1968. He stormed back looking for revenge on the man he blamed for his suspension: the Crusher.

The year ended with the never-say-die team of the Crusher and the Bruiser regaining the AWA World Tag Team Championship from Mitsu Arakawa and Doctor Moto on December 28 in Chicago. The Vachon Brothers immediately lined up to be the first challengers.

★ 1969 ★

The year started off with a showdown in St. Paul on January 5 between the Crusher and Firpo, and fans packed the auditorium to see the two pick up right where they had left off in 1966. In a second main event, Billy Red Lyons again attempted to stop Doctor X. The other feature on the card was a tag win for the Vachon Brothers against the team of Reggie Parks and Billy Red Cloud.

Fans in Minneapolis were treated to a World Tag Team Championship match on January 18, when new champs Crusher and Bruiser successfully defended the belts against former champs Arakawa and Moto.

Also on this card was a rare treat: Pampero Firpo against Doctor X. The masked man had cost the wild bull his chance to defeat Crusher back on January 5, when Doctor X interfered in their match. He had attempted to slug the Crusher, but missed and hit Firpo by mistake, and Firpo was ready for revenge. Suddenly, Firpo became a good guy. Fans cheered his wild tactics and were solidly behind his campaign to unmask Doctor X. Since Firpo hadn't changed his ring style, fans got to see two roughnecks go at each other. It made for some interesting matches.

On the singles front, Verne Gagne feuded with Mitsu Arakawa, and was said to be avoiding a showdown with Bill Watts. The two met in title matches later in the year.

Now that he didn't have to worry about Firpo, the Crusher tried to convince fans that Mad Dog and Butcher Vachon did not deserve a title shot. The Milwaukee strongman met the two Algerians in a handicap match on February 8 in Minneapolis, but came up on the losing end to their double-teaming.

In a shocking countermove, on February 16 the Crusher appeared with none other than Pampero Firpo as his surprise partner in a St. Paul run-in with the Vachons. They battered the brothers from one ring post to the other before being disqualified, and the match went in the record books as a win for the Vachons. Also on the card was Mike Riker, the real-life brother of Jay York, who had wrestled in AWA rings as the Alaskan back in 1967.

All these feuds led up to a big extravaganza in Minneapolis on February 22. Billed as a Tag Team Marathon, the program claimed it was the biggest tag card in history. The double tag team main event featured Verne Gagne and Cowboy Bill Watts against Larry Hennig and Lars Anderson in one match, and a six-man tag event pitting the Vachons teamed with Doctor X against Billy Red Lyons, Pampero Firpo, and the Crusher in the other. Firpo met X in a special singles encounter on the card as well, continuing his vendetta.

March 23 in Minneapolis saw champs Crusher and Bruiser battling Mad Dog and Butcher, and rematches between Anderson and Watts and Firpo and Doctor X. Of special note on this card was the long-anticipated and highly publicized return to the Twin Cities of Red Bastien, gone from local action for close to ten years.

Red Bastien had made a name for himself in Florida, Texas, California, and even Australia, but stated that he wanted to work in front of his hometown fans. Red had started in the business in the mid-1950s, working for about a year in preliminary matches on Minnesota cards before moving on to build up his reputation. New York wrestling magazines had closely followed his career, and often featured articles on his teaming with "brother" Lou in the early half of the decade. They also reported on his rugged battles with the likes of Johnny Valentine and others in Florida.

Bastien delighted his fans with a win over fellow redhead Larry Hennig on the March 23 card when the latter was disqualified. He then partnered with still another redhead, Billy Red Lyons. The two were touted as a natural team due to their similar ring styles, and they were a welcome addition to the tag team scene.

Fans got their first look at the new redhead combination on April 19 at the Met Sports Center in Bloomington, when they were joined by the Crusher in six-man action against the Vachons and Doctor X. Crusher went after both the Vachons and X, and Lyons also challenged the masked X. The match set the stage for an eventual showdown between the Vachons and the Redheads.

The main event at this match was Verne Gagne defending his title for the first time to his friend Cowboy Bill Watts. Their bout ended in controversy when the match was stopped by the ringside physician after Watts was cut. After the bout, when asked about a return match for Watts, Gagne only said, "There are other contenders." This callous statement by the champion put the fans in the Cowboy's corner, supporting his demands for a return bout.

Mad Dog and Butcher Vachon remained the top heel team, but Hennig and Anderson were right on their tails for the honor. The latter had many matches against Lyons and Bastien, but in each match the Redheads came out on top. The Hennig and Anderson duo was as hated as the Hennig and Race combination had been, and fans enjoyed seeing them in action no matter who their opponents were.

To further build up the Redheads, St. Paul promoter Eddie Williams signed them for his twenty-second Amateur Aid Fund benefit card on May 31. To prove their worth, Lyons and Bastien would be tested by arguably the territory's all-time best tag team—former AWA World Tag Team Champions Larry Hennig and Harley Race. The return of Harley Race and his reunion with Hennig was the talk of the town, and fans wondered if they would finally be the ones to derail the Redheads. Fans were thrilled when Lyons and Bastien out-wrestled and out-classed the former champs and once again ran Race out of town. The main event on this card saw Gagne successfully defend his belt against Lars Anderson.

The June 15 card in St. Paul's Midway Stadium was highlighted by a couple of high-profile grapplers from outside the territory. One was Tarzan Tyler from the Central States region, who made his only Twin Cities appearance in a victory over rookie Bob Kappel. The other was Stan Pulaski, who came in to lose to Stan Kowalski. The main event on the card was a match between Watts and Lars Anderson, with the winner promised a title match with Verne Gagne.

The referee for the Watts-Anderson match was introduced as Frank Crawford, a trouble-shooting arbiter who was chosen by the AWA to maintain law and order between the Cowboy and Lars. Crawford was actually the manager for Tarzan Tyler, from Omaha and the Central States region, under the name "Dandy" Jack Crawford. He often interfered in Tarzan's matches so he would come out the winner. Such little twists made wrestling especially interesting for those in the know.

Harley Race was only in town for one card, as was "Texas" Bob Geigel, who had returned to face Cowboy Bill Watts. Single appearances by wrestlers in a particular territory were called one-night stands. Often they were used to give an up-and-coming wrestler a big push by having him win over a former main event wrestler. In this case, Race teamed with Hennig to lose to Lyons and Bastien, and Geigel lost to Watts. ★ Race and Geigel were still top stars in the business, working at the time in the Central States region. In fact, Geigel was co-owner of the territory with former NWA World Champion Pat O'Connor. Later in the 1970s, Race would also become a partner.

On June 28, Bill Watts secured his second title try with Gagne, but again fell short of his goal when Larry Hennig entered the ring and knocked out the champion, thus ending the match early. Wilbur Snyder lost to Doctor X, and Lyon and Bastien got a win over the Vachons. Firpo triumphed over Stan "Moose" Morowski, who was back for this card, and a match harking back to 1960 saw Joe Scarpello going to a time-limit draw with the Big K.

Larry Hennig was threatened with suspension for his actions in the Gagne-Watts match—unless he agreed to meet Doctor X. That was one angle. The other was that promoter Wally Karbo hoped that X and Hennig would eliminate each other so he wouldn't have to put up with their rule-breaking tactics any longer. The match, on July 12, was everything the fans and Karbo had hoped for and then some. It ended in a wild no-contest decision when both grapplers were counted out of the ring for fighting on the arena floor.

The other big match on this card saw the debut of "the Chain Gang": Jack and Frank Dillinger, who claimed to be members of California's Hell's Angels motorcycle club. The rowdy "brothers" handed Billy Red Lyons and Red Bastien their first local loss. The Chain Gang's tactics raised fans' collective blood pressure to the boiling point, and left both the Redheads and the fans wanting another go with their long-haired foes. The Dillingers had seemingly come from nowhere to become leading contenders for the tag title, with the Vachons now number two.

On the next Minneapolis card on July 26, an elimination match of sorts took place. Mad Dog and the Butcher were pitted against Hennig and Anderson in a rare Battle of the Bullies tag team main event. Also on this card, Lyons and Bastien got back in the winners' circle with a victory over the returning Angelo Poffo, who had been wrestling in Detroit and Indianapolis. His partner for the night was Professor Steve Druk. The Redheads suffered another defeat to the Chain Gang in St. Paul on August 16, to the dismay of their followers.

Two additional Minneapolis cards took place in August, on the 23 and 30. Both were headlined by Verne Gagne in defense of his championship against the masked Doctor X. Of special interest on these cards was the return of Dick the Bruiser, who gained a win over Mad Dog Vachon, and also the return of Moose Cholak. Jim Valen made his local debut on this card, and eked out a win over veteran Johnny Kace.

On the September card in St. Paul, Lyons and Bastien were again defeated by the Dillingers, and their title hopes quickly dwindled. The Chain Gang showed fans they were the dirtiest players in the game—in fact, they'd proved it three times in a row over their red-headed opponents. A story in *Wrestling Facts* announced that Jack Lanza was hinting about a return to the Twin Cities. Cowboy had a new rougher and more aggressive ring style. He was now calling himself "Black Jack" Lanza.

On August 30, in a cage match in Chicago, Mad Dog and Butcher Vachon finally reached their goal of becoming AWA World Tag Team Champions when they walked out of the cage victorious over the Crusher and the Bruiser. The

Jim Valen eventually evolved into "Handsome" Jimmy Valiant and made a tremendous name for himself on the East Coast in the mid-1970s with "brother" "Luscious" Johnny Valiant. The arrogant blondes returned to the Twin Cities in 1975 for many tag team matches.

While in the AWA, Crazy Luke was only given a mid-card push. He gained victories over opponents like Bruce Kirk and Rene Goulet, but lost battles to grapplers like Lyons, Bastien, and Carpentier. In many fans' eyes, his advance build-up made him seem much better than he actually was. Truth be told, his ability as wrestler was limited. As a performer he was entertaining, but not someone the AWA would build major angles around. ★ Luke (James Grady Johnson) took the name Graham in the early 1960s because of his resemblance to Dr. Jerry Graham. The storyline was that because Jerry's "brother" Eddie, whose real last name was Gossett, was unavailable at the time, Dr. Jerry was bringing in their "younger brother" Luke, who had spent time in a mental institution—hence the "Crazy" handle. During interviews and matches, Luke would claim to hear voices and appeared to grab at flies when asked questions. He claimed he wasn't crazy but "fabulous." For a wrestling gimmick it worked well, because fans would chant "Crazy, Crazy, Crazy" whenever Luke was in a match. He would demand that the referee get the fans to stop, and the more they were asked to stop, the louder the chants became. Of course, that was the idea all along.

NAIL DOWN THE CHAIRS TONIGHT!

Billy Red Lyons was involved in a rare switching of opponents for tonight's big world tag team championship match, and the rugged 235-pounder from Toronto wouldn't have it any other way.

Lyons's partner, Red Bastien, was originally scheduled to go against Doctor X tonight, but after the recent turn of events in a televised match, he asked promoter Wally Karbo to arrange the tag battle with Lyons as his partner, and Karbo readily agreed.

You might even say Lyons was a victim of circumstances during the TV bout. He and Bastien agreed to go against Mad Dog and Butcher Vachon when the original opponents didn't show, and the Redheads were doing an excellent job until the going got rough.

Lyons registered the first fall against Mad Dog with his deadly figure-four leg hold, and was about to wrap up festivities a short time later with the same hold on the Butcher, when the lights went out.

Mad Dog, who had been thrown from the ring seconds before Lyons locked the Butcher into the hold, came charging back into action with a ringside chair for a weapon, and when he was finished swinging, Lyons was out cold and Bastien was wobbly.

"I've never seen two guys so anxious to get at the Vachons as Bastien and Lyons," Karbo said. "They wouldn't consider any other kind of bout against anyone. It had to be the Vachons."

So it boils down to a pair of scientific grapplers tangling with a couple who won't even admit the presence of a rule book, and the Redheads know exactly what's in store for them.

"The incident on television is a good example," Bastien commented. "We not only have to keep an eye on the man in action, but must spend as much time keeping track of his partner. All we ask is that they keep the foreign objects away from the Vachons. We'll take care of the rest."

— *Sports Facts*, September 20, 1969

Crusher was reportedly seriously injured and could be out of action for several months.

With the Vachons as champions, the focus immediately shifted to who would now challenge them for the belts. Fans demanded that Billy Red Lyons and Red Bastien, despite their recent losses to the Dillingers, be given the opportunity. The two teams meet in a match on *All-Star Wrestling* on September 13.

Red Bastien and Red Lyons feel winning the title tonight could mean purses of $100,000 in the next month. The two Redheads feel promoters in Madison Square Garden, Los Angeles' Forum, and Chicago's Amphitheatre would pay a high price to sign them to defend their crown.

"We'll be shooting for the moon," said Bastien. "This is a big money bout for us."

— *Wrestling Facts*, October 4, 1969

After each team had won a fall, the match ended in the third fall when Mad Dog and Butcher were disqualified.

Lyons and Bastien were granted many matches with the champions as a result of their television victory. However, in every bout, the hated title holders managed to hang on to their belts.

The 1969 talent roster remained impressive as the year unfolded. Leading the pack were top names like Cowboy Bill Watts, Black Jack Lanza, Larry Hennig, Lars Anderson, the Redheads, and Rene Goulet. The list of newcomers and young rookies also kept fans running to the ticket offices. French ace Edouard Carpentier returned to the Twin Cities for the first time in over a decade, and "Crazy" Luke Graham made his local debut. Crazy Luke came with great credentials, as he had already carved out a reputation in other territories. He was a former WWA World Champion in California, a WWA World Tag Team Champion with Gorilla Monsoon, and WWWF Tag Team Champion with "brother" Dr. Jerry Graham. Fans were well aware of Crazy Luke's reputation, as he was regularly featured in magazines of the day like *Wrestling Revue* and *Wrestling World*.

Among the rookies rounding out local cards were Bruce Kirk, Buddy Smith, Bob Windham, and Jim Valen. All four wrestlers went on to have legendary careers in the business.

Though the year was winding down, the action wasn't. On November 8 in Minneapolis Cowboy Bill Watts got his third chance to unseat champion Verne Gagne. On November 27 in Minneapolis the Redheads got another disputed win over the Vachons on the big Thanksgiving card.

A rematch for the tag belts was presented in St. Paul on December 6, with Mad Dog and the Butcher just squeaking by to retain their championship. Fans were also treated to the return of Hard Boiled Haggerty. He got the nod over "Big Luke" Brown in a special match on the card. Another highlight was the debut of the great Mexican grappler Pepper Gomez, who came out on top over Larry Hennig, who was disqualified.

The December 14 card at the Minneapolis Auditorium featured Watts's final

After leaving the AWA, Bruce Kirk changed his name to Frank Monte and became a "cousin" to Mike and Jay York. He and Mike wrestled as "the Alaskans" and gained tag team honors in Texas. ★ Canadian grappler Buddy Smith, whose real name was Dale Hey, became famous for his work as part of two outstanding tag team combinations. The first one was with Jerry Brown, when they were billed as "the Hollywood Blondes." Together they won the U.S. tag title in a tournament in Oklahoma, and later in Montreal they were Grand Prix tag team champions. For a short time in the mid-1970s, Dale was worked into an angle in Houston as a younger "brother" to all-time great Johnny Valentine. But he is perhaps best remembered as the third member of the "Fabulous Freebirds" tag team, along with Michael Hayes and Terry Gordy. Together they were NWA Georgia tag champs, NWA National Champions, and the World Class Championship Wrestling Champions in Texas. ★ Bob Windham arguably became the biggest name in wrestling of these three. He later wrestled as Black Jack Mulligan, and was a near-carbon copy of Black Jack Lanza. As a team, the Black Jacks won the WWA Indiana territory World Tag Team belts in 1971 from Wilbur Snyder and Paul Christy, and then became WWWF World Tag Team Champions in 1975 in a victory over Domenic DeNucci and Pat Barrett in Philadelphia. Windham was also used as a trouble-shooting referee.

The arrival of the fiery Mexican Pepper Gomez in the AWA was big news. Fans had heard about him for years from wrestling magazines. Pepper was to Texas what Verne Gagne was to Minnesota. He held the coveted Texas state title a record twelve times, overcoming Mister Moto, Duke Keomuka, Buddy Rogers, Gene Kiniski, El Medico, Tosh Togo (of the James Bond movie *Goldfinger* fame), Danny McShain, Don Manoukian, and Bill Watts. He also held the Texas tag team title with partners Luigi Macera, Rito Romero, Larry Chene, El Medico, Hogan Wharton, and Dory Dixon. ★ Californians remembered Pepper Gomez for the classic wars he and Ray Stevens engaged in for promoter Roy Shire in San Francisco. While wrestling for Shire, Gomez also held the NWA World Tag Team Championship seven times with partners Jose Lothario, Pedro Morales, Rocky Johnson, Pat Patterson, Al Madril, and even Ray Stevens.

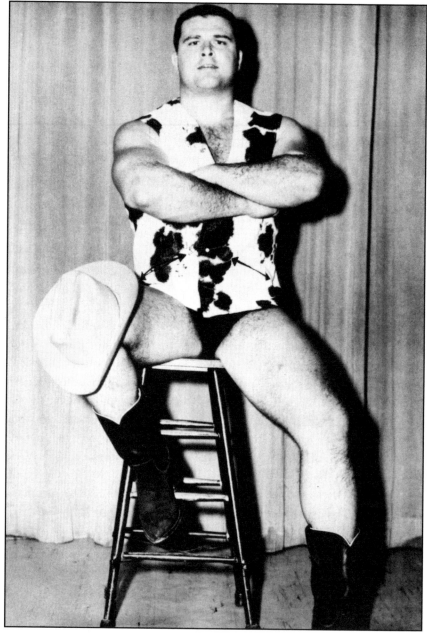

Voted by Wrestling News *magazine readers in 1968 as the AWA's most popular wrestler, the giant Cowboy Bill Watts was also a dominant force against foes like Larry Hennig, Lars Anderson, Doctor X, and even champion Verne Gagne.*

title shot against Gagne, which the champ won. It was the last fans would see of Bill Watts in the AWA for several years.

Another hot match on this card was a clash between Haggerty and Doctor X, which the Hard Boiled one lost when he was counted out while chasing the masked man around the ring. Doc made it back into the ring before the count

"SPORTS FACTS"

------------------------------ Published by ------------------------------
Minneapolis Boxing & Wrestling Club
605 DYCKMAN HOTEL   11   MINNEAPOLIS 2, MINNESOTA

Vol. 25, No. 10   BLOOMINGTON, MINNESOTA, SATURDAY, APRIL 19, 1969   25c PER COPY

Match of the Decade: Gagne vs. Watts for Title

Fans who are counting on strictly a scientific wrestling match tonight between champ Verne Gagne and Cowboy Bill Watts may be in for a mild surprise.

All indications are that the two main eventers will offer just that, but don't place too large a wager on that routine continuing for the entire match.

Neither Gagne or Watts is regarded as the pier-six type of brawler, but once tempers flare and planned strategy suddenly backfires, anything can happen.

"Yes, I'll admit that this could wind up as a brawl," Gagne offered.

Could This be a Brawl?

"This isn't my intention, and I doubt if Watts is thinking along these lines, but don't forget — there's a world championship at stake, and I certainly don't intend to release my grip on the title without the toughest fight I've ever shown," Gagne added.

It's history now that Gagne demanded and received the highest guarantee ever paid a wrestler in Minneapolis to go ahead with the title match against the Cowboy.

"Look, I'm not trying to fool anybody. Watts is big at 300 pounds, the guy moves like a cat, and his variety of holds and manuevers is unlimited. It's not like going against an alley fighter, where clever wrestling alone can do the job.

"This is going to take a supreme effort, and no one knows that better than I do. I admit that Watts is stronger than I am. He has a great sense of balance — and frankly my best manuever might just be to stay away from him for a while," Gagne stated.

Veteran wrestling fans figure it will be a showdown between the Cowboy's Oklahoma Stampede and Gagne's flying dropkicks, with the champ's sleeper not entirely forgotten either.

Watts knows what's at stake, and he knows what kind of an opponent he's meeting.

"Is it possible to say anything new about Gagne?" the Cowboy asked. "I do want fans to realize that I've waited a long time for this match and I don't plan to allow the opportunity to slip through my fingers. I think there's a way to beat Gagne. I'll find out soon, won't I?" he concluded.

* *   * *
Everyone Wants the Cowboy!

Apparently, there are more than a few promoters around the country who feel Cowboy Bill Watts has the ability to defeat Verne Gagne in tonight's big world championship bout.

Promoter Wally Karbo said this week that the phone in his Dyckman hotel office has been ringing constantly the last few days, and the callers are other big city promoters who want to book Watts in the very near future.

"These guys feel Watts can do it, and they want his name on a contract ahead of everyone else," Karbo said.

A few of those phone calls came from top wrestlers too. They wanted to be included on this card which is drawing national attention — but Karbo decided some time ago to use men who have been appearing here regularly, mostly because these grapplers represent the very best available anywhere.

CHALLENGER: COWBOY BILL WATTS

WORLD CHAMPION: VERNE GAGNE

April 19, 1969, Gagne versus Watts: wrestling's most anticipated and desired match. Bill Watts had defeated all comers in the AWA and Minnesota, and both he and fans wanted him to have his chance to defeat legendary champion Verne Gagne.

From the time of his debut in November of 1967, Cowboy Bill Watts got a monster push from the AWA, and rivaled Verne Gagne himself for sheer popularity with the fans. ★ Watts had celebrated runs in the WWWF in New York and the NWA in San Francisco before he came to the AWA. He gained national attention for turning on his partner in the WWWF, then-champion Bruno Sammartino. An article about him appeared in *Look* magazine in 1965: "The Rich Full Life of a Bad Guy." ★ Watts's stints in the WWWF, NWA, and AWA each lasted only a year or two. He would appear in a territory, be lavished with attention from promoters, and then disappear at the peak of his popularity. This was common practice with out-of-town wrestlers, who would stay in a territory only as long as they drew good crowds. ★ Watts appeared again in the AWA in 1973, but he was not given the same push as in his storied run of the 1960s.

Haggerty was in the Twin Cities to promote his part in the movie *Paint Your Wagon.* His appearances marked the end of his active ring career. Haggerty retired after his matches with Doctor X.

of ten, but Haggerty didn't. The rest of the card was rounded out with Billy Red Lyons beating Black Jack Lanza, a six-man tag team bout featuring Carpentier, Bastien, and Gomez getting the nod over the Vachons and Larry Hennig, and Luke Graham winning over Bob Brunelle in the opener.

The December 27 card saw Larry Hennig and Harley Race reunite for one final match in the Twin Cities. They were joined by Lars Anderson for a six-man tag bout against Billy Red Lyons, Red Bastien, and Pepper Gomez. The latter trio won the outing. The main event on the card was a final rematch between Haggerty and Doctor X, which the masked man won. When the decade ended, fans could only wonder if the 1970s could top it.

★ FOUR ★

THE 1970s

A NEW CHAMPION, DUOS DOMINATE

During the seventies, *All-Star Wrestling* on TV would begin telecasting in color and many of the old guard of wrestlers would give way to new names and younger talent.

★ 1970 ★

The hot news that kicked off the 1970s was the return of "the man who made Milwaukee famous," the one, the only, the Crusher! *All-Star Wrestling* reminded fans of the Crusher's injury back in August 1969, when he and Dick the Bruiser had their tag team belts lifted by Mad Dog and Butcher Vachon in Chicago. The injury, of course, was a "work," to give Crusher some requested time off from the ring. But he was ready to return, and the AWA was happy to have him.

St. Paul's Auditorium hosted the debut action of 1970. The main event was Pepper Gomez facing off with the still-unmasked Doctor X, but the semi-windup match was what fans came to see. The Crusher was back, and his opponent was one half of the AWA World Tag Team Champions: Butcher Vachon. Crusher got by the younger Vachon brother, and announced that Mad Dog was next on the list.

Their showdown was scheduled for January 17 in Minneapolis. Everyone expected Crusher to go 2 and 0 against the champs. An episode of *All-Star Wrestling* earlier in the day changed all that. The Vachons appeared on the show in a non-title match against Edouard Carpentier and young Bruce Kirk. When Kirk was injured, the Crusher charged in and attacked Mad Dog. The studio television audience and viewers at home saw Mad Dog's head open up with a wicked gash when Crusher rammed it into the ring post. When order was restored, Mad Dog was gone, reportedly rushed to a hospital for treatment.

Though fans were thrilled to see Crusher get a measure of revenge on his sworn enemy on *All-Star Wrestling*, they were disappointed at the main event later that evening, when Mad Dog canceled due to the injury sustained in the TV melee. The television encounter between Crusher and Mad Dog was meant as a build-up for their feud, but the injury to Vachon was real and unplanned. During the tussle with Crusher, Mad Dog proceeded to "blade" himself, but accidentally hit an artery and had to be taken to the hospital for stitches.

Crusher ended up teamed with Carpentier for the January 17 card to take on the tag combo of Larry Hennig and Lars Anderson. This helped cement the pairing of Crusher and Carpentier as a tag team with a shot at the Vachons and their championship belts.

Though the 1970s had just begun, the next *Sports Facts* blasted: "Crusher-Vachon Battles Could Be Classic Bloodshed of Decade." Promoters set up this rivalry to be the next major storyline, and fans loved it. On the January 28 card Crusher and Carpentier soundly defeated the Vachon brothers in a non-title match.

February 1 in Minneapolis saw a singles blood fest between Crusher and Mad Dog, giving the Milwaukee strongman more ammunition in his pleas for a title showdown. Hennig and Anderson had lost to Crusher and Carpentier on the previous card, but got a much-needed win over Gomez and Joe Scarpello in a special tag team feature. In another tag bout on the card, the Redheads got by the newly formed team of Black Jack Lanza and Doctor X. The Vachons were elusive about a title match, but Crusher defeated Mad Dog in the singles match. To add spice to the card, the still-masked Doctor X was back in the ring with his archenemy Billy Red Lyons, and came out on top.

A title match for the tag crown finally took place on March 1 in Minneapolis. It was an all-out brawl that saw the Vachons barely retain their championship and Carpentier become another victim of their ruthless tactics. It was later reported on *All-Star Wrestling* that the popular Frenchman sustained injuries that would keep him out of action for a couple of weeks. Crusher needed another partner, and promoters and fans enjoyed speculating about who it would be.

They got their answer on March 14 in Minneapolis, when it was announced that Crusher would pair up with none other than world champion Verne Gagne to face the Vachons. The four fought to an out-of-control no-contest, with all of them disqualified by the referee.

The action resumed in St. Paul on March 29—Easter Sunday—with a long-awaited main event clash between the Vachons and the Redheads. This was billed as a do-or-die match that might be the last shot at the championship for Lyons and Bastien. Though the popular Redheads won the match, they failed to gain the tag belts when they pinned the wrong Vachon brother. Butcher had entered the ring while the referee attempted to get Bastien back to his corner, and Lyons pinned Butcher instead of Mad Dog.

The Redheads weren't out of the action for long. At a St. Paul match on April 11, *Wrestling Facts* reported that promoter Eddie Williams wanted the fans to back him in his quest to recognize Lyons and Bastien as the champions because of their strong showing against the Vachons the week before.

Fans flooded the AWA with letters, and Eddie Williams and the fans got their rematch on April 18 in St. Paul. Mad Dog and Butcher again walked out of the ring with their title intact, and the fans saw Lyons injured (the storyline used to explain why Lyons would be gone from the AWA. Actually Lyons was leaving the territory to wrestle in Oklahoma for LeRoy McGurk) in the process. In another main event on this card, the Crusher tried, and failed, to reveal Doctor X's identity.

On the May 2 card in Minneapolis, Crusher was back for another shot at ripping X's hood off, but this match had a strange ending. Doctor X saved his mask thanks to the interference of a masked accomplice. Now there were two hooded grapplers on the scene. No one knew who the second masked man

Of note in the opener on the March 29 card was the debut of Jim Osborne, who wrestled to a draw against Bob Windham. Osborne played a major role later in the summer with Doctor X as his partner.

Whether he is suspended or not by the American Wrestling Alliance, promoter Eddie Williams is asking and hoping for the support of fans in his battle to recognize Red Bastien and Red Lyons as the world tag team champions. "I'll fight the AWA all the way," said Eddie. "But I need the fans behind me."

Williams suggested that the fans voice their opinions in letters to the AWA.

"It would be great if the fans flooded the AWA with letters backing me up," said Williams.

He suggests letters be written to the AWA in care of the Minneapolis Wrestling Club, 605 Dyckman Hotel, Minneapolis. The zip code is 55402.

Last Saturday on television, Williams argued his case in favor of the Redheads despite threats of violence by Mad Dog Vachon.

"You never know what Mad Dog will do. At one time I thought he was going to punch me," said Williams.

It was reported the following week on *All-Star Wrestling* that the wrestling club office was flooded with fans' letters in response to Williams' request. No doubt there were letters from fans who took the promoter's plea seriously, and it also showed the wrestling club that they still had another shot at presenting a Vachons vs. Redheads match.

— *Wrestling Facts,* April 11, 1970

was. Marty O'Neill posed the question to Doctor X on *All-Star Wrestling* and X replied, "You can call him Double X." One thing was for sure: whoever the guy was, he was a near–carbon copy of the Doc himself. And he was there to watch Doctor X's back.

The May 2 card also featured a six-man tag match. Pepper Gomez, Red Bastien, and Edouard Carpentier combined to face the Vachons and their partner for the night, Black Jack Lanza. The good guys won, with Bastien and Gomez gaining falls over both Vachons. The victory put them in line to be the next team to challenge Mad Dog and Butcher, on the assumption that if they were each able to beat a Vachon in the six-man match, they could probably do it again in a regulation match. With Lyons gone from the AWA, Bastien was in need of another partner, and Gomez fit the bill. The Red-Pepper combination got a chance to prove themselves in Minneapolis on May 9, but had to settle for winning only the match, not the title, when the Vachons were disqualified.

On May 16 in St. Paul, Bastien and Gomez got another disqualification win, this time over the masked X-men, and the Crusher spilled more of Mad Dog's blood.

Eddie Williams presented a world title match on the St. Paul card May 30. Verne Gagne agreed to defend his belt against Doctor X, but found he had to battle two opponents. The Doc's unknown friend Double X interfered, and his efforts disqualified the Doctor. Gagne decided that if the two X-men wanted to take their shots at him, he would get a partner and take them both on.

Gagne's choice was none other than popular and handsome Paul Diamond,

The popular Red-Pepper combination of Red Bastien and Pepper Gomez talking about an upcoming match against the Vachon Brothers with Marty O'Neill on All-Star Wrestling

who had defeated Doctor X in a TV match a few weeks earlier. Diamond had also defeated Double X on a previous card, so who better to be by the champ's side? The Gagne-Diamond combination did the trick against the masked duo on June 20 in Minneapolis, when they took two straight falls from them.

The summer of 1970 was a memorable one for wrestling fans. Gagne defended to Black Jack Lanza, the Red-Pepper combination continued to be a hot team, and Doctor X faced his toughest challenger to date: the legendary Bill Miller in his famous Mister M mask.

When the two clashed for the first time in St. Paul, the fans thought M had finally unmasked X. But it was later revealed that when the referee was knocked down—as part of the storyline of the match—X rolled under the

Huge Bill Miller stormed onto the wrestling scene hiding his identity as Mister M and claiming that if fellow wrestlers knew who he was, they wouldn't sign to fight him. His aggressive ring style took him all the way to the world championship.

ring and switched places with his partner Double X. So when Miller ripped the mask off, fans were surprised to see the face of Jim Osborne. The real Doctor X faced the giant M in a July rematch in Minneapolis, and managed to retain his identity.

In August, Doctor X had a falling-out with Black Jack Lanza and finally met his waterloo. Lanza, with the help of his manager Bobby Heenan, not only soundly defeated Doctor X, but left him bloodied and unmasked. But Doc threw a towel over his head to staunch the blood, and fans still didn't get a close look at his face. Out of this match, though, came something Doctor X had not received since he arrived on the Twin Cities scene three years earlier: the fans' support and cheers.

Finally, on the August 29 card in St. Paul, fans' three-year wait ended. Doctor X agreed to remove his mask if promoter Eddie Williams would grant him a return match against Black Jack Lanza. True to his word, X handed Williams his mask, revealing himself as Dick Beyer, from Syracuse, New York.

The real story was that Beyer was leaving the AWA, and it was his job to put Lanza over as the next big heel on the local scene. After this match, Beyer left the AWA for a world tour with his wife and children, wrestling as the Destroyer.

Another new tag team was unleashed that summer as well, as the Crusher joined forces with a newcomer to the AWA, Bull Bullinski. They made quick work of Larry Hennig and Lars Anderson, and claimed that the Vachons were next.

Larry Hennig with partner Lars Anderson bragging to announcer Marty O'Neill on TV's All-Star Wrestling

September saw Hennig and Anderson in a Battle of the Bullies showdown with the Vachons, but they fell short of winning the title. Next up for the hated Black Jack was a victory over Edouard Carpentier, in a match that promised the winner a title shot against Verne Gagne. Other notable feuds during the remainder of the year involved Hennig battling it out with Bull Bullinski, and the Crusher involved in a war with Lanza and his manager Bobby Heenan. Crusher referred to them as "Oil Can Harry" and "Irene"; together they were "the Odd Couple." Fans loved Crusher's antics and gave him their support.

The year ended with much controversy. Gagne and Carpentier met on October 17 and again on November 7 in Minneapolis, but the matches left fans uncertain which man should be champion. For the annual Thanksgiving card in Minneapolis on November 26, a Battle Royale was offered. New Japanese ace Shozo "Strong" Kobayashi managed to outlast the Vachons, Bastien, Gomez, Lanza, Diamond, Anderson, Hercules Cortez, and Bullinski to make his case as a challenger to Gagne.

As the year wound down fans were treated to the return of Hercules Cortez and also introduced to a cocky newcomer who would forever leave his mark on the AWA and in the Twin Cities. His name was Nick Bockwinkel.

Meanwhile, Verne Gagne was finally showing signs of age—at least according to the storyline. He had become the aging champion, and it was often reported that he could be slowing down. Speculation was rampant over who would eventually have the power to dethrone him.

Just who were the new challengers? Some of the 1960s contenders were still chasing Gagne, but now he had to match holds with guys like Baron Von Raschke, Lars Anderson, Black Jack Lanza, and a couple of foreign invaders who offered some especially exciting matches.

EXPERTS CLAIM 1970 COULD BE THE TOUGHEST YEAR YET FOR GAGNE

Champ Verne Gagne has been in and out of the Twin Cities lately, defending his world championship, and you can bet he didn't hear all the unfavorable comments that were being passed around last week.

Promoter Wally Karbo offered the opinion that 1970 might just be Gagne's toughest year since the popular ex-Robbinsdale High athlete joined the pro ranks.

"Gagne is another year older. His opponents are just as tough, and new, young wrestlers are moving up through the ranks. I think Gagne is in for a mighty tough year. His recent bouts with Cowboy Bill Watts indicate that big, tough wrestlers can take a lot out of a man," Karbo offered.

The list of challengers for Gagne continues to grow. The champ could keep busy right here in the Twin Cities meeting top men, but he feels the title should be available to anyone who can beat him on a coast-to-coast basis, not just here.

"It's the same old story, too," Gagne mused, "The young wrestlers build for that one big chance against the champion, while I have to methodically take 'em all, one at a time. Yes, I do get weary at times, but I'm in good condition and it hasn't created any real problems."

— *Sports Facts*, January 17, 1970

It didn't take Verne Gagne long to reply once he spotted the story in the January 17 issue of *Sports Facts*, pointing out that 1970 could be his toughest year yet, with the chance Gagne may not be in possession of the world heavyweight title belt a year from now.

"Yes, I saw the story and read it with a great deal of interest. Frankly, I was quite surprised to see Wally Karbo quoted the way he was. Karbo said I was another year older, my opponents are just as tough, and something has been taken out of me in bouts like the ones with Cowboy Bill Watts.

"Well, no one can argue that they are not another year older, it happens to all of us. But I think more concern should be placed on the fact I'm also a bit smarter as another year arrives.

"Sure, all the good young wrestlers want a crack at me to win the title. And I plan to meet them, too. But I can pace myself much better now, and actually, can be at full force when a younger opponent is tiring."

What does the champ see in 1970?

"Not much of a change from the pattern in effect now. I plan to continue wrestling all over the country. I will meet the top challengers offered by other promoters, and I feel confident I'll still have the title belt in January of 1971."

Gagne admitted that his biggest problem right now is coping with the rule book violations of the "pier six" type of wrestler.

"Everyone knows what these guys do. They gouge your eyes, carry hidden objects, kick, stomp, and what have you. This is the kind of wrestler who can put you in dry dock. I don't plan to fool with 'em anymore. They are trying to keep me from collecting a paycheck for my work. I'll put this type away early if it's at all possible," Gagne commented.

— *Sports Facts,* January 25, 1970

Shozo "Strong" Kobayashi came to the AWA at the urging of Gagne himself and was given Stan "Krusher" Kowalski as his American mouthpiece and manager. Gagne had wrestled Kobayashi when he toured Japan, and saw the potential for some great matches with the Japanese giant. Pairing him with Kowalski provided a built-in feud angle after the many battles the champ had over the years with Stan. But Kobayashi failed to win the championship and eventually left the AWA and the United States to return to his native Japan.

With Kobayashi gone from the local scene, Stan Kowalski was more determined than ever to find a wrestler who could finally end Gagne's long reign as champion. The next nominee had fans worried that perhaps Gagne's days with the belt were indeed numbered when Kowalski introduced the man known as "the Russian Bear," Ivan Koloff.

On January 18, 1971, Koloff had done the impossible and ended the nearly eight-year title reign of the legendary Bruno Sammartino in the WWWF, so he was a serious threat. Many of wrestling's elite had tried to topple Sammartino, including Kowalski himself, and all had failed. When Koloff pinned Sammartino at Madison Square Garden, you could have heard a pin drop. Fans all over Minnesota and the AWA wondered if their hero Verne Gagne could stand up to the Russian Bear.

"The Russian Bear," Ivan Koloff (at right), enjoyed the assistance of veteran Stan "Krusher" Kowalski as his manager and tag team partner.

★ 1971 ★

The talent roster in 1971 was similar to the previous year, and fans enjoyed outstanding wrestlers, interesting angles, and of course some great wrestling.

Larry Hennig and Lars Anderson got a hot push despite their losing record. They claimed to have a secret plan, and in every interview boasted that they were going to be the next World Tag Team Champions. Hennig had been to the top with two partners—Duke Hoffman and Harley Race—and not many doubted that he could do it again with Lars Anderson.

They started off the year by injuring Pepper Gomez during a confrontation on TV's *All-Star Wrestling*, which saw the popular Mexican star carried from the ring. To the fans' delight, giant Hercules Cortez came to Pepper's rescue, and he single-handedly cleared the ring of the Hennig-Anderson team.

With Gomez out of action, his partner Red Bastien lacked a teammate—but not for long. Hercules Cortez volunteered to fill his friend's commitments and partner with Bastien. The two teams would face each other for many months, in the Twin Cities and other AWA–promoted towns.

The really big news, though, was Nick Bockwinkel. Since the start of his career in 1954 he had played a babyface, but now the arrogant blonde was making his mark as a top heel. Bockwinkel started off strong by defeating popular Paul Diamond on January 16 in Minneapolis, the first of many victories.

Meanwhile, "Strong" Kobayashi, the Japanese ace, made it clear that he intended to take the world championship from Verne Gagne and return to his native country a hero. Stan "Big K" Kowalski was his mouthpiece, manager, and sometimes tag team partner. They posed a serious threat to Gagne and to the Vachons' tag team crown as well.

In the Twin Cities, Larry Hennig and Lars Anderson won another victory on the January 30 card in Minneapolis over Paul Diamond and Edouard Carpentier. This card featured one of the first showdowns between champion Verne Gagne and Kobayashi. Over 6,800 fans filled the auditorium to see the Japanese challenger get disqualified when the Big K interjected himself into the action.

On the February 7 card in Minneapolis, another showdown between Hennig and Anderson and Cortez and Bastien was on tap. Fans were assured that the winners would have their chance at tag champions Mad Dog and Butcher Vachon on the next St. Paul card on February 20. Hennig and Anderson were at their evil worst and were able to come out on top against their popular opponents—even though they won the match by using a chair.

They figured that because they were awarded the win, they had the title shot. But it didn't happen that way. Promoter Eddie Williams instead granted the match to Cortez and Bastien. Needless to say, this did not sit well with Hennig and Anderson.

The injury to Pepper Gomez during the TV match against Hennig and Anderson was a "worked" injury. He left the AWA and returned to wrestling on the West Coast.

In late 1970 Larry Hennig took a short tour of Japan with fellow AWA star Bob Windham. The two fared very well as a team. Not long after this tour Windham left the AWA and reappeared on the East Coast WWWF circuit as Black Jack Mulligan.

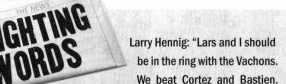

FIGHTING WORDS

Larry Hennig: "Lars and I should be in the ring with the Vachons. We beat Cortez and Bastien. Williams has joined forces with Karbo to connive against us. It's high time that these ruthless promoters be barred. We are the greatest tag team in wrestling and all the promoters know it. We are being pushed around because we refuse to bow to their demands for small purses. If we won the title we would be hard to deal with. That's why Williams refused to give us our rightful match with the Vachons."

Edouard Carpentier: "I never had a chance to protect myself in my match with Bockwinkel. This time I'll be ready for his charge. The defeat was embarrassing to me and I must gain revenge. My rival claims he will out-class me. I doubt that he can. I'll change his mind about a lot of things before our rematch is over. I'll be out to get him this time."

— *Wrestling Facts,* February 20, 1971

Pepper Gomez and Billy Red Lyons still nursing injuries suffered at the hands of Hennig and Anderson. — *Wrestling Facts*, February 20, 1971

Of course, the comment about Gomez and Lyons being injured was just another effort to support the notion in fans' minds that Hennig and Anderson were cripplers.
(Wrestling Facts)

As for Nick Bockwinkel, he brought national attention to himself when he whipped Carpentier in a record seventeen seconds. It was then, and today still is, considered a major upset, and proved that his campaign to get Gagne in a match had to be taken seriously.

Though Cortez and Bastien didn't come out victorious against the Vachons, they remained the most popular tag team on the local scene. They continued to meet Hennig and Anderson, as well as the combination of Kobayashi and

Hercules Cortez and Red Bastien became World Tag Team Champions in May 1971, but tragedy ended their reign when Cortez was killed in a car accident in July. During their time together, they were one of wrestling's most popular duos.

Big K. Red also linked up with Paul Diamond to get by the latter pair on March 7 in Minneapolis. On the same card, fans left disgruntled after seeing their hero, the Crusher, suffer a rare defeat at the hands of Black Jack Lanza.

On April 10, Hennig and Anderson were back in the ring against the Vachons in a match that saw them declared the winners—but they didn't get the belts. Mad Dog and Butcher were the crowd favorites by default against the rowdy Larry and Lars and were disqualified, thus retaining the championship.

The April 17 card featured something that had never been offered before in the Twin Cities: an eight-man tag team match. Hennig, Anderson, Bockwinkel, and Lanza (with the added advantage of Bobby Heenan in their corner) faced World Tag Team Champions Mad Dog and Butcher Vachon teamed up with Strong Kobayashi and the Big K.

Bockwinkel wanted to make a good showing to prove his challenge to Verne Gagne was legit. Hennig and Anderson wanted to keep their ranking as contenders to the Vachons' tag team title. Lanza wanted his own shot at Gagne, and was confident his chances could be improved by being on the victorious team.

As for the Vachons, they figured that if they could win, they might not have to defend their titles to Hennig and Anderson yet again. Kobayashi just wanted to get Gagne back in the ring for another shot at the title he came to the United States to get. The Big K added his years of tag team experience to the mix.

Who did the crowd put their support behind? At first, neither team was the clear favorite. But it didn't take long for the Vachons and their partners to garner some support. In the end, though, Hennig's team was victorious, but only after fans had witnessed one of the most exiting matches ever presented by the Minneapolis Wrestling Club.

On the May 22 edition of *All-Star Wrestling,* Marty O'Neill proclaimed at the top of the program: "Wrestling fans, we have new World Tag Team Champions! Last Saturday night, May 15, in Milwaukee, Red Bastien and Hercules Cortez defeated the Vachon Brothers to win the belts."

None of the wrestling organizations, including the AWA, issued official ratings, but articles ranking the top wrestlers were a staple in programs around the country. It gave fans a reason to support one team over another and often provided conversation between fans attending the night's card. After all, if they needed proof that their team was better than another, they had it in black and white in the program.

★ On the May 8 Minneapolis card, Cortez and Bastien lost to Kobayashi and Big K. But fans left the auditorium still convinced that their heroes were better. It was a psychological trick that worked in wrestling for years.

AWA RATES CORTEZ–BASTIEN TOP TEAM

The American Wrestling Alliance has named Hercules Cortez and Red Bastien the No. 1 challengers for the tag team championship held by Mad Dog and Butcher Vachon. The AWA ranks Larry Hennig and Lars Anderson No. 2, and Crusher and Bull Bullinski No. 3.

The lofty position pleased Cortez and Bastien, but Hennig blasted the ratings. "What a joke," snarled Hennig. "We aren't the No. 2 challengers to the champions."

— *Wrestling Facts,* May 1, 1971

The AWA sometimes assigned a special referee to officiate at championship matches. At the May 22 title match they sent Joe Blanchard. Blanchard was himself an outstanding wrestling star. In his native Texas, Joe was often in main events and was a former Texas state champion. But to the disappointment of Twin Cities fans, Blanchard never wrestled in Minnesota. Why Verne Gagne never used a star like Blanchard as a wrestler is unknown.

The June 19 card at the Minneapolis Auditorium marked the last publication of the popular wrestling program *Sports Facts.* After twenty-eight years, the Minneapolis Wrestling Club stopped publishing both *Sports Facts* and St. Paul's *Wrestling Facts.* It was the end of an era. Fans would no longer debate the programs' rating of the night's wrestlers or read stories about the matches they were about to see. Subsequent wrestling cards in the Twin Cities would offer only *Wrestling News,* a generic magazine with a typed lineup sheet insert for the current card. ★ To its credit, *Wrestling News* provided new and different photos, featuring the work of wrestling photographers such as Bob Ruiz, Bruce Krietzman, William Ondecko, Gloria Anthony, and Art Kristofferson. But the stories were repetitive, with little substance. Minneapolis and St. Paul weren't the only cities to suffer the loss of their programs. *Wrestling*

On the May 22 card in Minneapolis, Kobayashi got his last title shot against Verne Gagne in the main event. The Japanese challenger fell short of his goal.

On Saturday June 19, the Minneapolis Auditorium filled up with 8,229 fans to see the Crusher win a handicap match over his hated rivals Black Jack Lanza and his manager Bobby Heenan. This card also marked the debut of one of wrestling's most respected and talented grapplers, Billy Robinson, who defeated Kobayashi, to the delight of the crowd. Nick Bockwinkel took the measure of Bill Miller, who returned for this one show, and Hennig and Anderson kept their winning record intact by defeating the team of Paul Diamond and Sailor Art Thomas.

When the action returned to St. Paul on July 10, it featured new tag team champions Red Bastien and Hercules Cortez successfully defending their belts to Larry Hennig and Lars Anderson. In other matches, Billy Robinson continued to impress fans by beating the Big K, Art Thomas got the nod over veteran Jack Bence, and newcomer Don Muraco edged out Aldo Bogni.

Twin Cities fans had only that one opportunity to see Bastien and Cortez defend their championship. In the early morning hours of July 24, 1971, while driving back from Winnipeg, Hercules Cortez fell asleep at the wheel and lost control of the car. He was killed when the car went off the road, and partner Red Bastien suffered a leg injury. That night in Minneapolis, Cortez's place on the card was taken by Verne Gagne, who met Nick Bockwinkel in a non-title defense—a match the champ lost. The crowd was somber, but fans turned out in full force to show their support for Hercules with signs and banners.

This night also marked the Twin Cities debut of one of wrestling's biggest names: Ray Stevens. Fans often read about Stevens in the wrestling magazines. He was one of the biggest draws on the West Coast in 1960s wrestling, and Twin Cities fans were excited to finally see the blonde bomber in action. He won over TV jobber Jose Betancourt, who was a last-minute substitute for the injured Red Bastien.

With the AWA lacking tag team champions for the first time in its history, Hennig and Anderson made it clear they thought they deserved the title next, and they continued to defeat all their opponents. But the AWA announced in late August that Red Bastien should not have to forfeit the tag team title and allowed him to select a new teammate and retain the championship. His choice was none other than Milwaukee's favorite son, the Crusher. Naturally, this didn't sit well with Larry and Lars, who claimed once again that they had been robbed.

The new champions went on to successfully defend the AWA World Tag Team Title for the next five months before dropping it in Denver to the California team of Ray Stevens and Nick Bockwinkel. The pair had earned their shot at the championship by defeating the Crusher and Bullinski in several matches around the AWA, including a September 11 victory at the Minneapolis Auditorium.

★ 1972 ★

More than 7,300 wrestling fans filled the Minneapolis Auditorium for the year's inaugural card on January 15. They saw their hero the Crusher defeat Bockwinkel in the main event, and in a battle of scientific stars, Robinson got by Bastien in an exciting match. Fans also saw two new tag teams go at it: the Big K was now teaming with the Russian Bear, Ivan Koloff, and they defeated Bull Bullinski and Andre the Giant. Another newcomer to Minneapolis on the card was a young Dusty Rhodes.

In mid-January, Stevens and Bockwinkel became the new tag team champions when they downed the Crusher and Bastien in Denver. After the loss, the popular redheaded Bastien decided to leave the AWA and move his base of operations to Texas. Red immediately won over fans in the Lone Star State, and became the Texas champion.

The talent roster in the Twin Cities included Muraco, Koloff, Big K, the Crusher, Hennig, Rhodes, Robinson, Chris Markoff, and Doctor X, who had turned into a babyface and now enjoyed the fans' support. The Vachon Brothers returned for title matches against Stevens and Bockwinkel. Lars Anderson was suspended in the early months of the year, and former partner Hennig hooked up with Dusty Rhodes.

For the remainder of the year, Gagne defended against such challengers as Stevens, Koloff, and Bockwinkel. The new and popular team of Billy Robinson and Don Muraco were formidable opponents to champions Stevens and Bockwinkel. Doctor X continued as a fan favorite and was involved in many matches against Hennig, Rhodes, Koloff, and other heels.

As 1972 came to a close, fans packed the Minneapolis Auditorium on December 30 to see Ray Stevens and Nick Bockwinkel lose the AWA World Tag Team Championship to the popular combination of Verne Gagne and Billy Robinson. Stevens and Bockwinkel cried foul—of course—and a rematch was immediately ordered between the two teams. Promoters Wally Karbo and Eddie Williams assured Twin Cities fans that they were doing everything possible to get the match.

★ 1973 ★

The rematch was signed to take place in the St. Paul Civic Center on January 6. Promoter Eddie Williams told fans that he had to outbid every other top promoter in the country to get the match, but that the great fans of Minnesota deserved to see it, and money was not an issue if he could get the four grapplers to agree to terms.

As expected, Stevens and Bockwinkel were at their evil worst, and they were able to bring the belts back to their camp. In actuality their loss of the

News replaced the programs for the entire AWA. As a result, it no longer mattered whether you were in Minneapolis, Denver, Winnipeg, Milwaukee, or any other AWA promoted town: with the exception of the night's lineup sheet, *Wrestling News* was the same everywhere.

If fans had traveled to Milwaukee on July 10, they would have seen AWA World Champion Verne Gagne defending his title to Edouard Carpentier, Nick Bockwinkel winning by count-out over Dick the Bruiser, and both Wilbur Snyder and Baron Von Raschke disqualified in their match against each other. The AWA often presented cards on the same night in different cities.

For a couple of weeks after Cortez's death, while Bastien recuperated from his leg injury, the AWA had the Crusher and Bull Bullinski fill the champions' bookings. The AWA announced that they were going to give Bastien time to fully recover, and then decide what to do with the tag team title situation.

title on December 30 was done more to spark interest in the two teams' feud than anything else.

The other big news of the new year was a newcomer by the name of "Superstar" Billy Graham. Billy was a heel with an unbelievable physique and a talent for working the crowd with the microphone. Graham was supposedly the youngest brother of the famous Graham clan, Eddie, Dr. Jerry, and "Crazy" Luke, and claimed to be the best of them all. "Superstar" said that he was "the reflection of perfection, the number one selection," and told fans that they'd "seen the rest, now you're seeing the best!" His cocky and self-absorbed attitude made Billy a star the fans loved to hate.

The AWA gave Graham his first major push. He had worked briefly on the West Coast with "brother" Jerry Graham, but he soon tired of playing second fiddle. The Minneapolis Wrestling Club brought him to the Twin Cities, a move that proved successful for both Billy and the AWA.

Lars Anderson left the AWA in early March 1972 to wrestle in San Francisco for promoter Roy Shire. His suspension from the AWA explained his absence and showed fans that the AWA wouldn't tolerate his roughhouse tactics. Lars enjoyed the same success in California that he did in the Twin Cities, and became the NWA World Tag Team Champion with Paul De-Marco. They defeated Anderson's old nemeses Pepper Gomez and Rocky Johnson—father of modern movie star and WWE wrestler "the Rock"—for the honors.

"The reflection of perfection, the number one selection"—these were the words spoken by the arrogant "Superstar" Billy Graham.

Hailing from one of wrestling's dominant families, Eddie, Dr. Jerry, and "Crazy" Luke Graham left trails of broken bones behind them in the ring. Dropping his 275 pounds onto the Minnesota scene in the late 1960s, Luke was especially hated by fans.

Minneapolis fans had still more to buzz about, because football star Wahoo McDaniel was working the AWA territory. Wahoo's football career was legendary, and by this point he had already carved out a memorable wrestling career as well. Fans who were able to follow Texas wrestling were already acquainted with the Indian star, and they were confident he could take care of business. He didn't let them down.

During 1973, Wahoo and Billy Graham waged a war that ranked among the blood fests of the decade. Wahoo even challenged his blonde foe to the famous Indian Strap match. In this type of match, both contestants are connected at the wrist with a leather strap. To win, a wrestler must touch all four corner posts of the ring while still tied to his opponent. Wahoo won the war when he got to all four posts while dragging a helpless Graham behind him.

The big Russian Bear, Ivan Koloff, was still on the scene, and he and Graham wasted no time forming a formidable tag team combination. They had many battles against Wahoo, who was joined by partners including the Crusher and Bill Watts. These wrestlers were at the peak of their careers, and the fans were the real winners in getting to see them in action.

Five young newcomers appeared on the Twin Cities wrestling scene for the first time in 1973. Verne Gagne had trained another group of hopefuls, and this class would prove to be perhaps his most talented and successful ever. They became household names to longtime followers of Minnesota wrestling: Jim Brunzell, Ric Flair, Bob Bruggers, Ken Patera, and Gagne's own son, Greg Gagne.

All of Gagne's 1973 protégés except Bob Bruggers went on to win major championships in professional wrestling. Bruggers's career was cut short by injuries in a 1975 airplane accident.

Ed Francis became Hawaii's promoter in the 1970s. Both of his sons later joined the pro ranks and made their own marks in the game. The older son, Russ Francis, is also remembered for his days on the football field with the New England Patriots. Billy Francis stayed in the wrestling business longer than Russ, but the brothers were very popular wherever they wrestled. They would team in the AWA in the later 1970s. ★ Lord James Blears is probably better remembered for his role as a promoter in the 1974 movie *The Wrestler*, where he introduced Billy Taylor (played by Billy Robinson) to promoter Frank Bass (Ed Asner of the *Mary Tyler Moore Show*). In the movie, Blears backed Taylor to beat the aging champion Mike Bullard (Verne Gagne). ★ Blears is also remembered by Minnesota fans as a troubleshooting referee for several title matches later in the 1970s and early 1980s. During his illustrious career, Blears held many championships and tag team titles. In his day, he was as hated as any wrestler could be for his vile ways in the ring. In real life, he was a liked and well-respected gentleman of the game.

On the tag team scene, Dusty Rhodes decided to bring in his former "Texas Outlaw" partner, Dick Murdoch. The pair had held the coveted NWA World Tag Team Championship for the Michigan and Ohio territory for six months in 1970.

After the loss of their titles, Rhodes and Murdoch each went solo for awhile. When Dusty found his way to the AWA in 1972, he was quickly snatched up by Larry Hennig, who was in need of a partner after Lars Anderson was suspended. Early in the year, though, Hennig announced that he wanted to try the solo route for a bit, and in fact boasted that he felt it was time to retire Verne Gagne and take his title. This paved the way for Dick Murdoch, who was a better match for the colorful Rhodes, and together the Texas Outlaws were tops on the fans' hate parade for most of 1973.

Billy Robinson was still teaming with the young Hawaiian Don Muraco, and they came close on many occasions to relieving Stevens and Bockwinkel of their title belts. Billy and Don also were the odds-on favorites in matches against the Outlaws.

Two other all-time Hawaiian greats graced Twin Cities rings during 1973: former Hawaii State Champion Ed Francis and the colorful Lord James Blears.

An interesting team challenged Stevens and Bockwinkel for their title: the Crusher and Billy Robinson. Because of their wildly contrasting ring styles, Crusher—a brawler—and Bill—a scientific grappler—made a potent combination. Many times during 1973, they attempted unsuccessfully to snatch the belts away from the champions.

Throughout the year the array of stars performing in the Twin Cities grew; the list included veterans and favorites like Rene Goulet and Joe Scarpello and newcomers like Horst Hoffman and Vic Rossitani. Fans got what they had always been promised in the introduction to *All-Star Wrestling*: "the greatest wrestlers from around the world."

One particular tag team battle, on April 8 in St. Paul, drew a lot of fan attention because it was between two heel teams. Promoters rarely pitted heel against heel, but on this particular night, fans were treated to champions Stevens and Bockwinkel defending their championship to the rugged combo of Rhodes and Murdoch. In heel versus heel matches, fans usually side with one team over the other eventually, and on this night, they were solidly behind Dusty and Dick. It came down to who could dirty-wrestle the other more, and in the end, Ray and Nick proved they were the nastier of the two teams and retained their titles.

To determine the number-one contender for the singles world championship, a big sixteen-man Battle Royale headlined the May 6 card in St. Paul. Over 8,000 spectators were on hand for the action. Entered in the Royale were Khosrow Vaziri, Horst Hoffman, Geoff Port, Dick Murdoch, Jim Brunzell, Billy Graham, Rene Goulet, Ray Stevens, Wahoo McDaniel, Ken Patera, Mark Starr, Dusty Rhodes, Don Muraco, Billy Robinson, Vic Rossitani, and Reggie Parks. The winner was popular Billy Robinson, which made the fans happy—but not Verne Gagne. For many months, Billy had been asking for a title shot, and

Verne always seemed to have an excuse why he couldn't or wouldn't wrestle the English star. Though champ Gagne was popular with the fans, many felt that he was dodging a showdown with Robinson, a match fans wanted to see.

The question now was whether Robinson would get his title shot at Gagne. Promoters put the fight on hold with various excuses, and the more the promoters claimed they were finding it difficult to put the match together, the more the fans wanted to see it. Few doubted that when the match finally did happen, it would become a classic.

While he was waiting for his title shot, Billy continued his winning ways. Fans were thrilled when Robinson put Larry "Pretty Boy" Hennig out of action again with another broken leg.

Geoff Portz, a newcomer to the AWA, wrestled in the same "hooker" style as Robinson. Geoff resembled Verne Gagne in appearance, and a few fans even thought they would have made a good tag team. It was Robinson, though, who took on his fellow Englishman as a partner, and together they gave some exciting moments to the tag champions and other teams in the AWA.

Also returning in 1973 was St. Cloud great Lars Anderson, who made an announcement during an interview on *All-Star Wrestling:* "My name is Larry Heiniemi and I've got a secret," shouted Lars/Larry. "You may not remember me as Heiniemi, but that is my name, and I'm going back to my given name because I'm sick of being associated with all the stupid Swedes and Norwegians named Anderson!"

He went on to say, "I'm back to get Billy Robinson for putting my friend Larry Hennig out of action, and the other news is, I'm going to be joined shortly by a new partner, whose name will remain a secret at this time."

With that, Heiniemi ended the interview, but he left the fans with more questions than answers. They were curious about who Larry's tag team partner would be, and still weren't sure why he went back to his real name. As always, the comments were a way for promoters to build fan interest. Heiniemi had been gone from the territory for almost two years by then, and they probably felt he needed a different gig to gain popularity with the fans.

In late August, Heiniemi's new partner was unveiled. It was none other than his old college roommate from St. Cloud University, Les "Buddy" Wolfe. Wolfe was the one who got Larry interested in the grappling game; professional wrestling was the furthest thing from Larry's mind when he was in college. He had had an outstanding amateur background in the American Athletic Union (AAU) and collegiate ranks. But all that changed when Buddy Wolfe told him that he should try wrestling professionally. Larry sought out Verne Gagne and started training with him. Working with Verne at the time in his training camp was an unpretentious wrestler named Gene Anderson, who had a major impact on Larry shortly after he turned pro.

Another tag team came together this same year: the combination of Wahoo McDaniel and Billy Red Cloud, who would go on to challenge Heiniemi and Wolfe.

Unbeknown to Minnesota fans, Heiniemi and Wolfe had already teamed together in the Omaha territory back in 1972. At the time, Larry was still working as Lars Anderson, and he and Buddy were billed as "cousins."

Friends outside the ring and a dominant tag team inside, Larry Heiniemi and Les "Buddy"
Wolfe billed themselves as "cousins" and won matches all over the Midwest.

One of the biggest events of the year unfolded on September 15 in St. Paul, with not just one, but two simultaneous Battle Royales. As was always the case in a Battle Royale, a wrestler could only be eliminated by being tossed over the top rope to the floor. Pin falls and submission falls did not count.

For the first time in Twin Cities history, the Royale was staged with two rings set up side by side. With twelve wrestlers in each ring, the fans had double the action to keep track of. The winner in each ring would meet in a head-to-head showdown for a $50,000 purse. The entrants were both wrestlers already working the Twin Cities and several who came in for the chance to deposit the big prize into their bank account. There were twenty-three grapplers: Larry Hennig, Billy Graham, Buddy Wolfe, Ivan Koloff, Bill Miller, Hans Schmidt, Frank Valois, the Big K, Ric Flair, Bill Howard, Joe Scarpello, Billy Robinson, Wahoo McDaniel, Ken Patera, Geoff Portz, Red Bastien, Bill Watts, Andre the Giant, Sailor Art Thomas, Man Mountain Mike, Mighty Igor, Reggie

Parks, and Jack Pesek. Ray Stevens was also set to appear, but he had been injured earlier in the evening in a match against Billy Robinson.

The winner in Ring 1 was Andre the Giant, and in Ring 2, Billy Graham. The Superstar prevailed when he flipped the Giant over the top rope while Andre was attempting to fight with Graham's partner Ivan Koloff. Fans didn't leave the Civic Center happy that night as $50,000 walked out in the hands of a heel.

A lot of noise was made about the return once again of Larry "Pretty Boy" Hennig to Twin Cities rings. He had reportedly suffered yet another broken leg, this time at the hands of Billy Robinson, and Larry made no bones about the fact that he would make Robinson pay for the wages he'd lost while out of the ring. Joining the big Redhead in seeking revenge was his longtime friend and partner Larry Heiniemi, and their friend Buddy Wolfe.

When the fall season got under way in 1973, Superstar Billy Graham was still running roughshod over all opponents. On October 6 in St. Paul he was pitted against the one wrestler who was, in the fans' minds, the best bet to stop him: the Crusher. The match was a blood fest that saw Superstar disqualified for his unruly tactics. The Crusher may have been bloodied by his opponent, but he returned the favor in spades. Graham had a face of crimson and had to be all but carried from the ring when the Milwaukee strongman was finished.

By this time, the Heiniemi and Wolfe combination had been around for a while, and they didn't even have to win to remain a top draw. In most of their matches, they would be disqualified, or simply lose, but they still remained at the top of fans' hate lists. They were billed as "the Minnesota Wrecking Crew," which came from Heiniemi's days of working with "brother" Gene Anderson in southern rings under the same billing.

In November, it was announced that amateur mat great Chris Taylor was

THE MINNESOTA MAULERS

Luscious Larry Heiniemi, Beautiful Buddy Wolfe, and Pretty Boy Larry Hennig have signed a pact to not take over all of the titles in professional wrestling but also destroy and run out of the game a number of wrestlers.

As we have mentioned previously, Heiniemi recently imported Wolfe, a friend and teammate from their college days, to form a tag team. In addition it must be pointed out that Hennig not only has had ring experience with both men but has held the AWA World Tag Team Title on more than one occasion, so any combination of the three is not only dangerous but sure to be very effective.

Besides winning titles the three would love to run a few wrestlers out of the game, including Verne Gagne. Both Hennig and Heiniemi received early training from Gagne but today hate the champion with a passion. Both feel a victory over Gagne would be especially sweet as it would bring the victor not only the most prized title in wrestling but prove to the fans that the student is now the master of the teacher.

— *Wrestling News,* Fall 1973

going into training to become a professional wrestler. Chris was an Iowa State graduate, and he was trained by Verne Gagne. Taylor represented the United States in the 1972 Olympics in Germany in the heavyweight-plus division in both freestyle and Greco-Roman, winning a bronze medal. Fans learned on *All-Star Wrestling* that Gagne felt Chris would be unbeatable as a professional, and that he had also considered partnering Taylor with fellow Olympian Ken Patera.

A card on December 8 in Minneapolis saw another battle between the Crusher and Superstar Graham. This one ended when Graham received help from Larry Heiniemi and Buddy Wolfe, who jumped the Crusher, making it three-on-one. The bout was ruled a no-contest by the referee. For this card, Red Bastien had returned again to his hometown of Minneapolis and was teamed with Billy Robinson in a losing effort against champions Ray Stevens and Nick Bockwinkel. Red and Billy had earned the title match by gaining a non-title win over the champions on *All-Star Wrestling* in a two-of-three-falls battle.

To end the year, it was only natural for the Crusher to seek revenge on Superstar Graham. Crusher advised promoter Wally Karbo that he would get a partner and take on Graham, who could have either Heiniemi or Wolfe as his partner. Fans speculated about who the Crusher was going to team with. Marty O'Neill asked on TV if it might be the Bruiser, and the man from Milwaukee told him that his partner had to be meaner than Bruiser. Fans were both shocked and ecstatic when Crusher brought out none other than Mad Dog Vachon. This would be a classic team-up, but of course the question on everyone's mind was could these two even trust each other? Fans were reminded of the many wars and the bloodshed between the two. Graham partnered with Larry Heiniemi, but they were unable to defeat the determined Crusher and the Dog. The crowd of over 9,000 screaming fans saw the Superstar handed one of his rare defeats.

★ 1974 ★

The wild tag match in December paved the way for the first card of 1974. On January 4 in St. Paul, Mad Dog Vachon battled Superstar Graham to a bloody no-contest. In the main event on the same card, Ray Stevens and Nick Bockwinkel barely saved their championship belts again when they got by Robinson and Bastien. Big Chris Taylor made his first appearance in a pro ring on this card, and fans were impressed.

The Crusher and Mad Dog Vachon had caught on as a team, and they were given a shot at Stevens and Bockwinkel on February 17 in St. Paul. They won the match, but not the belts.

An especially interesting match took place early in the year between Germany's Horst Hoffman and England's Billy Robinson. Besides the international flavor it offered, the match showcased two of the game's most talented grapplers.

Who owns the tag team title belt? Nick Bockwinkel and Ray Stevens insist they are still champions, but Crusher and Mad Dog Vachon have the belts and refuse to part with them.

In a wild finish, with more than 7,000 fans howling at the St. Paul Civic Center Sunday, Mad Dog Vachon counted Bockwinkel and Stevens out after referee Chuck Svenson was knocked out. The title match found both teams battling outside the ring and forgetting the rules.

After Vachon and Crusher grabbed the belts and ran to their dressing rooms, the revived Svenson ordered them to return to the ring. When they refused he gave the match to the champions. However, Crusher and Vachon are protesting Svenson's decision. Stanley Blackburn, president of the American Wrestling Alliance, was to be in the Twin Cities Tuesday and will make a decision.

Promoter Eddie Williams said it will be up to Blackburn to determine who the champions are.

— *St. Paul Pioneer Press*

Though he probably had the ability to upset Robinson, Hoffman tossed out the rule book and was disqualified for his efforts. A brutal battle was also staged between Wahoo McDaniel and Larry Heiniemi that saw Larry's partner Buddy Wolfe get involved. Double-teamed, the popular Indian star lost the match.

On the same card, on February 17 in St. Paul, Chris Taylor scored another win when he beat veteran Moose Morowski. Greg Gagne won over Bob Re-

Mad Dog Vachon and the Crusher, battered and bloody, proudly display championship belts in a short-lived celebration. The belts were soon returned to rightful owners Ray Stevens and Nick Bockwinkel because of a disqualification.

mus, Baron Von Raschke toppled Italy's Tony Rocco, and Ric Flair pinned Paul Pearchmann in the opening bout.

For the March 9 card in Minneapolis, Wahoo McDaniel won the main event over Buddy Wolfe, who was disqualified when Heiniemi interfered. In other bouts the German team of Von Raschke and Hoffman won a controversial decision over the Olympians Ken Patera and Chris Taylor, who had been teamed up by Gagne.

McDaniel was still looking for revenge against Heiniemi and Wolfe. He was joined by the Crusher on March 24 in St. Paul and came out victorious when Larry and Buddy left the ring after having their heads handed to them by Crusher and Wahoo. In another tag bout on the card, the Von Raschke–Hoffman duo moved a notch closer to the top as they won over challengers Robinson and Bastien.

Dusty Rhodes returned to the Twin Cities on April 13, this time as a fan favorite. He was joined by Ken Patera in a losing battle against the unlikely team of Nick Bockwinkel and his partner for the night, Superstar Graham.

A newcomer to the Twin Cities was also on tap—Ivan Putski, who was a near–carbon copy of the Mighty Igor. Billed as hailing from Poland, just like Igor, Putski wore the same cut-off underwear under his trunks as Igor had, and had the same long hair and beard. His physique was similar to Igor's too.

Putski was immediately thrust into an "arm wrestling contest" with Superstar Billy Graham, and the two met many times during the remainder of the year. *All-Star Wrestling* promoted Ivan by showing video clips of him performing various feats of strength: holding back a speeding car with his legs while sitting against a wall, lifting the back of an automobile off of the ground, having a cement block placed on his head and then smashed with a sledgehammer. These were the same feats performed by "cousin" Igor years earlier, and fans were as amazed by Ivan's awesome power as they had been by Igor's. Ivan Putski was a hit.

For the previous few months, Larry Hennig had been working in the East Coast's WWWF territory, where he had grown a beard, dropped his "Pretty Boy" persona, and become Larry "the Axe" Hennig. When Larry returned to the AWA and the Twin Cities, his eastern adventures were the talk of every town he appeared in. With a new hold, name, and image, he was given a monster push as a top heel. The big redhead bellowed that he was now more confident than ever that he was going to eliminate hated rival Verne Gagne once and for all. Larry also announced that he intended to stop Greg Gagne as well. The feud between Hennig and the Gagnes was a hot ticket for the summer months of 1974.

The younger Gagne's career had been developing, and he had also formed a potent tag team combination with Jim Brunzell, who in his own right was developing into quite a wrestler. Jim, like Greg, had been trained by the elder Gagne, and his high-flying dropkicks were considered by some in the business to be the best they'd ever seen. Brunzell was a local boy from White Bear Lake, Minnesota, and had been a state high-jumping champion in high school. Due to

Ivan Putski never denied that he stole the Igor gimmick. He had been in the business just a couple of years and had only moderate success under his real name of Joe Bednarski in Florida. When the AWA was unable to lure Igor back to their rings, Ivan Putski was created. He used the name for the remainder of his active career. Since Putski and Igor didn't normally wrestle in the same territory, it didn't matter if Bednarski's character was a direct rip-off of Igor's successful Polish strongman gimmick. ★ The Minneapolis Wrestling Club did offer an explanation for the likeness between Igor and Putski. They explained that Ivan was a younger "cousin" to Igor.

In the early 1970s, Minnesota fans followed the friendly and powerful Ivan Putski as one of their favorites. Putski took on many battles with "Superstar" Billy Graham in an effort to prove who was the strongest wrestler in the AWA.

In 1974, Verne Gagne released *The Wrestler,* a movie based on his own life. He played the part of Mike Bullard, an aging champion who was always trying to bring wrestling's different leagues together in order to have just one "unified" champion. ★ The promoter in *The Wrestler* was Frank Bass, played by Ed Asner of *Mary Tyler Moore Show* fame, who was secretly working behind the champ's back to find a challenger to defeat him. Putting additional pressure on Bass was Bullard's wife, who didn't want her husband to die in the ring like Ray Gunkel, who had been the same age as Bullard. ★ The movie also starred Billy Robinson as Billy Taylor, a young hotshot brought in to challenge Bullard. The movie was crammed with many of the top AWA wrestlers of the time: Nick Bockwinkel, Ray Stevens, Wahoo McDaniel, "Superstar" Billy Graham, the Crusher and the Bruiser, Dusty Rhodes, Dick Murdoch, Wilbur Snyder, Eddie Graham, Hard Boiled Haggerty, and a very young Ric Flair all made appearances. Verne Gagne's close friend Joe Scarpello played the part of Jack Cutter, who dies when he is hit by a Ray Stevens knee drop off the top rope. In the end, as one would guess, the showdown between Mike Bullard and Billy Taylor comes to pass, and as he did so often in real life, the champ won.

his alliance with Greg Gagne, Brunzell was now on Hennig's hit list. As a team Greg and Brunzell were dubbed "the High Flyers" by the fans and the AWA.

Larry "the Axe" Hennig attempted to take on both Greg and Brunzell in handicap matches on more than one occasion. In one such encounter on June 29, he agreed to beat both wrestlers within twenty minutes or forfeit the match. He was able to get by Jim Brunzell, but when he failed to pin Greg before the time limit ran out, Hennig had to settle for the match going into the record books as a loss. This only intensified his desire to stop Greg and his partner.

Then Larry Hennig made another challenge, and this time it included

Verne Gagne too. "I'll team with Larry Heiniemi and Buddy Wolfe, and we'll destroy all three of you if you're not afraid to suffer humiliation in front of all your fans," Hennig said. Greg and Jim wasted no time in accepting the challenge, and neither did Gagne. The match was signed for Minneapolis on July 13. The battle line had been drawn, and this time Larry Hennig told all who cared to listen on *All-Star Wrestling* that he and his partners would once and for all eliminate the Gagne family and Jim Brunzell.

The first fall of the match gave the fans reason to be concerned: Buddy Wolfe was able to pin Greg's shoulders to the mat for a three count. But in his second fall, Greg came back to avenge himself when he pinned Wolfe. During the final fall of the match, Hennig and his partners had some communication and timing issues. Words were exchanged between the three brawlers, and then the unthinkable happened. In an attempt to drop one of his devastating "Axe" elbow smashes onto Greg Gagne, Hennig missed the target and accidentally landed on his own partner Larry Heiniemi. Taking advantage of Hennig's mistake, Greg was able to quickly roll the redhead onto the mat, pin his shoulders for a three count, and win the match. It was then that Heiniemi and Wolfe turned on Hennig and started to double-team their own partner. It was announced later that Heiniemi had suffered a broken wrist from the elbow drop Hennig delivered.

The other big news on the tag team front was that on July 21 in Green Bay, Wisconsin, the Crusher and Billy Robinson teamed together and defeated Ray

Hated Japanese star Kinji Shibuya delivers a karate chop to Wilbur Snyder, who holds partner Mitsu Arakawa in a painful abdominal stretch.

Larry "the Axe" Hennig, Luscious Larry Heiniemi, and Beautiful Buddy Wolfe were once known as the three Musketeers and in fact were regarded as one of the most deadly trios to ever form a friendship in wrestling.

Their friendship recently came to an abrupt ending when Hennig broke Heiniemi's wrist during a wild six-man tag team match. The incident occurred when Hennig landed on Heiniemi with one of his infamous elbow drops after an opponent escaped Heiniemi's grip.

Heiniemi and Wolfe claim that Hennig's move was deliberate. Luscious Larry, who at one time was Hennig's regular tag team partner, claims that the big redhead is jealous of the victory streak that the team of Heiniemi and Wolfe had run up.

Hennig on the other hand says that the thing was an accident but he certainly isn't going to back down from the challenges being thrown his way. The Axe says that he helped the pair from St. Cloud break into the game and that he is still capable of teaching them a few tricks.

Wolfe, who was standing in the corner when the incident took place, is certain that Hennig did it on purpose and claims that he will pay dearly for it. Wolfe said he will never trust another man at his side other than Larry Heiniemi. Beautiful Buddy also wants it known that he intends to break both of Hennig's arms and gain revenge for his longtime friend and partner Heiniemi.

— *Wrestling News,* Summer 1974

Stevens and Nick Bockwinkel for the AWA Tag Team Championship. To no one's surprise, the former champs cried foul, and demanded a rematch.

During an episode of *All-Star Wrestling*, promoter Wally Karbo decided to pit Stevens and Bockwinkel against the young "High Flyers," Greg Gagne and Jim Brunzell. But before the match could begin, the former champs called announcer Marty O'Neill to the center of the ring so that they could deliver some news. The TV studio audience was silent as the California duo began to speak, and then they were shocked when Ray and Nick announced that in an effort to get their championship back, they felt they needed a manager. Enter Bobby "the Brain" Heenan. Bobby told the fans that from now on he was going to handle everything for Stevens and Bockwinkel and that all they had to do was wrestle. He would handle their bookings, travel arrangements—everything.

Greg and Jim lived up to their billing as High Flyers in the match, and gave the former champions plenty to handle. The referee was accidentally hit and knocked unconscious by Brunzell, and that's when Bobby Heenan decided to make it a three-on-two battle. Nick, Ray, and Bobby launched an attack on their victims, and it appeared that two young careers were about to end.

Several wrestlers from the dressing room were called upon to restore order, but to no avail, as they were tossed out of the ring as quickly as they entered by Heenan and his team. One of them was big Larry "the Axe" Hennig. Fans naturally figured that he too would go after the High Flyers, but those watching—not to mention Stevens, Bockwinkel, and Heenan—got the shock of their lives when Hennig went completely berserk on the Heenan team and sent them running out of the ring. The big redhead then picked up the injured

Greg Gagne and carried him away. The studio audience was stunned, as were the viewers at home. Why would Hennig come to the rescue of his longtime ring foes?

In an interview after the match, Larry explained that though he had never had any love for the Gagnes or Brunzell, he couldn't in good conscience stand by and allow the mauling that was taking place. He further stated that he had a young son that maybe would enter the pro ranks someday, and that he wouldn't want him to be attacked in the way that Gagne and Brunzell were.

Just like that, Larry "the Axe" Hennig was now a babyface, and the most heroic wrestler in the eyes of the fans. For the remainder of the year, Larry was cheered not only in matches against his former partners Heiniemi and Wolfe, but also against the former champions Stevens, Bockwinkel, and their manager Bobby Heenan. And to further shock fans, he also joined Greg Gagne and Jim Brunzell in tag matches against all of his former friends.

With Hennig joining the good guys' camp, he, along with the Crusher, Billy Robinson, Ivan Putski, the High Flyers, and champion Verne Gagne, finished out 1974 as the fan favorites. In the heels' locker room were Stevens, Bockwinkel, Heiniemi, Wolfe, the tag team of Horst Hoffman and Baron Von Raschke, and Superstar Graham leading the charge for the bad boys.

Verne Gagne successfully defended his title to Horst Hoffman in St. Paul's Civic Center on September 28, and son Greg and Jim Brunzell copped a non-title win over Stevens and Bockwinkel, who were still in the hunt for a return match with the Crusher and Billy Robinson. On this card, fans saw the popular Englishman Billy Robinson defeat rugged Stan Pulaski, and also saw a young Bob Backlund from Princeton, Minnesota, go to a draw against veteran Bill Howard.

Back in Minneapolis on October 8, the tag team belts were on the line. To the delight of the crowd, Crusher and Robinson dispatched Stevens and Bockwinkel, despite having Bobby Heenan in their corner. Another tag bout on the card saw Gagne and Brunzell whipping Stan Pulaski and Yugo Babich, and in a special grudge bout, Larry Hennig battled to a torrid no-contest decision against his former friend Larry Heiniemi.

The action was back in St. Paul on October 12 with a main event that saw Larry Hennig and his former rival the Crusher pitted against Stevens and Bockwinkel. Rules for the match stipulated that the first three rows of ringside seats would be removed and that pins would count on the floor if the four brawlers fought their way out of the ring. The first fall ended with Nick holding Hennig's shoulders down for a three count. The Crusher evened things up in the second fall when he stopped Stevens. In the third and final fall, all hell broke loose when Greg Gagne and Jim Brunzell interfered to get at Stevens and Bockwinkel, and the referee disqualified everybody. Though they didn't win, Crusher and Hennig, along with Greg and Brunzell, got their licks in on Stevens, Bockwinkel, and Heenan.

On October 24 in Winnipeg, having Bobby Heenan at their side finally paid off when Stevens and Bockwinkel recaptured the AWA World Tag Team Cham-

Larry Hennig's babyface turn remains to this day one of the most remembered and talked-about angles that took place on *All-Star Wrestling.* For over a dozen years, Hennig had been the guy fans loved to hate, and he went out of his way to fuel their hatred. His babyface turn was first hinted at when he had his falling out with Heiniemi and Wolfe, and then materialized when he came to the aid of the fallen High Flyers. For the remainder of his active ring career, Larry Hennig was one of Minnesota's most popular grapplers.

The tag team match between the High Flyers and Pulaski and Babich was filmed, and was used as one of the opening scenes for the introduction to *All-Star Wrestling.*

pionship. Bobby Heenan was arguably more despised than the champions, and promoters had no trouble serving him to fans whenever he was available.

Three days later, on October 27, Minnesota wrestling fans witnessed something they thought they would never see: Verne Gagne and Larry Hennig in the same corner of a ring, as partners, to take on Stevens and Bockwinkel. The Civic Center in St. Paul played host to 6,223 fans who came to see the two former archenemies soundly defeat the arrogant new champions.

In November, Bobby Heenan introduced a new member in his "family" of wrestlers. His new charge tipped the scales at a whopping 320 pounds and was said to be from Russia. He was Boris Breznikoff, who Heenan claimed would not only protect him, but act as a policeman for the tag champions.

Twin Cities fans were in for another shocker before year's end. It happened on November 16 in St. Paul during a six-man tag team war. On one side was Larry Hennig, Ivan Putski, and Chris Taylor, and on the other were the hated Germans, Von Raschke and Horst Hoffman, and their partner Superstar Billy Graham. With the match even, the German duo suddenly turned on their blonde partner in the final fall, leaving Superstar prey to Hennig's devastating elbow smash and the resulting pin. The Baron and Hoffman threw up their hands and left the ring. Could Superstar Graham possibly be turning babyface? The question was on many fans' minds after the card.

On a cold night on December 7 at the Minneapolis Auditorium, they got their answer. Billy Graham faced off in a grudge match against the hated Baron Von Raschke. He would have won, too, had it not been for the Baron's partner hitting the Superstar with brass knuckles and knocking him senseless. Then the two Germans proceeded to do a double-team number on him. Fans were told on the next installment of *All-Star Wrestling* that Horst Hoffman had been suspended for his actions.

★ 1975 ★

Graham demanded that the AWA not suspend Hoffman, because he wanted to take both him and Von Raschke on in a grudge match to make them pay for their attack. For the revenge match, the Germans faced Superstar and his surprise partner, the American Dream, Dusty Rhodes. Big Dust had been gone from the local scene for a while, but fans who read the national wrestling magazines were kept abreast of his ring battles. Dusty had become a fan favorite, too, and was one of the top babyfaces in southern rings.

The fans were firmly on the side of Graham and Rhodes, hoping that they could not only thrash the Germans, but send them packing out of town as well. In Minneapolis on January 25, the "Dream Team" got in plenty of licks, but the ruthless tactics of the Baron and Hoffman proved superior—at least for this night. Of special note on this card was the first appearance of Russ Francis. Young Russ was known to pro football followers from his days with

Boris Breznikoff had an extensive wrestling background before coming to the AWA. He was better known in other territories, first as Bepo Mongol on the East Coast in WWWF rings, and later as Nicoli Volkoff in the same territory. He is not to be confused with the wrestler from the 1950s who wrestled as Nicoli Volkoff along with his "brother" Boris Volkoff.

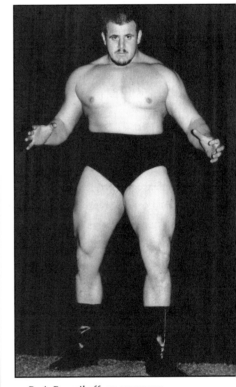

Boris Breznikoff, an enormous Russian managed by Bobby "the Brain" Heenan, acted as policeman for Nick Bockwinkel when Nick wore the world championship belt. Many an opponent found it hard to get past Breznikoff, and with Heenan in his corner the challenge was doubly tough.

the New England Patriots, and now the young Hawaiian was trying his hand at pro wrestling during the off-season.

The February 8 card back at the Minneapolis Auditorium saw two singles grudge matches on tap. In the main event, Horst Hoffman won by disqualification over the Superstar when Rhodes entered the action to assist his partner. In the other special main event, Von Raschke was able to get a win over Dusty when Hoffman interfered and hit Rhodes with a loaded glove. Nick Bockwinkel also appeared in a singles match and was able to come out on top over Larry Hennig. In a tag team match, the High Flyers won over Bobby Heenan and Boris Breznikoff.

Greg Gagne and Jim Brunzell were rewarded for that win on February 15 in Minneapolis. A crowd of 4,214 paying fans saw the High Flyers come incredibly close to upsetting champions Ray Stevens and Nick Bockwinkel, only to fall short when Greg was disqualified for coming off the top rope. In the other top match, Dusty Rhodes used the ring ropes to his advantage in gaining a pin fall over Horst Hoffman.

Action returned to St. Paul on March 8 with a Battle Royale as the main event. Andre "the Giant" Rousimoff, 7'4" and over 400 pounds, was in town, and he was the odds-on favorite to win the Royale. Promoter Eddie Williams signed thirteen of the top grapplers in the AWA to challenge him, with each posting $1,000 to enter. Williams matched their payments to make up the big prize of $25,000. The order of elimination went like this: Chris Taylor, Geoff Portz, Buddy Wolfe, Jim Brunzell, Larry Hennig, Boris Breznikoff, Superstar Graham, Ray Stevens, Dusty Rhodes, Nick Bockwinkel, and Billy Robinson. The Giant then tossed both Von Raschke and Hoffman out of the ring at the same time to win the purse. A huge crowd of 7,751 was on hand for the action.

Another battle in the war between Rhodes and Graham and the Germans was waged on April 12 in St. Paul, when each team added a third partner to the fold. The "Dream Team" had the services of Andre the Giant, and the Germans aligned with Boris Breznikoff: 5,340 fans saw the good guys win.

Naturally, this feud was hot enough to allow for another clash between the two teams, and on May 10 in St. Paul, promoter Eddie Williams added a twist to encourage fan interest. All four grapplers would be allowed to wear a glove on either fist. In past encounters Von Raschke had used a loaded glove to try to maim either Rhodes or Graham, but this time the playing field would be level. Only 3,341 fans attended the show, though. One reason could have been the lack of a solid supporting card. Those who did attend once again saw the Germans go home on the losing end of the battle.

Fans clamored for a title shot for Dusty Rhodes and Billy Graham, but it never came to pass. Superstar had finished up his tour of duty in the AWA, and he would soon be gone. On May 31 in Minneapolis, the champs defended their belts to Dusty, but he had his former partner Larry Hennig at his side instead of Graham. Hennig and Rhodes had been booed when they previously teamed

Before the February 15 card, Larry Heiniemi stunned viewers with his announcement on *All-Star Wrestling* that, win or lose against Billy Robinson on the upcoming card, he was retiring from professional wrestling. He told fans that after ten years in the business he had decided it was time to get out while he still had his health. The Luscious One went on to lose to Robinson that night in Minneapolis. And, true to his word, he was gone. ★ Apparently what Heiniemi forgot to mention was that he was only retiring from the AWA. He worked in other territories under the name of Lars Anderson for many years, and in the early 1980s took over promoting in Hawaii.

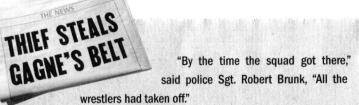

Verne Gagne successfully defended his American Wrestling Association world title against Nick Bockwinkel, but he lost the trophy, a $10,000 belt, to a thief.

During the bout Wednesday night at John O'Donnell Stadium, the belt rested on the time-keeper's table. After Gagne's triumph he strode to the table where officials were preparing to present it to him.

However, a thief ran by, grabbed the silver and diamond belt, and fled.

Police indicated Thursday that they had a few leads on the theft. They said they considered the report accurate and not a publicity stunt.

"By the time the squad got there," said police Sgt. Robert Brunk, "All the wrestlers had taken off."

He said Gagne claimed that "a young male Mexican with a ponytail took it and left in a car."

Gagne said he won the belt in 1960 but lost the title for a few years. He said he has been the recognized world champion for the past four years and had defended his title about once a month.

The wrestler from Minneapolis left about midnight Wednesday in his private plane. Police continued their investigation.

— Davenport, Iowa, newspaper, July 17, 1975

in 1972; now there were cheers everywhere they appeared. They gave a good account of themselves, but Nick and Ray were able to keep the title in the best-two-of-three-falls bout.

Major changes unfolded for Twin Cities fans over the remainder of the year. Nick Bockwinkel got a push in singles matches, and he lost a couple of close matches to Billy Robinson. Verne Gagne was on hand to meet Baron Von Raschke on June 28 in St. Paul, and Chris Taylor won a big one over Mad Dog Vachon when the latter was counted out of the ring. Their match made national headlines when it was telecast over ABC's *Wide World of Sports,* thanks to Taylor having become the biggest Olympian ever at a hefty 412 pounds. He competed in freestyle wrestling in Munich in 1972.

July ushered in the AWA debut of the Valiant Brothers, "Handsome" Jimmy and "Luscious" Johnny. The blonde "brothers" came to the territory boasting an explosive reputation on the East Coast, where they had been WWWF champions for a year, from May 8, 1974, to May 13, 1975. Every newsstand wrestling magazine had covered Jimmy and Johnny's exploits, and now they set their sights on the AWA World Tag Team Championship.

Fans got a taste of how good the Valiants were when they were co-winners of a Battle Royale in Minneapolis on July 25. Throughout the entire match, Jimmy and Johnny stayed close together and eliminated both big Chris Taylor and Larry Hennig. After Hennig was gone, Dusty Rhodes charged in and chased the boisterous blondes from the ring.

Twin Cities fans constantly saw old wrestlers leave and new ones come in. Such was the case with the Valiants, who were joined in the AWA by newcomer Joe LeDuc and the returning Pampero Firpo. Others rounding out local cards included the usual faces like Bull Bullinski, the High Flyers, Hennig, Tay-

Arrogant and obnoxious, "Luscious" Johnny and "Handsome" Jimmy Valiant never hesitated to declare their superiority. When they strutted to the ring, loudly booing fans always made clear how much they hated the blonde brothers.

lor, Putski, Stevens, Bockwinkel, and Buddy Wolfe. Wolfe got a new partner by the name of Kim Duk.

On August 16, 1975, in Chicago's International Amphitheatre, the beer-drinking cousins Crusher and Bruiser were back together, and they took back the AWA World Tag Team Titles from Ray Stevens and Nick Bockwinkel.

Nick Bockwinkel got a big push as a singles wrestler and demanded a shot at Gagne's world championship. Bobby Heenan imported Big Bad Bob Duncum to assist Nick when he needed it, or to be his partner when Ray Stevens wasn't available.

To get the ball rolling toward a title showdown with Gagne, Nick was joined by his manager Bobby Heenan on September 13 in St. Paul against Verne Gagne and son Greg. The Gagnes were disqualified when Greg managed to take a pair of brass knuckles from Heenan and was caught with them by the referee. To the fans' delight, after the Gagnes were disqualified, they used the knuckles on both Bockwinkel and Heenan.

Another of the big rivalries was between master of the claw hold Baron Von Raschke and Argentina's Pampero Firpo, who was using a claw hold of his own that he called "El Garfio." Von Raschke was also feuding with Billy Robinson for the right to a championship match with Gagne.

Jimmy and Johnny Valiant were now considered the number-one challengers to new champions Crusher and Bruiser. Minneapolis promoter Wally Karbo gave the arrogant brothers a stiff test on his September 27 card at the auditorium. They battled to a no-contest against the Canadian team of Joe LeDuc and Mad Dog Vachon. All four wrestlers were counted out of the ring by the referee.

The biggest happening of the year unfolded on November 8 in St. Paul. On that night, Verne Gagne lost his coveted world title to Nick Bockwinkel, a title Nick had dreamed about since his arrival in the AWA back on December 10, 1970.

The next card in Minneapolis was the annual Thanksgiving show. New champion Nick Bockwinkel make his first local title defense in front of 5,140 spectators against Larry "the Axe" Hennig. The other main event for the night was a Texas Death Match between Baron Von Raschke and Pampero Firpo, which the Wild Bull of the Pampas won.

On December 6, the Crusher and the Bruiser were in town to meet Stevens and Bockwinkel in a rematch. Because Bobby Heenan always liked to stick his nose into Ray and Nick's business, Crusher and Bruiser told fans that Firpo would be in their corner to counter Heenan should he get out of his chair at ringside. The first fall of the match saw Bruiser get the win over champion Bockwinkel. In the second fall, Nick returned the favor by stopping Bruiser. In the final fall, Heenan tried to help his team, but was held back by Firpo, allowing Crusher to pin Stevens.

The last card for the year was on December 14 in St. Paul. In the main event, Verne Gagne battled with Bob Duncum in a match ruled a no-contest when Greg Gagne and Bobby Heenan came in to help their respective partners. In a tag team match on the card, the Valiant Brothers were disqualified against the Crusher and Pampero Firpo when Jimmy used brass knuckles on the Crusher, busting him open. The feature event on the card was also a bloody one. Larry Hennig had to settle for a no-decision with Joe LeDuc when the latter hit the Axe over the head with a chair.

Verne Gagne wanted to take time off from his normal wrestling schedule and attend to business behind the scenes. In order to do that, he had to find a new champion to fill his shoes, and Nick Bockwinkel fit the bill perfectly. In Bockwinkel he had a man he trusted and knew would be a good representative for the AWA. Nick was a solid wrestler, a great worker, and talented on the mic, and he had paid his dues since he started wrestling in 1954. Though he and Gagne were enemies in the public eye, behind the scenes they were friends and had the greatest respect for each other. ★ For the next five years, Nick Bockwinkel represented the AWA as its world champion. And though he was unpopular with the fans, he was an excellent technical wrestler when he wanted to be. He defended the belt on average three nights a week, not only in AWA-promoted cities, but also in towns outside the AWA.

Of special note on the March 21 card was the debut of the latest rookies to emerge from Verne Gagne's training camp: Dick Blood, Buck Zumhofe, Jan Nelson, and Scott Irwin. Three of these grapplers went on to have outstanding ring careers. ★ After leaving the AWA, Dick Blood went to the Atlantic Coast territory and became the legendary Ricky Steamboat. He won the NWA world title and also the Intercontinental Championship in the WWF in the 1980s. He retired to run a highly touted wrestling school along with former wrestlers Harley Race and Les Thatcher. ★ Scott Irwin wrestled under various names before finishing his career under his given name. As "Thor the Viking" he had a huge heel push in Florida, and in the WWWF he was Eric of the Yukon Lumberjacks. But Scott had his greatest success under a mask. He and his real-life brother Bill Irwin donned hoods to become the Super Destroyers in Texas. Then in the early 1980s, Scott and Bill, minus their masks, were the Long Riders in the AWA. ★ Buck Zumhofe remained a constant in the AWA and got a minor push in matches against Bobby Heenan and his family of wrestlers. Buck was also involved in a feud for the light heavyweight title with Steve Regal and Mike Graham. ★ Sadly, Jan Nelson, who was predicted to be a bright star, died shortly after he got into the wrestling business.

Many of the feuds that ended 1975 were still being waged in the early months of the new year. Any combination of the Heenans against the Gagnes and Jim Brunzell still had the fans' interest, and the Valiant Brothers were still trying to prove themselves worthy of a title shot against Crusher and Bruiser.

The Valiants had stiff competition for the top spot, though. Other teams included the High Flyers and three new teams. Black Jack Lanza returned to rejoin manager Bobby Heenan and was teamed with Bob Duncum. Baron Von Raschke formed an alliance with Mad Dog Vachon, and former opponents Hennig and LeDuc joined forces.

Andre the Giant was brought back in for a first-of-its-kind Two-Ring Twenty-Two-Man Battle Royale on March 21 in Minneapolis. Eleven wrestlers entered each ring, and the two winners battled it out for the $25,000 purse. The winner in ring number one was Black Jack Lanza, and huge Olympian Chris Taylor prevailed in ring number two. Lanza lost to Chris in the singles match that followed the Royale.

After winning the Battle Royale, Chris Taylor was rewarded with a title shot against Bockwinkel on April 10 in Minneapolis. The big guy had the champ on the run, but was disqualified when he lost his temper and rammed Nick's head into the steel ring post. In a rematch on May 8, again in Minneapolis, Chris won when Bockwinkel was disqualified.

On this same card Jimmy and Johnny Valiant met Larry Hennig and Pampero Firpo in a bout that stipulated that the losers would have to leave the AWA. Though Hennig and Firpo were the winners, Firpo never again appeared in an AWA ring. As for the Valiant Brothers, their bid to be AWA champions ended with the loss, and they were gone.

Fans got to see two favorites return for the May 22 card in Minneapolis when Red Bastien unsuccessfully challenged Bockwinkel for the AWA world title, and former champion Wilbur Snyder won by disqualification over Japan's Kim Duk.

A bloody battle between Joe LeDuc and Mad Dog Vachon was on tap in St. Paul on June 5, with former AWA and NWA world champion Gene Kiniski officiating as a special referee. Russ Francis was also back for this card to join the High Flyers in victory over Bobby Heenan, Black Jack Lanza, and Bob Duncum. In a singles match on the card, Francis also emerged victorious over Duncum.

Buddy Wolfe received a title match with Bockwinkel on July 17 in St. Paul, and the Crusher was back in town for the card. So, too, was Indian star Billy Red Cloud.

A big event took place on June 25. In a televised main event, Japanese champion Antonio Inoki met the great world champion boxer Muhammad Ali in a Martial Arts Championship Match. The match was shown in cities all over the United States and Japan via closed-circuit television, with each territory also presenting their own supporting card. Twin Cities fans filed into the

St. Paul Auditorium to see a card that was fought in Chicago. It featured Verne Gagne meeting Nick Bockwinkel in a rematch for the AWA world title, and Crusher and Bruiser defending their tag belts to Lanza and Duncum.

On July 23, Lanza and Duncum managed what they failed to accomplish in Chicago the month before, taking the AWA World Tag Team Title from the Crusher and the Bruiser. The list of challengers to the new champions was staggering. The fan favorites, heavily pushed by the AWA, were Greg Gagne and Jim Brunzell, followed by Mad Dog Vachon and Baron Von Raschke, and Larry Hennig and Joe LeDuc. But the Crusher and the Bruiser were first in line.

The rematch for the tag team title took place in St. Paul on September 24, but the Crusher and the Bruiser failed to recapture their belts when they were disqualified. In a special non-title bout on the card, Russ Francis surprised champion Nick Bockwinkel with a rare defeat. In another feature bout, Mad Dog Vachon lost to "High Chief" Peter Miavia, a newcomer to the AWA. Miavia was an instant sensation and battled all the major heels, even earning a title match against Bockwinkel.

The October 29 match in St. Paul was co-promoted by Eddie Williams and Wally Karbo. The main event featured Bockwinkel and Ray Stevens back together against Verne Gagne and the Crusher. Gagne bolstered his chances for a rematch with Bockwinkel when he pinned the champ to win the match. Peter Miavia kept his winning streak alive by downing Baron Von Raschke, and it earned him a shot at the championship on the next card.

The title match took place in St. Paul on November 12. Though he didn't win the title, every fan in the building left convinced that Miavia was better than Nick Bockwinkel, at least for the night. The other big news for this card was the local debut of former WWWF champion Pedro Morales, who at the last minute substituted for Greg Gagne in a tag match against the new team of Moose Morowski, who had returned to the AWA, and his French partner Pierre Poisson. Pedro and Jim Brunzell made quick work of them.

The Crusher and Mad Dog Vachon ended their partnership and were battling once again. Back to his heel ways, Vachon teamed up with Von Raschke to form one of the most ruthless tag teams ever to appear in Minnesota. Crusher and Mad Dog met two times in November, and each match was a bloodbath reminiscent of their earlier wars in the mid-1960s and early 1970s.

What is considered one of the all-time best matches in AWA history took place on December 17 in St. Paul. On that night, Jim Brunzell went solo and wrestled champion Nick Bockwinkel to a sixty-minute draw. Surprisingly, neither Bobby Heenan, Nick's manager, nor Greg Gagne, Brunzell's partner, interfered in the match to help their partners.

The entire match was a seesaw battle of holds and counter-holds. If fans had any doubts that Bockwinkel was an excellent ring technician if he wanted to be, this match dispelled them. When the hour had expired, both Jim and Nick were totally spent.

Though the Ali versus Inoki match-up was highly publicized, the match was considered a flop. Inoki was on his back the entire match, and used his feet to keep the champ away. The long and boring match was eventually ruled a draw. It did mark a milestone, though: the use of closed-circuit TV would become the future of professional wrestling. Less than a decade later, cable television forever changed the wrestling business with pay-per-view events.

Modern-day Hollywood star and WWE wrestler the Rock is the grandson of Peter Miavia.

During a trip to Japan for a tournament, Brunzell and Bockwinkel joined up as a tag team. Because in the United States they were enemies, their partnership was never acknowledged. Jim Brunzell wanted to become a heel, but the AWA never let it happen. Had he been allowed to turn on partner Greg Gagne, it would have been a hot ticket.

Nineteen seventy-seven brought a newcomer to Minneapolis and St. Paul: a masked grappler calling himself the Super Destroyer, billed as coming from Parts Unknown. Also making his AWA debut was former Canadian football player Angelo "King Kong" Mosca. Later in the year, he and the masked man combined their talents to form a formidable team and become challengers for the tag team championship.

For the first card of the year, on January 16, the action was at the Minneapolis Auditorium. Billy Robinson failed in another bid to become world champion—he won the match, but not the belt, when Nick Bockwinkel was disqualified.

In a shocking turn of events during the early months of 1977, viewers of *All-Star Wrestling* saw "the Crippler" Ray Stevens refuse to play second fiddle to manager Bobby Heenan and his family of wrestlers. When Heenan was presented with a Manager of the Year trophy but rudely pushed away Stevens's congratulations, the grappler punched Heenan and grabbed the trophy. Saying, "This represents my contract," he shattered the trophy on the corner ring post. Stevens then grabbed the microphone and told the TV audience that he was tired of being treated like an idiot by Heenan.

Bobby Heenan bellowed that Stevens was an ingrate, and that he needed to be taught a lesson. He sent Black Jack Lanza against the Crippler on the January 16 card. Stevens came out the winner and enjoyed the cheers of the crowd.

The second chapter in the Stevens-Heenan feud played out on February 20 in St. Paul. This time around the Crippler stopped Bob Duncum. Now fans had seen him clearly defeat both tag team champions in consecutive singles matches. The buzz was that Ray's former partner Nick Bockwinkel could very well be next. And if Ray found the right wrestler to join him, he might even defeat Lanza and Duncum for their title, too.

Quick to offer his services to Stevens was Larry "the Axe" Hennig. He still had his own scores to settle with the Heenan family, and what better way to salve his wounds than to team with Stevens? They were scheduled against Lanza and Duncum for a title shot on March 6 in St. Paul. However, at match time Bobby Heenan claimed that Black Jack was unable to wrestle due to an injury. Thinking his team would be relieved of their match obligation, the crafty manager was shocked when the promoter told him that he would have to wrestle in Lanza's place. Though he protested, he was further advised that if he didn't get in the ring, Lanza and Duncum would be stripped of their belts. Fans were treated to a donnybrook that saw Hennig and Stevens solidly trounce Heenan and Duncum.

Fans rushed to get tickets for the Minneapolis card on March 20 when it was announced that Stevens would get a chance at his former friend Nick Bockwinkel. Even though Nick's title would not be on the line in the grudge battle, fans anticipated the champion getting a thrashing by the Crippler. They definitely got their wish.

On this same card, the High Flyers went to a draw against a tag team new to the AWA: veteran Roger Kirby and his teammate from the Central States region, Lord Alfred Hayes. Hayes advised everyone that he was taking over the masked Super Destroyer's contract, thus becoming his manager.

Billy Francis and his brother Russ returned to the AWA to add their names as challengers for the World Tag Team Title. They got by Bob Duncum and Angelo Mosca in Minneapolis on the May 1 card, which featured the second meeting between Stevens and Bockwinkel in the main event. This time, with the title at stake, Nick was able to come out on top.

Wrestling returned to Bloomington on May 20 at the Metropolitan Sports Center, which was home to the Minnesota North Stars hockey team. In the main event, Verne Gagne was joined by Billy Robinson and former rival Ray Stevens in a victory over Bobby Heenan's championship family, AWA world champ Nick Bockwinkel and the AWA World Tag Team titleholders Bob Duncum and Black Jack Lanza. Also on the card, Miavia continued his winning streak by defeating Angelo Mosca, Pedro Morales edged out Roger Kirby, and in a rare babyface battle, Jim Brunzell had a thirty-minute broadway against Billy Francis.

On the June 24 card in Minneapolis, Verne Gagne teamed up with Stevens again to try to win the tag belts from Lanza and Duncum. When the match ended, fans believed Gagne and Ray had won, as Gagne had effectively applied his sleeper hold to Black Jack and put him out. But the decision was reversed when AWA president Stanley Blackburn ruled that Duncum should have been in the ring, not Lanza.

The Heenan clan weren't the only ones who wanted to stop Stevens and his newfound popularity. The Crippler was joined by another of his former rivals: Milwaukee strongman the Crusher. Together they battled Lord Alfred Hayes's team of Mosca and Super Destroyer, but they were defeated on August 5 at the St. Paul Civic Center.

Billy Robinson was still getting the mega push as the number-one challenger to Bockwinkel. He had wrestled to a draw against the champ, and also scored the winning pin falls in a number of six-man tag matches, with Nick being the

THE CRIPPLER AND THE AXE

Ray "the Crippler" Stevens has joined with former enemy Larry "the Axe" Hennig to put Heenan and his men Lanza, Duncum, and Bockwinkel out of action by this time breaking their bones. And the fans are behind the Crippler all the way.

— *Wrestling News,* August 1977

When mentioning the top wrestlers in the world one name is always on the list of every promoter in the country, and that man is the huge product of Robbinsdale, Minnesota, Larry "the Axe" Hennig. At close to three hundred pounds, the big redhead has remained a force to be reckoned with on the AWA mat circuit.

Hennig began under former world champion Verne Gagne about twenty years ago, and to this day can hold his own with the best in the game. At first he appeared as one of the top referees in the sport, and then ventured into what has become a very explosive career.

Now calling himself "the Axe" and sporting a full red beard, Larry Hennig remains not only popular but a never-ending title contender as well.

— *Wrestling News*, August 1977

victim of those pins. Billy further gained momentum on the August 5 card when he scored an impressive win over former WWWF champion Pedro Morales.

On July 7 in Winnipeg, the High Flyers saw their dream as a team become reality when they captured the World Tag Team Title from Black Jack Lanza and Bob Duncum. They celebrated on *All-Star Wrestling* by telling their fans that they would defend the belt with honor to all worthy contenders.

Another war heated up between the Crusher and the Super Destroyer. Crusher called him "Super-Dummy" on *All-Star Wrestling,* infuriating the masked man and his manager Lord Alfred Hayes. They had several grudge battles with nothing settled.

In a move meant to embarrass Hayes and Super Destroyer, the Crusher challenged them to a handicap match. The Milwaukee favorite had been attacked on TV by the duo and wanted revenge. But he was told by promoter Wally Karbo that he would have to get a partner—so Crusher went over to the ring, reached underneath it, and pulled out grubby, dirty George "Scrap Iron" Gadaski. George was a capable wrestler, but never a regular winner in the ring. His primary job was to referee and set up the ring.

Crusher told Karbo that if he had to have a partner, Gadaski would fit the bill because he had dirt under his fingernails. This didn't sit well with the dapper Lord Alfred Hayes, who claimed that it was beneath him to get in the ring with a common man like Gadaski. But the partnership was accepted over his objections.

For the big annual Thanksgiving card on November 24 in Minneapolis, fans cheered on Crusher and his new partner and saw them win when Super Destroyer was pinned by Crusher. In frustration, Hayes stormed from the ring, leaving his partner behind.

As the year was winding down, fans were treated to a flashback to 1976 when Nick Bockwinkel defended his title to Jim Brunzell. Though the champ took the only fall, those in attendance couldn't help but be impressed with the performance of the high-jumping Brunzell.

A rematch was set to take place on this card between Crusher and Gadaski and Hayes and Super Destroyer. However, on the day of the match, it was announced that Crusher's mother had passed away, so his place was taken by Larry Hennig. This one went to Hayes and his buddy when the masked man got a pin fall on the big redhead and Gadaski was knocked out with a foreign object wielded by Lord Alfred.

To end the year and give the fans a Christmas present, Wally Karbo presented a Tuxedo Match between the Crusher and Lord Alfred Hayes. The first wrestler to completely tear off the other's tuxedo would be the winner. Naturally, Crusher won over his overdressed opponent. The other big bout for this card saw a successful title defense by Greg Gagne and Jim Brunzell over Super Destroyer and Angelo Mosca, winning by disqualification.

★ 1978 ★

Since the Crusher had disposed of Lord Alfred Hayes on the last card of 1977, it was only fitting that he should be on the first card of 1978 to face Hayes's charge, the Super Destroyer. To make it interesting, and to further humiliate Hayes, George Gadaski was again recruited, but not for the actual match this time. Scrap Iron was there to see that Lord Alfred didn't interfere—and to make sure he didn't, the crafty manager was handcuffed to George at ringside. A crowd of 4,675 fans was on hand on January 13 in Minneapolis to see the Crusher give the masked Super D a sound beating, and Hayes could do nothing to prevent it.

A couple of newcomers showed up on the card, too. Though they were new faces to Twin Cities fans, they both came with solid reputations in the business. One was charismatic Rufus R. Jones from Dillon, South Carolina. Rufus was well known in the Central States region and St. Louis, where he formed a team with former world champion Pat O'Connor that had the distinction of never being defeated.

The other newcomer was a second-generation grappler by the name of Bob Orton, Jr. His father, the elder Orton, was a major player in the game during the 1950s and 1960s, holding many championships during his storied career. In his early matches in the AWA, Bob Jr. switched back and forth from scientific to roughneck wrestling. Fans were unsure what to make of him in his early outings.

Another new face in AWA rings was someone every fan who read any of the national wrestling magazines had heard about: Pat Patterson, whose reputation on the West Coast was legendary. Pat and Ray Stevens had been the top tag team in San Francisco for many years before Ray moved his base of operations to the AWA in 1971. They had held the NWA World Tag Team Title twice. Now that Stevens was a fan favorite, everyone wondered if his former partner would challenge him, or if they would re-form their once-feared combination and pick up where they left off.

The question was answered on the February 26 card in Minneapolis. Stevens was signed to face Rufus R. Jones, and though fans had expected to see a clean match, they soon found out that the Crippler had returned to his heel ways. To further prove this point, Pat Patterson interfered in the match, causing Stevens to be disqualified.

Fans knew about Rufus's outstanding tag team combination with Pat O'Connor, and how they had never lost a match. When Jones was double-teamed by Stevens and Patterson, Rufus decided to seek the help of the former world champion and challenge the two blondes to a match. On March 19 in St. Paul, Stevens and Patterson did what no other tag team had ever done: they defeated Pat O'Connor and Rufus R. Jones. And one other thing was accomplished: Ray Stevens and Pat Patterson were a heel team again.

Jones, frustrated by his defeat, decided that to counter the roughhouse tactics of Stevens and Patterson, he needed someone who could fight as dirty as they did. Enter the Crusher. With Milwaukee's favorite son at his side, the colorful Jones was able to stop the California duo on April 7 in Minneapolis when Rufus pinned Stevens. The duo vowed to be even more ruthless in future matches.

Fans still weren't sure what to make of Bob Orton, Jr. Was he someone they should support, or was he a rule breaker? Bobby Heenan provided the answer when he announced he was taking the young Orton under his wing and teaming him with Black Jack Lanza. The two cowboys became instant threats to the High Flyers' hold on the tag team title, and Heenan anticipated getting the title back in his family.

Verne Gagne fell short in an effort to regain his world title on June 30 in St. Paul. The former champion put Nick Bockwinkel to sleep with his dreaded sleeper hold in the first fall of the match, but the wily champion got himself disqualified in the second fall. Thus Gagne won the war, but not the title.

A new masked man was on this card, too. Lord Alfred Hayes introduced him as hailing from Gibraltar and weighing in at an incredible 320 pounds—the Super Destroyer Mark II.

The new Super D Mark II was joined by manager Hayes to give him credibility in a tag match against young Evan Johnson and his partner, the greatest AWA masked man of all time, Doctor X. For the July 14 card in Minneapolis, Dick Beyer reprised his X role and helped defeat Super D Mark II.

In the main event on this card, Stevens and Patterson used every foul trick in the book in a bid to take the tag team title from Gagne and Brunzell. When the latter tired of being fouled by the blondes, they lost their tempers and got disqualified, losing the match but keeping the title.

An old favorite returned for this card, too: the Mighty Igor, who was now working without his longtime manager/mentor Ivan Kalmikoff. Igor was appearing in front of a new generation of fans. His childlike Polish strongman gimmick had been around for fourteen years, and had even been copied to great effect by Ivan Putski a few years earlier, but to these fans it was fresh.

All-Star Wrestling announced that the Crusher had unmasked the original Super Destroyer in a Denver match, and that he then left the AWA. That was only a partial truth. Super Destroyer did leave, but not after a match in Denver with the Crusher. In fact, no such match or unmasking ever took place. ★ In reality, the AWA told Super Destroyer that they thought it was time his identity was revealed. Super D disagreed, feeling that it wouldn't benefit his career, and he walked out on his future AWA commitments. This left Lord Alfred Hayes without a masked man, so the new Super Destroyer Mark II was unveiled.

Verne Gagne and Billy Robinson challenged Stevens and Patterson's winning streak on the July 28 card in Minneapolis, but had to settle for a victory by disqualification. Another new feud broke out on *All-Star Wrestling* between Larry Hennig and Super Destroyer II, and they clashed on this card as well. Hennig came out on the short end of things when he was counted out of the ring for fighting with Lord Alfred Hayes.

Another meeting between Gagne and Robinson and Stevens and Patterson took place before 4,179 fans on August 25 in Minneapolis, and this time the Blonde Bombers from California managed to squeak out a win. But the good guys won out in another tag bout on the same card: Hennig teamed with Rufus R. Jones to bounce Hayes and Super D II. In the main event, Bockwinkel successfully defended his title to Greg Gagne.

Jim Brunzell injured a leg in a charity softball game before a card on September 8 in Minneapolis, and was unable to fulfill a title defense with partner Greg Gagne against challengers Stevens and Patterson. Rookie Steve Olsonoski took Brunzell's place in the match, but Ray and Pat proved too much for them.

Brunzell's injury ended up costing the High Flyers their championship. On September 22, AWA president Stanley Blackburn sent a telegram from his office in Corpus Christi, Texas, to the Minneapolis Wrestling Club. He wrote: "After much consideration and review of all facts regarding Brunzell's injuries which were unrelated to wrestling and because of hardships it has created to the many promoters of AWA, I have no other alternative but to strip the tag team title from Gagne and Brunzell and through default award it to Pat Patterson and Ray Stevens."

The year 1978 came to a close with things left unsettled between Larry Hennig and the Super Destroyer II and Hayes. With a solid lineup, and especially with the tag team championship in the hands of a pair of heels, the AWA had plenty with which to draw fans in the coming year.

Stripping the title from the High Flyers was a promotional move, to avoid having Greg and Jim lose their belts. Handing the championship to heels Stevens and Patterson further incited the fans' hatred of the new champions, because they didn't win the title in the ring.

★ 1979 ★

The new year started off strong with the tag champions defending on the first card of the year, on January 14 in Minneapolis. Their opponents were the Crusher and Igor Vodik. This card also marked the return of Doug "Mr. High" Gilbert, who was back after a long and successful tour of Georgia and various southern cities, where he forged a name for himself while wrestling under a mask as "the Professional." Of course none of this was revealed to Twin Cities fans.

In February, three huge Japanese stars made appearances in the AWA. On a Minneapolis card on February 11, Giant Baba challenged champion Nick Bockwinkel for the title, but had to settle for a disqualification win. In a tag team match, the High Flyers were back together and whipped Tommy "Jumbo" Tsurata and his partner Tenyru. Billy Robinson, who had been billed as the "Brit-

It was common in professional wrestling to use a "suspension" to explain why a wrestler was no longer working in a particular territory. In the case of Bobby Heenan, Verne Gagne—who was the real AWA boss—sent Bobby to Atlanta for a while to work for promoter Ole Anderson. Black Jack Lanza also left the AWA, complaining of shabby treatment by promoters, to work with Heenan in Atlanta, as did the Crusher, and Heenan and Lanza carried their feud with Crusher to Atlanta.

Like him or hate him, it is hard to argue that Bobby "the Brain" Heenan wasn't the greatest wrestling manager ever. In the AWA, he managed top stars like Black Jack Lanza, Bob Duncum, Ray Stevens, and Nick Bockwinkel. His numerous battles with the Crusher are still remembered as classics.

ish Empire Champion" since he first arrived on the scene back in 1971, found himself defending that title to Cecil DuBois (the AWA name of Alexis Smirnoff) from Montreal.

A big announcement that fans widely approved of came via another telegram from AWA president Stanley Blackburn to promoter Wally Karbo: "As of January 10, 1979, wrestling privileges and all managerial activities extended to Bobby Heenan by AWA have been suspended and revoked indefinitely by this governing body. The last unacceptable action by Bobby Heenan has been reviewed by a special committee and its conclusion is adamant and there will be no reconsideration."

There were more suspensions that year. The big Texan Stan Hansen had come to the AWA to team with Bob Duncum, and together they were pushed as monster heels. But during a TV match in which Duncum and Hansen mauled Steve Olsonoski and Tom Stone, promoter Wally Karbo jumped up on the ring apron to signal the referee to stop the match. When Wally did this, Hansen ran over and clobbered him so hard that Karbo was carried unconscious to the dressing room.

The AWA immediately suspended Hansen for his actions. Stan pled innocent, claiming that he didn't know who Karbo was. "It was my first time in town. All I saw was someone jumping in the ring. I thought he was a crazed fan who may have had a gun or knife." Duncum, on the other hand, said that the whole thing was a plot arranged by Karbo and the AWA to break up his great new team.

On another tag team front, Stevens and Patterson were still feuding with Verne Gagne and Billy Robinson. They managed to injure the popular English star and temporarily put him on the shelf. Frustrated with the constant back-alley tactics displayed by the Californians, Gagne decided to take some drastic measures. He announced that in order to defeat wrestlers like Stevens and Patterson, he would obviously need a wrestler at his side who could give Ray and Pat a taste of their own medicine—and asked his longtime enemy Mad Dog Vachon to be his partner!

This was genius promoting at its best. The formula had worked many times over the years—not just in the Twin Cities, but in other territories as well. Take two sworn enemies and have them bury the hatchet to destroy two mutual foes, and the fans would love it. Everybody was buzzing about the new team and whether Gagne could trust the Dog at his side.

At the first encounter between the two teams, in Minneapolis on April 15, the champions would only agree to get in the ring with Gagne and Mad Dog if their title was not on the line. The challengers responded that if that was the only way to make the match happen, then it was okay with them. Actually, this was yet another promotional angle: this way, Stevens and Patterson could lose and still retain the championship. And lose they did.

The Gagne-Stevens-Patterson feud almost overshadowed the arrival of a wrestler who would play a major role in the future of the AWA and the Twin Cities—indeed, the entire state of Minnesota. His name was Jesse Ventura. He was initially compared to no less than the late, great, and colorful Gorgeous George. Jesse boasted of his great strength and claimed that he was the strongest wrestler to ever hit these parts. His ring style and appearance were reminiscent of one "Superstar" Billy Graham, whom fans still remembered from a few years earlier. In fact, Ventura claimed that Graham had been his hero and an inspiration to him when he decided to become a professional wrestler.

With Jesse bragging of his strength and physique, it was only natural that he be challenged by Paul Ellering, who though a relative rookie in the business had one of the best builds in wrestling at the time. They clashed in a "pose down" contest on the June 3 card in St. Paul, and when the fans voted that Ellering had the better body, Ventura was even more determined to prove his superiority.

On June 6 in Winnipeg, Gagne and Vachon again got their hands on Stevens and Patterson, and snatched the AWA World Tag Team Championship away from the blonde bad boys in the process. Fans rejoiced when they heard that the nearly year-long reign of terror by Stevens and Patterson had come to an end. The unlikely combination of Gagne and the Dog jelled, and they went on to defend the championship for over a year.

Top among their challengers were, of course, Stevens and Patterson, who were gunning for a rematch. When the two teams faced each other again on August 5 in Minneapolis, fans saw the champions prove their title win wasn't a fluke as they defeated Ray and Pat a second time.

In the fall, action in Twin Cities rings remained hot as Gagne and Vachon dealt with team after team of challengers. They were assisted by Billy Robinson, who had returned fully recovered from his injuries.

Lord Alfred Hayes's masked protégé Super Destroyer Mark II added his name to the list of contenders for the tag team title when his Lordship introduced Super Destroyer Mark III, giving Hayes an opportunity to manage them to the title. Still another new combination was formed when Jesse Ventura joined forces with newcomer Adrian Adonis.

As the year came to a close, fans were treated to a visit from Andre the Giant, who held Bockwinkel to a one-hour draw on November 4 in Minneapolis. The card also saw the debut of powerful and popular Dino Bravo from Montreal.

In his second Minneapolis match on November 22, Bravo showed fans what he was made of when he got the best of Lord Hayes. In the main event, his Lordship's pair of masked Super Ds failed in their bid to unseat Gagne and Vachon for the championship.

Then in a startling turn of events, Super Destroyer Mark II was defeated in a TV match on *All-Star Wrestling* by the mighty Dino Bravo. The masked man blamed his manager Lord Hayes for the loss and fired him on the spot. But that wasn't all: Super D II announced that his new manager was none other than Bobby Heenan, who had recently been reinstated by the AWA.

On the big Christmas card in Minneapolis. Dino Bravo did further damage by defeating Mark III and unmasking him. Then Mad Dog Vachon managed to pull the mask off Mark II in their wild contest against each other. Mark II, however, was able to cover his face and run from the ring, remaining unidentified. But in the real surprise of the evening, the Crusher buried the hatchet with Hayes and they trounced world champion Nick Bockwinkel and Bobby Heenan in a tag match.

In the opening match, a wrestler billed as "Farmer" Blackwell dropped all of his 468 pounds on his opponent Ricky Hunter. Blackwell was going to be very big—no pun intended—in the next year.

★ FIVE ★

THE 1980s AND 1990s
WRESTLING GOES NATIONAL

A sea change came to professional wrestling in the 1980s, though not everybody could see it at the time. Crowds in the Twin Cities and all over the AWA increased at an incredible rate, and those crowds were made up of younger fans. Many factors contributed to the attendance increases, but the primary reason was a new breed of wrestler. Hulk Hogan and other colorful characters like Jesse Ventura, Jerry Blackwell, and Sheik Adnan El Kaissey were major draws.

Larger-than-life personalities brought in fans who otherwise would have had no interest in professional wrestling. Their cockiness, arrogance, and jive-talking caught the attention of these new ticket buyers, who came out in droves to cheer, boo, shout, and have a good time at the wrestling matches. It became normal for cards to draw 15,000 for an average show, and when something extra spectacular was on tap, those numbers soared closer to 18,000 or 20,000.

Wrestling's popularity soared all over the country in the 1980s. In the mid-South, stars like the Junkyard Dog, Hacksaw Duggan, and Ted DiBiase were to their fans what Hulk, Ventura, and the Sheik were to the AWA. Wrestling had become big business, and the cool place to be.

★ 1980 ★

Verne Gagne was the first big story of the decade in Twin Cities wrestling, capturing the coveted International Wrestling Alliance (IWA) title while on tour in Japan by defeating Japanese star Rusher Kimura. After the match, Gagne told reporters that he also planned to win back the AWA world title from Nick Bockwinkel. To add to his honors, Gagne still held the World Tag Team Title with Mad Dog Vachon. Before his big win in Japan, there were rumors that Gagne was thinking about retiring, but instead the former University of Minnesota grappler was only getting better.

Gagne's rivals in the Twin Cities wanted him back home defending his titles, not traveling halfway around the world for more glory. Ray Stevens and Pat Patterson were considered the best bet to topple the tag team champs if they got the chance. The team of Jesse Ventura and Adrian Adonis was also getting attention with a string of victories.

The biggest noise came from "Farmer" Blackwell, who had debuted on the last card of 1979. In an explosive TV interview Blackwell issued a challenge: "Have you ever seen a four-hundred-pound stone dropped on something? Well, I'll tell you just what happens when something of that great size is dropped on an object—it's crushed! And that's just what I intend to do to any wrestlers who step in the ring with me—crush them." Calling himself a "crusher" was a sure bet to provoke a certain grappler from Milwaukee. If that wasn't challenge enough, Blackwell also offered $5,000 to any wrestler who could body slam him. He claimed that it had never been done.

On March 23 in St. Paul another classic feud played out between Hayes and Heenan and their partners—Super Destroyer III and Crusher for Hayes, Bockwinkel and Super Destroyer II for Heenan—in a six-man tag match. Bockwinkel, Heenan, and Super D II lost to Hayes, Crusher, and Super D III when III pinned II.

The match rules stipulated that the losing side's masked man would be forced to unmask. On the next *All-Star Wrestling* program, Heenan got an ultimatum from promoter Wally Karbo: remove Super D II's mask or they'd both be suspended. Super D II had lost his mask on the last card of 1979, but he was able to cover his face and keep his identity secret. This time, though, he had no choice, and Heenan made his man take off his hood, revealing the grappler underneath it as "Matt Burns."

In St. Paul on June 1, Gagne and Vachon saved their tag team championship when challengers Ventura and Adonis, calling themselves the East-West Connection, were disqualified. From the way they tore at each other in the match, there was little doubt the two teams would meet again.

An interesting contest between Dino Bravo and huge Jerry Blackwell took place on this same card: an arm wrestling match, with the winner to receive $5,000. Things were going Blackwell's way until the one and only Crusher entered the ring to dispute Jerry's claim to the Crusher name. The distraction gave Bravo the win over Jerry, who attempted to take out his wrath on the Crusher. Fans had anticipated this feud since the moment Blackwell first set foot in an AWA ring, and this was just the beginning.

On June 22 in Minneapolis, fans were treated to a title defense by Nick Bockwinkel against Japan's Jumbo Tsurata, which saw the cocky champion save his title by disqualification. Other notables on the card were Giant Baba and Mexican newcomer Tito Santana.

Bockwinkel's days as world champion came to an abrupt end when former champion Verne Gagne finally got him back in the ring in Chicago on July 18. On this night, fans saw an unusually aggressive and persistent Gagne completely dominate Bockwinkel to regain the title he had lost to Nick back in 1975.

Winning the AWA world title indirectly cost the new champion the World Tag Team Title he held with Mad Dog Vachon when AWA president Stanley Blackburn issued a ruling that would strip Gagne and the Dog of their belts.

After defeating Bockwinkel for the singles title, Gagne decided to take a well-deserved vacation in Europe for three weeks, which was approved by Mr. Blackburn. However, trouble was brewing in Denver while Gagne relaxed. Earlier in July, he and Mad Dog had fought a wild title match against Jesse Ventura and Adrian Adonis that ended with much controversy. Denver promoter Gene Reed had long sought a rematch for his city, and the AWA championship committee agreed. Somehow, though, Gagne wasn't notified of the Denver rematch, which was set for July 27. When he failed to make the match, the East-West Connection was awarded the decision, and by default, the tag team title.

On July 20 in Minneapolis, the original Crusher and the would-be Crusher, Jerry Blackwell, clashed in a Battle of the Crushers main event that was one of the bloodiest and wildest encounters ever staged in the Mill City. When the two brawlers got completely out of control, the referee ruled the match a no-contest, and disqualified them both.

The name "Matt Burns" was an inside joke. Wrestlers often got mat burns, similar to rug burns, from the canvas in the ring. Mark II's real name was Bob Remus, and he had been trained by Verne Gagne in 1974. Remus had wrestled in the AWA under his real name, but few fans remembered him. Later in his career, Remus would return to the AWA as Sergeant Slaughter.

All-Star Wrestling broke the news about Gagne and Vachon being stripped of the tag team title, angering fans and ensuring sympathy for the pair and hatred for Ventura and Adonis. Most importantly, it allowed Gagne and Vachon to lose the belts without having to be defeated in the ring. Gagne was then free to defend his newly won singles championship, and Mad Dog kept busy feuding with the East-West Connection, either with other partners or in singles matches.

Sworn enemies all through the 1960s, oftentimes fighting over the AWA world title, Mad Dog Vachon and Verne Gagne buried the hatchet in the late 1970s because they hated Ray Stevens and Pat Patterson more than they despised each other. Their efforts paid off when they defeated the blonde team to win their championship belts.

A big-name grappler new to the AWA made his presence known on this same card. He was Big John Studd, who had already carved out a reputation in the WWWF. Trained by Killer Kowalski, John and his dreaded heart punch had stopped many a wrestler in their tracks. This night, his victim was young Steve Olsonoski.

Wrestling promoters often acted as though wrestling fans wouldn't remember anything that happened more than a month ago. On the October 12 card in St. Paul, Super Destroyer Mark II returned as a babyface for a six-man tag match, teamed with Greg Gagne and Dino Bravo against Bobby Heenan's trio of Nick Bockwinkel, Ray Stevens, and Pat Patterson. It hadn't been long since Stevens had turned his back on Heenan and his family of wrestlers, but promoters didn't mention that. On this night, Ray was back to his usual evil self and reunited with Heenan, and they emerged victorious.

A Battle Royale was on tap for the November 2 extravaganza in St. Paul. Fifteen of wrestling's best tore into each other for the $50,000 prize. The participants were Andre the Giant, the Crusher, Mad Dog Vachon, Greg Gagne, Dino Bravo, Angelo "King Kong" Mosca, Buck Zumhofe, Jerry Blackwell, Nick Bockwinkel, Bobby "the Brain" Heenan, Jesse "the Body" Ventura, "Golden Boy" Adrian Adonis, Steve Regal, Chris Markoff, and Evan Johnson. As an added incentive, the victor was promised a shot at Verne Gagne for the title.

Huge Jerry Blackwell outlasted his adversaries and pocketed the money. The Mountain from Stone Mountain got his title crack at Gagne on the next card, held in Minneapolis on December 12. Experience and superior wrestling allowed the champ to retain his belt.

Gimmick matches were a reliable way to lure fans to the box office. For the final card of 1980, Mad Dog Vachon challenged Big John Studd to an Algerian Death Match. Mad Dog had had a couple of run-ins with Studd and his dreaded heart punch the previous month, so the Dog came up with this match to even the score. Vachon had supposedly never lost this type of match. Both wrestlers entered the ring wearing a full hood over their heads, similar to an executioner's mask. There were no eyeholes, so neither wrestler could see the other. Once the hoods were in place the referee turned each man around three times, and then the match began. Usually whoever found his opponent first had the advantage. In this case Studd found Mad Dog and gave him the expected beating, but in the end Vachon managed a comeback and won out over his giant foe.

★ 1981 ★

The High Flyers, Greg Gagne and Jim Brunzell, reunited early in 1981, pushed as the top challengers for the tag team title that they had technically never lost. The Minneapolis Auditorium hosted the first card for the year on January 11, and though Greg and Jim showed their usual outstanding teamwork, they had to settle for the victory by disqualification over Ventura and Adonis. Fans also saw John Studd avenge his Algerian Death Match defeat by Vachon when he stopped Mad Dog with his heart punch.

Another Gagne training-camp graduate made fans sit up and take notice in the early months of 1981: Brad Rheingans, a 190-pound 1975 NCAA champion, six-time AAU champion, winner of the 1976 Wrestling World Cup in Toledo, Ohio, gold medalist at the Pan American games, fourth at the Olympics in Montreal in 1976, and third at the 1979 World Tournament in San Diego, California. He served as the assistant wrestling coach at the University of Minnesota in 1976–77.

Verne Gagne taught Brad to make the transition from amateur to professional rules, which are more wide open, aggressive, and grueling. Having Rheingans join the pro ranks was a coup, as Verne always prided himself on his students' mastery of the fundamentals and Rheingans had an exceptionally sound amateur wrestling background.

Nick Bockwinkel, still hoping to regain the title from Verne Gagne, put a new spin on the rivalry by adopting his own version of Gagne's controversial sleeper hold. Many of Gagne's foes claimed it was really a choke hold and should be banned; debate over the sleeper being a choke had played out on *Sports Hot Seat* back in April of 1960, when Gagne had demonstrated the hold on St. Paul promoter Eddie Williams in front of a panel of top sportswriters. The final verdict back then was that Gagne's sleeper was both effective and legal.

To counter the Gagne sleeper, Nick Bockwinkel announced that, after a jaunt to the Orient, he now had a sleeper hold of his own. The tables were turned, and Dino Bravo, after a match against Nick, claimed that Bockwinkel's new hold was definitely a choke hold.

Now Gagne had one more thing to worry about when he defended the championship to Bockwinkel. Their feud began anew in a February 20 match, in which Gagne was able to come out on top.

In a special tag match on the card, the High Flyers faced off against Jerry Blackwell and John Studd, with the winners to get a title shot. Greg Gagne and Jim Brunzell used their high-flying dropkicks to take the measure of their bigger, slower opponents.

In March, Mad Dog Vachon got tired of the constant attacks and beatings he had to endure at the hands of Blackwell and Studd, and imported his former partner Baron Von Raschke to assist him. Fans found it strange to be cheering the Mad Dog and the Baron instead of jeering them. Until now, they had always been two of the top heels in the AWA. The two ring ruffians battled the much younger and bigger Blackwell and Studd for much of the year in both tag team and singles matches.

Twin Cities fans were introduced to another newcomer to the game in March. Like many before him, he was brought into the business under the watchful eye of Verne Gagne. He was Curt Hennig, son of the legendary Larry "the Axe" Hennig. The younger Hennig was an immediate hit with fans and demonstrated the potential to become even better than his father. Larry was as proud as any father could be to see his son carving out his own career, and he was often at ringside with Curt to offer advice and encouragement.

In an effort to keep his title hopes alive, Bockwinkel was signed to face former world champion Pat O'Connor on the March 22 card in St. Paul. Fans were somewhat disappointed when the aging O'Connor seemed to be an easy target for the crafty Bockwinkel.

Mad Dog Vachon was "injured" in one of the matches against Blackwell and Studd, so his partner Baron "the Claw Master" Von Raschke was joined by the Crusher to avenge the Dog. Of course, pitting Crusher against Blackwell fueled their ongoing battle over who was the rightful "Crusher." The original Crusher and the Baron hammered out a bloody victory over their massive foes on April 19 in the Minneapolis Auditorium.

Of special note on this card was a match between young Curt Hennig and Adrian Adonis. After watching Adonis bend the rules for several minutes, Larry Hennig, who was seated at ringside, decided that he was tired of seeing his son endure illegal tactics. The Axe jumped into the fray, and to the delight of the crowd, cleaned up on Adrian. Unfortunately, Curt was disqualified for his father's actions.

On May 10 the eyes of the entire wrestling world turned to the St. Paul Civic Center. Verne Gagne was defending his world title for the last time. Win or lose, the champ had vowed that this would be his last match. He was going to retire after thirty-two years in the game. Naturally, he wanted to go out on top and be the first wrestler ever to retire as champion. Trying to prevent Gagne from accomplishing his dream was his opponent for the night: former champion Nick Bockwinkel.

More than 18,000 people filled the Civic Center for this once-in-a-lifetime event. On the champ's side were Jim Malosky, Bud Grant, and Billy Bye, who had all been in Gagne's corner for his very first match back in 1949. The three had played football together at the University of Minnesota and remained close friends through the years. Also on hand to second Verne for the night was his old buddy and sometime tag team partner Leo Nomellini, who was there to counter Bobby Heenan in Bockwinkel's corner. The referee for the match, assigned by AWA president Stanley Blackburn, was all-time favorite Doug "Mr. High" Gilbert, and Blackburn himself was at ringside to see the match.

The tension level in the Civic Center was higher than it had ever been for a Twin Cities wrestling match. The fans were solidly behind Verne Gagne. Bockwinkel had his supporters too, though they were in the minority.

The match went back and forth, and fans agree that this was among Gagne and Bockwinkel's best performances. It was clear that although they had squared off so many times over the last decade and exchanged the championship, Verne and Nick had the utmost respect for each other.

Both Gagne and Bockwinkel were masterful technicians in the ring. Each wrestler had the advantage at one time or other, each achieved near falls, and both got a chance to demonstrate their different sleeper holds. Finally, with both Verne and Nick spent with exhaustion, the great Verne Gagne scored the victory. The cheers were deafening as the champ's friends piled into the ring to congratulate the greatest wrestler Minnesota ever produced.

The tag team scene in the Twin Cities in 1981, led by champions Jesse Ventura and Adrian Adonis, was as exciting as it had always been. Gunning for the East-

May 10 was an important date for Gagne. It was the date of his first match, all the way back in 1949, the date he graduated from college, the date he joined the army, and the date he was discharged from the army. Governor Al Quie even declared May 10, 1981, Verne Gagne Day in Minnesota.

West Connection and a title shot were the Crusher and Baron Von Raschke, John Studd and Jerry Blackwell, Greg Gagne and Jim Brunzell, and Ray Stevens and Pat Patterson. The latter two combinations had both held the tag belts in the past, and were touted by the Minneapolis Wrestling Club as the top prospects to eventually dethrone Jesse and Adrian.

On June 14, in Green Bay, Wisconsin, Gagne and Brunzell got the job done and started their second reign as the AWA's tag team champions, an honor they held for almost two years.

When Verne Gagne retired undefeated as champion, the AWA decided to avoid a long, drawn-out tournament and announced on May 19 that they were awarding the title to Nick Bockwinkel. Nick had been the champion before Gagne and was the number-one contender at the time of Verne's retirement. Still, this was not a positive move in the fans' eyes. Once again a championship was handed to a wrestler who hadn't won it in the squared circle. To counter the resentment, the AWA made an inspired promotional move. They signed new champion Nick Bockwinkel to defend against the evil and much-hated Sheik Adnan El Kaissey, who hailed from Baghdad and wore a sword at his side.

Their first encounter took place on August 9 in Minneapolis, and it was one of the rare times Nick had the fans 100 percent behind him. The Sheik started off the bout by attacking manager Bobby Heenan. This took him out of the equation so no one could say the match was two on one, as was usually the case whenever Bockwinkel was in a match. With Heenan out of the way, Kaissey battered Nick bloody, but in the process the champ gained the fans' respect. Not only was Bockwinkel fighting to keep the title, he was fighting to keep the title in America. Kaissey won the match when the champ was disqualified. A subsequent match on August 30 in St. Paul was much the same, with Nick finally winning when the Sheik was disqualified.

The matches succeeded in getting fans to forget how Bockwinkel had gotten the title. All he, and the fans, cared about now was making sure that it didn't leave the country in the hands of the Sheik.

When Hulk Hogan arrived in town in August, he was given an immediate push in the top matches. Hulk's real name was Terry Bollea. World Wrestling Federation owner Vince McMahon gave Hulk his nickname when he fought in the East Coast territory the year before, and the name stuck. Hulk was blonde and golden-tanned, tipped the scales at 325 pounds, and stood a gigantic 6'8" tall. In his initial outings he was given not one, not two, but three opponents to face simultaneously during his television matches, and the muscular star from Venice Beach, California, beat his foes in record time without even working up a sweat. He was a braggart who boasted that he could and would beat any man alive in the wrestling business—all he needed was the chance. He didn't come alone to the AWA, either. His mouthpiece—as if he needed one— was "Luscious" Johnny Valiant, who was brought in to be his manager. The AWA intended to push Hogan as the next big heel.

But even the best plans sometimes need to be changed. No matter what a

The referee for the second Bockwinkel-Sheik match was one Larry Lisowski, the son of Milwaukee's favorite son, the Crusher. Over the next couple of years Larry worked as a referee at many top matches around the AWA. No acknowledgement was ever made of his relationship to the Crusher, and Larry never pursued a wrestling career of his own.

Next page: In 1981, after Nick Bockwinkel was named AWA World Champion for the second time, he fought off the hated Sheik Adnan El Kaissey from Bagdad, Iraq. Though a battle between heels, fans threw their support to the champ, hoping he would rid wrestling of the Sheik.

One of professional wrestling's most awesome competitors, the Hulk, is scheduled to invade AWA rings in the month of August. The Hulk is a towering gi- ant of a man, who is known as a real ring strongman. Be sure to watch AWA *All-Star Wrestling* on TV for more details about the Hulk's arrival and who he will be wrestling.

— *Wrestling News,* July 19, 1981

The announcement of the Hulk's arrival in the AWA wasn't met with any unusual fanfare. In time, though, Hogan would transform fans, promoters, and the wrestling business itself.

wrestler wants to be in the ring, ultimately his persona depends on how the fans receive him. In the case of Hulk, the dirtier and cockier he tried to be, the more the fans cheered him. Promotion was trying hard to make Hogan their biggest heel, and fans were not letting it happen. Finally, the AWA realized that if the fans wanted to cheer Hulk Hogan, they were going to do it regardless of how he was promoted, and switched gears. Johnny Valiant disappeared, and Hulk began to challenge the AWA's most hated grapplers.

In the main event on the September 13 card in Minneapolis, with Baron Von Raschke as special referee, the third installment of the Nick Bockwinkel versus Sheik Adnan El Kaissey battles took place. This match proved to be the wildest of the lot. Before the bell even sounded, the Sheik slashed manager Bobby Heenan with his sword. Nick then went after Kaissey and rammed him into the ringside table, opening a gash on his head. When they finally got into the ring, one of the most aggressive bouts ever staged in the Mill City truly began. Heenan returned with a chair to clobber the Sheik, but the Baron got to Heenan first and knocked him out of the ring. Nick then went after Von Raschke with the chair, but when the Baron ducked, the champ hit the Sheik instead, knocking him out. Nick fell on him for the count of three and retained his title.

On October 4 in Minneapolis, Hulk Hogan battled with Jerry Blackwell over who was the biggest and strongest wrestler in the AWA. Blackwell had long offered $5,000 to anyone who could body slam him. Hulk left the ring with Jerry's money.

The card in St. Paul on October 25 featured what had become an annual event: a big $50,000 Battle Royale. Among the highlights was the return of Andre the Giant, the odds-on favorite to emerge the winner. In all, eighteen wrestlers entered the ring to pound, kick, stomp, and do whatever it took to be the last man standing. On this particular night, the predictions were correct, as Andre took it all—but not before he was double- and triple-teamed by many of the other contenders.

The supporting matches presented as a prelude to the Royale helped persuade fans to plop down their $10 to $15 admission. A slam contest between Hulk Hogan and Jerry Blackwell once again left the big man from Stone Mountain frustrated when Hulk took his money. Sheik Adnan El Kaissey won by

The Incredible Hulk Hogan, perhaps the most recognizable wrestling star of all time, got his first big break in the AWA, where "Hulk-a-Mania" began. Minnesota fans still recall his fierce battles with Bobby Heenan and his stable of wrestlers.

disqualification over a frustrated Baron Von Raschke, who lost his temper over the Sheik's illegal tactics. Bobby Heenan's new team pairing strongman Ken Patera and Bob Duncum, known as the Black and Blue Express, was able to stop Billy Robinson and Rene Goulet, to the fans' dismay. Heenan himself didn't fare as well, as he lost a grudge battle to Mexican favorite Tito Santana.

With both Andre the Giant and Hulk Hogan on the scene fans speculated about what would happen if they either faced off or teamed up. Promoters thrived on such talk, and on November 8 in St. Paul, one of those speculations became reality: the Hulk and the Giant were partners.

The big question was who could beat them. Andre had issues with Jerry Blackwell, as did Hogan. The Hulk was also fed up with the insults thrown his way by Jesse "the Body" Ventura and his abrasive partner Adrian Adonis. The answer was obvious: Hulk and Andre against Ventura, Adonis, and Blackwell. This was a dream main event. The babyfaces didn't disappoint, and dispatched their three foes.

When Thanksgiving night rolled around on November 26, world champion Nick Bockwinkel, still a much-hated heel in his own right, managed to prevent the even-more-hated Sheik Adnan El Kaissey from taking the championship back to Iraq. Jesse and Hulk faced off, this time in an arm wrestling challenge. The Body was again frustrated when the Hulkster put his arm down.

On Christmas night at the Civic Center, Bockwinkel again defended his title, this time to perennial challenger Billy Robinson. Two tag team bouts were also on the card. The first saw Patera and Duncum incite their opponents, Tito Santana and Hulk Hogan, into losing their tempers for a disqualification. In the second the Sheik joined Blackwell in upsetting champions Greg Gagne and Jim Brunzell in a non-title match.

★ 1982 ★

Nineteen eighty-one set records for attendance and provided the AWA with one of its most profitable years since its inception in 1960, and 1982 would prove to be even better.

Back-to-back title defenses by the High Flyers to the Sheik and Jerry Blackwell were presented on January 17 and February 7 at the Minneapolis Auditorium. Even though Gagne and Brunzell were the champions, they were the underdogs in these matches thanks to Kaissey's treachery and Blackwell's huge size. In the February 7 contest, Gagne and Brunzell retained their belts only because they were counted out of the ring by special referee Leo Nomellini.

Hulk Hogan was still feuding with Jesse Ventura, and now former Olympian Ken Patera was in the mix too. He felt that with his credentials and experience he was superior to Hulk, and he was aggressively trying to prove it. With Bobby Heenan in his corner, Patera held a slight advantage due to Heenan's constant interference. In their February 7 battle, Hogan was disqualified when he lost his temper after being fouled by Patera and constantly taunted by the Brain.

Other news in the new year was the return of Rene Goulet, but he was no longer the popular favorite he had once been. The Frenchman decided the rough route was the way to go, and adopted a new name and gimmick. He was now Sgt. Jacque Goulet of the French Foreign Legion. One of his first foes was the popular Claw Master, Baron Von Raschke. The two had reversed their roles from the early 1970s, with Goulet cheered by fans and the Baron jeered.

The Sheik and Blackwell were persistent in their bid to unseat the High Flyers, and they got another opportunity on March 14 in St. Paul. Leo Nomellini was again called upon to officiate, as no regular referee could control these four when things got out of control. Leo took no guff from the heels. He eventually tired of their continuously flaunting the rules and disqualified them, allowing Gagne and Brunzell to retain their championship.

This donnybrook between the two teams failed to settle anything, so drastic measures were employed. On April 18 at the Civic Center over 18,000 screaming fans saw the High Flyers finally prove their right to be champions when they bloodied and battered the Sheik and Blackwell in a cage match, with Lord James Blears brought in to officiate. It was Greg and Jim's night.

Blears also refereed a title match on April 24 pitting champion Nick Bockwinkel against the opponent everyone wanted to see: Hulk Hogan. Hulk was the crowd favorite thanks to his babyface turn. But once again, with the help of Bobby Heenan, Nick was able to survive the test with Hulk and keep his belt. It was the first of many encounters between Bockwinkel and Hogan.

Hulk sought a rematch, and said that if Heenan wanted to add his two cents worth, he should join in the action officially. He demanded both Bockwinkel and "the Weasel"—Hulk's name for Heenan—meet him in a handicap match. The Hulkster vowed to beat them both. He got his wish on May 2 in Minneapolis, and proved his invincibility when he battered the champion and his manager all over the auditorium.

The Sheik and Blackwell still claimed that they were robbed by the High Flyers of their chance to win the tag team title. They boasted that they deserved another crack at them and would go through any team to prove it. They did just that on the May 2 card when they handed a rare defeat to former champions Ray Stevens and Pat Patterson, who had title hopes of their own.

All-Star Wrestling had been hinting for weeks that Jerry Blackwell had put Mad Dog Vachon out of wrestling action for two years and that Vachon wanted revenge. On May 23 at the Civic Center in St. Paul, the Sheik and Blackwell again saw the High Flyers retain their belts when Mad Dog returned and attacked Blackwell. Referee Leo Nomellini did not see the infraction.

Since 1963, the World Wide Wrestling Federation (WWWF), later renamed the World Wrestling Federation (WWF), had been managed by Vince McMahon. In 1982, he sold the company to his son, Vince McMahon, Jr., who had worked behind the scenes at his father's company for years.

The younger McMahon had a vision for the WWF: he wanted to go national. This had never been done before in wrestling. A gentlemen's agreement among promoters had always prevented them from crossing over into each other's territories to run wrestling cards. In the days before cable TV and the Internet, fans did not have access to wrestling in other cities. But with the advent of cable television, Vince Jr. saw a way to promote wrestling across the country while keeping his talent on the East Coast. All he needed was a mega-star, a wrestler who could play not just to live crowds, but also to the much larger television audience. With the right talent roster, Vince could conquer every territory in the nation. His choice? Hulk Hogan.

Sylvester Stallone of *Rocky* movie fame provided a huge boost to Hogan's already soaring career when he recruited the Hulkster to portray a wrestler named Thunder Lips in *Rocky III,* making Hogan a movie star. He appeared on the *Tonight Show* with then-host Johnny Carson, and on many other television talk shows. Hogan was becoming a true celebrity, and the more popular he became, the more people wanted to see him wrestle.

The fans thought it was time for the Hulk to become world champion, and they demanded another match with Bockwinkel. Even uninformed fans knew that by the true definition of the word, Hogan was not a "wrestler," but that didn't matter to them. Hulk was the biggest thing to ever hit the wrestling business, and it seemed logical that he should be the champ.

When Hogan finally got a shot at Bockwinkel—and Heenan—on June 20 in St. Paul, fans left the Civic Center frustrated again. Their hero won, but didn't get the title because Nick saved himself again by being disqualified.

On this same card the new tag team of Tito Santana and Rick Martel delivered a loss to Heenan's Black and Blue Express, Duncum and Patera. This was fans' first chance to see the flashy and talented Martel, who brought with him a solid reputation he would go on to uphold in the AWA.

Promoters were so impressed with Martel and Santana's smooth style that they signed them to challenge champions Greg Gagne and Jim Brunzell in a rare babyface versus babyface match on July 18 in St. Paul. The bout was fast-paced and gave fans a chance to witness a classic wrestling match between the two teams. The High Flyers won when Tito was counted out after he fell out of the ring.

In a spectacular six-man tag team match on the same card, a newcomer called Otto Wanz joined Baron Von Raschke and Hulk Hogan in a victory over Duncum, Patera, and Jesse Ventura. Verne Gagne had brought Wanz into the AWA from Austria, and this was his first trip to the United States. His appearance was a step in Gagne's plan to prove that the AWA was a global organization.

Gagne himself was lured out of retirement for a tag team match with Mad Dog Vachon as his partner, facing Sheik Adnan El Kaissey and Jerry Blackwell. Fans were reminded that Blackwell had "injured" Mad Dog, and the revenge-minded Vachon begged Gagne to come out of retirement because, as he said on *All-Star Wrestling*, "You owe me a favor, Verne Gagne." Mad Dog was referring to a time in 1979 when Verne asked him to be his partner against then–tag team champions Ray Stevens and Pat Patterson, with whom Gagne was feuding at the time.

After much prodding, Verne Gagne made an appearance and reluctantly agreed to be Mad Dog's partner, because he felt Vachon was right about owing him a favor. When they appeared together on *All-Star Wrestling*, Vachon poked at Gagne's chest and shouted, "What took you so long?" Verne coolly replied, "Calm down, Mad Dog. You've called me, sent telegrams, called me names, and everything else. I wouldn't take that from anyone but you. I've decided that I owe you this one favor, but when this match is over, you go your way and I'll go mine."

Gagne came out of retirement for this match for a couple of reasons. The first, obviously, was that this was great promoting and would draw huge crowds. The other, some said, was to build his own ego, so that he could once again come off as a savior. Whatever the reasons, it was a great main event, held on August 8 in St. Paul. The 18,000 fans weren't disappointed as Verne and Mad Dog handed the Sheik and Blackwell a sound beating.

In St. Paul on August 29, the real reason for Otto Wanz's visit to the AWA was revealed. He pulled off the upset of the year when he took the AWA world title belt from the waist of longtime champion Nick Bockwinkel. Fans were in equal parts pleased and confused. Otto Wanz had come from out of nowhere to do what dozens before him had been unable to.

The August 29 card also spotlighted another scientific encounter between High Flyers Jim Brunzell and Greg Gagne and the Martel-Santana duo. This one concluded with Brunzell scoring the pin fall over Santana to retain the championship. In a big six-man tag clash on the same card, Larry "the Axe" Hennig was joined by Baron Von Raschke and Brad Rheingans for a wild no-contest decision over Ken Patera, Bob Duncum, and Jesse "the Body" Ventura.

Of special interest to fans was Ray Stevens seeking revenge on Bobby Heenan in one of the preliminary bouts. This confrontation resulted from Heenan's attack on referee Stevens during the arm wrestling contest between Hulk Hogan and Ken Patera on the August 29 card. This bout once again brought Ray Stevens over to the babyface side of the ring as he battled his former manager Bobby Heenan.

On the September 19 card in St. Paul, Bockwinkel was granted a rematch with Wanz, but he again fell short of defeating the big Austrian. Another bout on this card saw Larry Hennig defeat Adrian Adonis in a grudge match. Adonis had supposedly sidelined Larry's son Curt, and the big Axe was going to make Adrian pay for it. He did just that in quick order when he landed his famous elbow smash to Adonis's head, and Adonis went down. The fierce rivalry between Mad Dog Vachon and Jerry Blackwell was in the forefront too, as they fought to a torrid no-contest decision. Jerry's partner, the hated Sheik, had to settle for a draw against Rick Martel.

Otto Wanz actually paid Verne Gagne $50,000 to take the rank of world champion. At the time, it was a winning situation for both of them. Otto, after dropping the belt back to Bockwinkel on October 10, would return to his native Austria able to boast of having captured the AWA championship. And Verne Gagne was able to market the AWA as a global player. ★ Fans did not respond well to Otto Wanz winning the title, and he never really captured the fancy of the public.

Professional wrestling's popularity was growing by leaps and bounds in the early 1980s, and the simultaneous growth of cable television gave fans everywhere a chance to see wrestling from other territories. Twin Cities fans could now view wrestling from Atlanta on Super Station TBS, or World Class Championship Wrestling (WCCW) from the Dallas Sportatorium promotion. Some cable TV providers in the Twin Cities allowed fans to see wrestling from the Universal Wrestling Federation (UWF) out of Oklahoma. ★ Fans were becoming more and more aware that Minnesota wrestling wasn't the only show in town. Furthermore, these other promotions let fans watch wrestlers they had never seen before, who might even be better than "their" wrestlers in the AWA.

In the early 1980s, Otto Wanz from Austria brought his 300 pounds to the Minnesota and AWA scene, surprising everyone when he seized the AWA World Championship from Nick Bockwinkel.

Nick Bockwinkel persisted in demanding still another match with Wanz. It finally happened on October 9 in Chicago. Nick was at his nastiest on this night, and he left little doubt as to why he had been so successful over the years. He regained his belt, ending Otto's six-week run as champion.

For the remainder of 1982, the year's clashes and feuds continued to rage, with things mostly unsettled between everyone involved.

Hot was the word for the January 16 main event at the Civic Center in St. Paul, as Nick Bockwinkel defended his title to the explosive Rick Martel. The champ survived the battle only because Martel let his French temper get the best of him and was disqualified.

In a makeshift tag team contest, Jesse Ventura hooked up with Ken Patera to hand a disappointing loss to Hulk Hogan and his partner Mad Dog Vachon. This was the first of many clashes between Jesse and Hogan. The two were intense rivals, and told anyone who would listen about their mutual hatred.

Indian great Wahoo McDaniel returned in one of the feature matches on the January 16 card to triumph over Bob Duncum.

Wahoo's next match, on February 13 in St. Paul, was another win, this time over John "the Golden Greek" Tolos, who was also returning to the Twin Cities. McDaniel was heavily pushed as a solid contender for the world title. The great Memphis grappler Jerry "the King" Lawler made quick work of rookie Tom Lintz in the opening match on the card. Rounding out the event were three grudge bouts: Mad Dog Vachon won by disqualification over Jerry Blackwell, the Hulk scored the win over Ventura, and Von Raschke avenged an earlier loss to Sgt. Jacque Goulet by thrashing the Frenchman with his dreaded claw hold.

April 24 was billed as Super Sunday (long before the term was trademarked by the National Football League) for an extravaganza at the St. Paul Civic Center that was given statewide attention. Hulk Hogan was signed to meet Nick Bockwinkel in a world title match.

The Civic Center and adjacent St. Paul Auditorium were packed with 29,000 fans. They were convinced that this was the night that the title would change hands, and they paid increased ticket prices to see that happen. As soon as the match was announced it was completely sold out, a full two and a half weeks before the card, with fans paying a total of $300,000 to watch the seven bouts.

As for the title match itself, when the smoke cleared, Nick had apparently lost, and the Hulk had won. But it wasn't that simple.

The match was a back-and-forth battle, but Hulk ultimately dominated the action, and had his hand raised in final victory. Then AWA President Stanley Blackburn entered the ring to talk with the referee, Lord James Blears. Blackburn advised Blears that he was changing the decision because during the match, when Blears's back was turned, Hulk had thrown Nick over the top rope to the floor. As this should have been an immediate disqualification, Blackburn said he had no other alternative but to render his decision and declare Bockwinkel the winner by disqualification. Blackburn was the most hated man in the building that night, as he received the jeers of every fan who had just seen their hero Hulk win the title.

The fans saw Blackburn overturning that victory as nothing short of robbery. This single match has often been identified as the reason professional wrestling would undergo such an enormous change over the next several years.

The April 24 match is still referred to as the match that sealed the demise of wrestling in the Twin Cities and the AWA.

In addition to the Hogan/Bockwinkel debacle, there were other outstanding bouts on the card. Wahoo McDaniel continued his winning streak, beating "Dizzy" Ed Boulder; Jerry Lawler handed John Tolos his second straight loss in as many matches; and Greg Gagne, Jim Brunzell, and Rick Martel lost a six-man tag war to Ken Patera, Jesse Ventura, and Black Jack Lanza.

In a second main event on the card, Mad Dog Vachon brought Verne Gagne out of retirement for the second time to bloody and batter the Sheik and Jerry Blackwell. In this match the Sheik had an arm broken, and it was later stated that he could no longer wrestle.

The Sheik's injury was of course a "work," and set the stage for Kaissey to become a full-time manager of Jerry Blackwell. The two referred to themselves as the Sheiks and began wearing similar ring outfits.

There was never a shortage of angles in professional wrestling, and one of

Shortly after the reversed decision against Bockwinkel, Hulk Hogan announced to fans that he felt he had let them down, and he was leaving the AWA. This was just a promotional angle to explain Hulk's absence while he was wrestling in Japan.

The hated Mad Dog and Butcher Vachon (left) are introduced to the crowd, while their opponents, the popular Redheads, Red Bastien and Billy Red Lyons, wait their turn. The teams' fervent feud started on All-Star Wrestling *and stretched across Minnesota and the AWA.*

the most interesting and clever angles of the decade began when Sheik Adnan El Kaissey summoned Bobby "the Brain" Heenan to TV's *All-Star Wrestling*.

Kaissey shocked everyone with an offer to buy Ken Patera's contract from Heenan for $250,000. Sheik then told Bobby that he would also give Patera $250,000 to join him. Naturally the Brain accepted the lucrative offer, and then pulled a surprise of his own. He called out Patera and presented him with a robe exactly like the one worn by the Sheik.

This angle was especially shocking because Ken Patera, who had represented the United States in the Olympics, had just turned his back on his country and aligned himself with the Sheik from Iraq. This move angered every decent U.S. wrestling fan—as it was meant to. Promoters were continually finding new ways to make professional wrestling more dramatic and play on fans' emotions.

The Sheik's ulterior motive was getting Patera to team with his other "Sheik," Jerry Blackwell, and go after the High Flyers for the World Tag Team Title. His investment paid off on June 26 when Kaissey's Sheiks defeated Gagne and Brunzell at the St. Paul Civic Center, and became the new champions.

With Hulk Hogan gone from the scene, Wahoo McDaniel was next in line for a title match with Nick Bockwinkel in the main event, but lost in his first bid to capture the champ's belt.

The Twin Cities' ever-changing roster of personalities added some new talent and one returnee on the next card, in St. Paul on July 24. In a rematch, McDaniel gave Bockwinkel everything he could muster and battled the cagey title holder to a frenzied no-contest. Dick the Bruiser was back in town as Mad Dog Vachon's partner, but they were disqualified against the Sheik's new team of Ken Patera and Jerry Blackwell. Black Jack Lanza fell to Baron Von Raschke. In what fans thought of as an upset, Rick Martel lost out to newcomer Mr. Saito from Tokyo, Japan.

Florida's Mike Graham, son of legendary Eddie Graham, was also in town. He was recognized as the light heavyweight champion as soon as he entered the AWA, but immediately lost that title to Buck "Rock and Roll" Zumhofe. Finally, David "Redneck" Shults, another newcomer who would become a key factor in later Twin Cities matches, was disqualified against Jim Brunzell. The opener saw still another newcomer, "Rebel" Bill White, go to a time-limit draw with popular Brad Rheingans.

The Sheik's investment in acquiring Ken Patera and uniting him with big Jerry Blackwell paid off on June 26 when his team finally dethroned the High Flyers, Greg Gagne and Jim Brunzell, to capture the AWA World Tag Team Title.

Hulk Hogan made big news that summer when he agreed to return to the AWA in September. For a big card on September 26 in St. Paul, the Incredible Hulk took on two enemies at once: David Shults and Mr. Saito. After being double-teamed throughout the match, the Hulkster was given the victory when the referee disqualified his opponents.

This match was the result of an *All-Star Wrestling* escapade that saw Hulk

Mr. Saito, who debuted on the July 24 card, wasn't familiar to Minnesota fans, but he was an accomplished athlete and respected wrestler in the business, having held titles in both the NWA and WWWF. Though he played the heel role, his credentials verified that he could wrestle when he wanted to. He wrestled for Japan in the 1964 Olympics and won a silver medal. The crafty mat man played an interesting role later in AWA history.

attacked by Saito after the latter had presented Hogan with a trophy congratulating him on his successful tour of Japan. When Hulk bowed to thank Saito, the sneaky Japanese grappler threw salt into Hogan's eyes and then brutally attacked him with the trophy. It marked the first time anyone had blemished Hogan's tanned and heavily muscled frame. The angle only increased fans' support of Hogan as they welcomed him back to the Twin Cities.

One of the anticipated highlights of the year was the annual Battle Royale in St. Paul. On October 23, some 19,500 fans jammed the Civic Center to see Mad Dog Vachon outlast twenty-two of his fellow grapplers to grab the top prize of $50,000, plus a chance at Nick Bockwinkel. In other bouts on the card, Hogan got a measure of revenge when he defeated David Shults, Vachon teamed with Rick Martel to win a non-title tussle with the Sheik's champions Patera and Blackwell, Otto Wanz scored a splash victory over "Rebel" Bill White, and Billy Robinson toppled Chris Markoff.

In a surprise turn of events, Bobby Heenan had a falling out with longtime partner Black Jack Lanza. The wily cowboy had tired of the Brain's constant demands and interference and turned on him. This led to Lanza challenging Heenan to a series of "bunkhouse" matches across the AWA. A bunkhouse match had both wrestlers dressed in cowboy attire, with the ring surrounded by fellow wrestlers who would toss either one back in if they fell out or tried to escape.

On the October 23 card Lanza was joined by former Heenan family member Ray Stevens, and they whipped Bobby and his partner for the night, Mr. Saito.

The Christmas card on December 25 in the St. Paul Civic Center turned out to be a monumental event for the AWA. Promoters trumpeted for weeks in advance that Hulk Hogan would be part of a rare eight-man tag team match. Hulk's partners were to be High Flyers Greg Gagne and Jim Brunzell and Ray "the Crippler" Stevens. Their opponents would be four of their most hated foes: Ken Patera, Mr. Saito, Jerry Blackwell, and David Shults.

Days before the big clash, word began leaking in wrestling magazines that Hogan would not appear for the show. In fact, the AWA knew he wouldn't appear because he had told them so just days before the card, but the AWA never publicly acknowledged this fact. Fans didn't find out until the night of the match.

A large crowd of nearly 18,000 were in their seats when eight wrestlers filed into the ring—but Hogan wasn't one of them. Fans were told that the Hulkster had missed his plane connections to the Twin Cities and would be replaced by Baron Von Raschke. To say the audience was disappointed would be an understatement.

What the AWA didn't tell their fans was that Hulk Hogan had jumped to the WWF. Hulk's departure was the beginning of the end of wrestling's territory system. Hogan was lured to the WWF by Vince McMahon, Jr., who promised to make him the WWF World Champion. That promise was fulfilled on January 23, 1984, when Hulk defeated short-time title holder Kosrow "the Iron Sheik" Vaziri, who had only a month earlier taken the belt from Bob Backlund.

David Shults failed to appear at the Christmas match for the same reason as Hulk Hogan. The AWA claimed on TV that Shults had been suspended indefinitely, and announced that Sheik Adnan El Kaissey would stand in for the Redneck in the match.

McMahon planned to take professional wrestling to a national level. With Hogan as "his" champion, he now had a hugely popular wrestler on his side to draw in the fans. The plan worked, and over the next dozen or so years, one by one, wrestling's great promoters and the territories they ran were drained of talent. The WWF convinced fans that they were the best because they had all the stars, and eventually this boast became reality.

★ 1984 ★

Fans were confused and excited at the beginning of 1984. Suddenly they had to make a decision: should they go to the AWA card or the WWF card? Up until this point, fans who followed professional wrestling in Minneapolis and St. Paul had only read about the WWF in wrestling magazines. Now they could see it in their hometowns. For any hardcore fan, the chance to see this much wrestling was like dying and going to heaven. But while the WWF seemed harmless enough on the surface, fans would soon learn that the invader from New York didn't intend to coexist; it intended to show fans that its stars were bigger, better—and the best.

This attack on Verne Gagne's territory was the first time an enemy had challenged his stronghold in the Twin Cities, or for that matter the entire Upper Midwest region that made up the AWA. At the onset, though, fans only saw this as a dream come true, a golden opportunity to see more wrestling than ever before.

The AWA was first out of the chute in 1984 with their January 15 card at the St. Paul Civic Center. Headlining was AWA World Champion Nick Bockwinkel, teamed with huge Black Jack Mulligan. Their opponents were the original Crusher and his former rival Mad Dog Vachon. It was Mulligan's first time in a Twin Cities ring since the early 1970s, when he had appeared as rookie Bob Windham. Since then, Big Bob had carved out a solid reputation as a near-lookalike partner to Black Jack Lanza. This time, though, Mulligan was wrestling on behalf of Bobby Heenan, not only in the main event against Crusher and Mad Dog, but also to protect Bobby from Lanza. Heenan and Lanza had had a falling out, and Lanza was hell-bent on destroying his former manager. So for protection, Heenan brought in Mulligan.

Fans were shocked when they saw Black Jack Lanza appear during the match and approach his former partner Black Jack Mulligan. After exchanging words, Lanza convinced Mulligan to side with him, leaving Bockwinkel alone in the ring with the Crusher and Vachon. After some double-teaming on the champion, Crusher pinned Nick and won the match. Fans had seen the world champion defeated and the Black Jacks reunited.

The rest of the January 15 card wasn't bad either. Black Jack Lanza threw his former manager Heenan around the ring like a rag doll in a bunkhouse

Both the Crusher and Black Jack Mulligan were suddenly on the AWA scene because Verne Gagne, having recently lost Hulk Hogan to the WWF, persuaded the Crusher to come out of his semi-retirement to try to fill the void. As for Mulligan, he had a national reputation, so his work in the AWA had drawing power. ★ In keeping with kayfabe, the wrestlers' code of secrecy, no mention was made of the fact that Mulligan was also Bob Windham.

Look-alike bad-guy cowboys, the team of Black Jacks—Mulligan and Lanza—carved out victories from Minnesota to New York to Texas. Their blood battles with the Crusher and the Bruiser live on in fans' memories even today.

match, to the delight of the fans. In a special tag team match, scientific masters Billy Robinson and Brad Rheingans gave it a good effort, but were counted out against Jesse "the Body" Ventura and Mr. Saito. High Flyer Jim Brunzell came out on top over the returning "Superstar" Billy Graham, who was now a shell of his 1970s self. Gone were the long blonde locks and colorful tie-dyed tights and boots. In their place was a new martial arts look, complete with a shaved head. For fans who remembered Superstar from his glory days, it was a disappointment.

The opening bout on the card saw Steve "Mr. Electricity" Regal win over Buck "Rock n' Roll" Zumhofe in what was advertised as a world light heavyweight championship match. A scheduled match between Greg Gagne and Sheik Adnan El Kaissey did not take place, and no reason was given.

Only two days later, on January 17, the WWF made its Minnesota debut in Bloomington at the Metropolitan Sports Center, then home of the Minnesota

North Stars. For this initial splash, the WWF brought in their top guns: Hulk Hogan and David Shults. Just as in their AWA appearances only a short time before, they knocked heads with each other in one of the feature matches. In all, nine outstanding matches were presented. The main event was an eighteen-man Battle Royale won by former AWA grappler Big John Studd.

Many other former AWA favorites were also among the participants: Rene Goulet, Dick Murdoch, Adrian Adonis, Tito Santana, Andre the Giant, Ivan Putski, Tiger Chung Lee (known as Kim Duk in the AWA), and Alexis Smirnoff, who had formerly appeared as Cecil DuBois.

One more AWA face appeared on this WWF card: none other than Mad Dog Vachon, two days after his appearance on the first AWA card of the year.

In just a two-day span, over 30,000 Minnesota fans attended these two shows. The talent roster on both cards was mind-boggling, to say the least. The war between the AWA and the WWF was on.

Verne Gagne wasn't fighting to keep a wrestling title. He was fighting to keep wrestling a sport. Gagne had always put the word *wrestling* first and foremost on the marquee, but now Vince McMahon had added more flash and splash to the mix. McMahon, in Gagne's eyes, had made wrestling a performance, and this raised Gagne's ire.

To rub salt in the wound, McMahon had also stolen Gagne's TV and ring announcer, "Mean Gene" Okerlund. Gene had an almost cult-like following in the AWA. His presentation was hypnotic as he pitched a big card. Vince recognized Okerlund's microphone talent and realized what Mean Gene could do for the WWF.

Not surprisingly fans were confused by some of the things they were seeing—and not seeing. Since the AWA sometimes taped their TV programs two to three weeks in advance, for the first couple of weeks in January fans saw Gene Okerlund on both the AWA and the WWF television shows. The only difference was that the WWF show was more current, because Gene left the AWA in late December 1983—the same time that Hulk Hogan bolted.

In business, competition is usually good, and for the most part that was true of the AWA being challenged by the WWF. It forced both promotions to be at the top of their game and consistently provide the best wrestlers and produce a great television show.

In the early months, AWA fans still enjoyed many of their old favorites, including Bockwinkel, Lanza, Crusher, and others. In February, eight-time NWA World Champion Harley Race made his return to the Twin Cities, with Bobby Heenan as his manager.

On February 22, in Tokyo, Japan, the AWA became truly international when Nick Bockwinkel lost his world championship to Tommy "Jumbo" Tsurata, with former NWA World Champion Terry Funk as the referee. Announcers back in Minnesota emphasized the international flavor, bragging that the AWA was big all over the world—and of course promising that the AWA would bring Tsurata to the Twin Cities for a rematch.

Hulk Hogan made it a point to tell everyone that he was now in the Big Apple, along with the best wrestlers in the world, and that he was going to win the WWF World Championship. This wasn't a stretch; every fan in Minneapolis, St. Paul, and the Upper Midwest had already seen him defeat Nick Bockwinkel in the disputed title match. True to his word, and Mc-Mahon to his, Hulk captured the WWF title from the Iron Sheik on January 23 in New York's famed Madison Square Garden.

Gene Okerlund began his broadcasting career as a deejay on radio station KOIL (1280 AM) in Omaha, Nebraska. In the Twin Cities, radio listeners might remember Okerlund on local station KDWB (630 AM) under the name Gene Leeder.

★ Okerlund got his start in the wrestling business by accident. He was a marketing representative for television station WTCN Channel 11, now KARE, which aired the weekly *All-Star Wrestling* program. In the mid-1970s, when longtime wrestling announcer Marty O'Neill was out on strike, Verne Gagne approached Okerlund, who was in the studio, and asked if he would do the announcing for the show.

★ Gene replaced Marty for the duration of the strike, and when O'Neill passed away, Gene became the voice of *All-Star Wrestling* and the host of the show. When he first replaced Marty, though, Gene received loud boos from the audience. ★ Jesse Ventura gave Gene Okerlund the "Mean Gene" moniker. Jesse would say, "Let me tell you something, Mean Gene," and then rant about an upcoming match or opponent. Other wrestlers began to use the nickname too. Hulk Hogan would shout, "Well, you know something, Mean Gene?" Ric Flair called him "Meeeean Gene," or sometimes "Mean, by God, Gene." ★ Okerlund became as important a part of *All-Star Wrestling* in the AWA as the wrestlers. When he suddenly appeared on WWF shows with his carnival-barker shtick, fans were even more confused, and it went a long way

"The Mountain from Stone Mountain" is how announcers and promoters introduced 450-pound Jerry Blackwell. Jerry insisted on being called Crusher Blackwell, however, leading to many grudge matches with Crusher Lisowski of Milwaukee, much to fans' delight.

New to the AWA were a couple of heartthrob babyfaces meant to attract women to the matches. They were Stan Lane and Steve Keirn, who called themselves "the Fabulous Ones." They dressed in top hats, bow ties, and vests, and entered the ring to the sound of Kenny Loggins's "Footloose" playing over the speakers. Lane and Keirn, though still young, had already earned a solid following in Florida and Tennessee, among other places. While in Florida,

Lane held the NWA Florida Tag Team Title on three different occasions, and Keirn held the same title with popular Mike Graham six times, and also with partners Bob Backlund and Jimmy Garvin.

The Black Jacks, Lanza and Mulligan, were reunited on the May 13 card in St. Paul in a bloody no-contest with Jerry Blackwell and his imported partner Abdullah the Butcher, who was known worldwide as one of the most vicious and bloodthirsty wrestlers ever to appear in the ring. He had become part of Sheik Kaissey's army, along with "King Kong" Brody. The biggest news on this card was the crowning of a new world champion when Rick Martel upended Tommy Tsurata. Verne Gagne and several other wrestlers were on hand to congratulate the young and flashy Martel.

On May 6 in Green Bay, Wisconsin, the Sheik had a temporary setback when his team of Blackwell and Ken Patera dropped the AWA World Tag Team Title to the Crusher and Baron Von Raschke. In some fans' eyes, it would have been more logical to put the belts on either the Black Jacks or the Fabulous Ones. But the AWA went with two wrestlers who had been loyal to them over the years and they felt they could count on during this promotional war.

The AWA pulled out all the stops during the first half of 1984, especially for the June 10 card in St. Paul. The main event was a $100,000-purse Battle Royale—the largest dollar prize ever presented—and competing in it were some of the best the wrestling game had to offer.

The unthinkable happened when Jerry Blackwell, who had been one of the most despised wrestlers in the AWA for several years, was the last man in the ring. His win had unfortunate consequences when his buddies the Sheik, Brody, and Abdullah the Butcher turned on him. The beating that ensued is talked about to this day as the single most brutal treatment ever given to a wrestler in the Twin Cities. Twenty thousand fans cheered "Jer-ry! Jer-ry! Jer-ry! Jer-ry!" as Blackwell was brutally beaten and stomped on in the ring. The Fabulous Ones and Dusty Rhodes returned to the ring to assist the big Mountain from Stone Mountain, and were finally able to clear the ring of the Sheik and his cohorts. As a result of this one match, Jerry Blackwell instantly became the AWA's top babyface, and fans couldn't wait to see him get his hands on the Sheik, Brody, and Abdullah.

In July, fans had their first look at the Road Warriors (Minneapolis body builders Joe Laurenitus and Mike Hegstrand, called Animal and Hawk, respectively, by Ole Anderson). Without question, this was the single most devastating combination ever to grace a wrestling ring. They attacked with unrelenting force. With their manager Paul Ellering, they ran into the ring with Led Zeppelin's "Iron Man" blowing out the speakers. The heavily muscled Animal and Hawk were intended to be heels to battle Lane and Keirn, the Fabulous Ones, but the AWA quickly changed their minds. Animal and Hawk were so dominant that fans inevitably cheered and approved of their tactics, so they became babyfaces.

On August 12, Animal and Hawk battled to a no-contest with champions

toward convincing them that the WWF must be better than the AWA. Okerlund was the lead voice of the WWF for the next nine years and an integral part in the early success of the WWF television shows, bringing in old fans and attracting plenty of new ones.

In conjunction with the June 10 card in St. Paul, the AWA cooperated with me and Mick Karch in putting together a fan gathering called SuperVention 84. The big event started off with a showing of the movie *The Wrestler* at a Minneapolis theater, followed by a wrestling flea market and trivia contest, which was refereed by Kenny Jay. On the day of the card, an awards banquet was held at the Prom Center in St. Paul. Mick Karch and I hosted the event. The ceremony featured Wally Karbo, Verne Gagne, Greg Gagne, Nick Bockwinkel, Curt Hennig, Steve Keirn, Ken Resnick, and Minnesota Gopher announcer Dick Jonkowski. Fans enjoyed a great dinner and a chance to get pictures and autographs.

Author George Schire with TV wrestler Kenny Jay and ring announcers Mick Karch and Dick Jonkowski at SuperVention 84, a huge fan convention and wrestling event put together by Schire and Karch.

Crusher Lisowski and Baron Von Raschke, and in a rematch in Las Vegas on August 25, they beat them and took the tag team titles.

Nick Bockwinkel, no longer world champion, aligned himself with Mr. Saito and they began a feud with the Fabulous Ones. The two teams met many times all over the AWA, after Nick and Saito—with the urging of Bobby Heenan—attacked the Fabs on *All-Star Wrestling*, setting up a series of grudge matches.

Meanwhile Curt Hennig had returned to the AWA, no longer the novice he had been when he last appeared in the Twin Cities. For some reason, Harley Race took it upon himself to try to injure Curt during a TV match on All-Star Wrestling. This didn't set well with Larry Hennig, who was watching his son from the sidelines, and the big Axe entered the ring and got in Harley's face. This was a thrilling moment for longtime wrestling fans, who recalled all the years Hennig and Race had been the best tag team in the business. Now their friendship was tested as Harley attempted to manhandle Larry's boy.

As exciting as a showdown between Larry and Harley would have been, it never happened. Harley left the AWA with no reason given, and there was no further mention of the incident on TV. The speculation was that Race wasn't happy with his money arrangement and pulled out. This was a big loss for the AWA; matches between Hennig and Race could have been a big draw, and the

AWA needed every fan it could get in its war with the WWF. So far the AWA was still holding its own in attendance, with crowds ranging between 10,000 and 15,000 per show. These were respectable numbers, considering the competition from the WWF.

For the October 21 lineup at the Civic Center in St. Paul, the AWA produced the first-ever Tag Team Battle Royal, with a $100,000 purse. New hero Jerry Blackwell was teamed with Boom Boom Bundy to outlast Brody and the Sheik, Bockwinkel and Saito, the Fabulous Ones, Larry and Curt Hennig, Billy Robinson and Larry Zbyszko, Steve Regal and Jimmy Garvin, the Crusher and Von Raschke, the Road Warriors, and Jim Brunzell and Tony Atlas. The Road Warriors continued their dominance by winning over the Fabulous Ones in a standard tag team match, former champion Nick Bockwinkel wrestled to a draw with Curt Hennig, and Tony Atlas won by disqualification over Mr. Saito.

Then, in a meeting billed as unsanctioned by the AWA, Blackwell and Brody faced off in a Lights Out Match after the regular wrestling card had ended. Promoter Wally Karbo stated before the match that AWA president Stanley Blackburn would not sanction another match between Brody and Blackwell because their previous meetings had gotten completely out of control. So after the regular card ended, the lights in the arena were turned off for a few minutes, then turned back on for an "unsanctioned" match between the two grapplers. Fans were advised that if the two got out of control again, Karbo would be responsible. Blackwell proceeded to pound Brody into defeat.

The annual Thanksgiving night card in St. Paul on November 22 saw nearly 15,000 fans pack the Civic Center. The main event on this much-anticipated night took place inside a steel cage. Greg Gagne faced the Sheik, and won out over his Iraqi foe when he turned the Sheik's face into a crimson mask from battering the cage. The tag team title was also on the line as the Road Warriors defended to Blackwell and Bundy, with both teams getting their share of cheers. Rick Martel defended his AWA world title to Billy Robinson, who had adopted a heel role in recent matches and was wrestling a much more aggressive style in his attempt to finally take the crown. Martel proved the better bet that night. Also on the card were Jimmy Garvin (with his wife Precious as his manager), Mr. Saito, Curt Hennig, Steve Regal, and Crazy Luke Graham. And a new face, or rather mask, debuted on this card: the masked Superstar.

After all was said and done, the AWA had survived the first year of its promotional turf battle with the WWF. Fans were still the winners, as each promotion worked hard to win their support.

1984 IN THE WWF

What of the WWF's first year in AWA territory? They started off strong with a January Battle Royal. The program was much more professional and impressive than similar AWA programs, but the WWF didn't capture the Twin Cities

The *Wrestling News* magazine sold at all Twin Cities matches since June 1971 was replaced by *Verne Gagne's Pro Wrestling Report* beginning with the October 21, 1984, card in St. Paul. The new publication had a newspaper format and presented excellent photography, interesting stories, and trivia. It was a vast improvement over the generic and repetitive *Wrestling News*. Subscriptions were also offered, something the previous publication lacked.

The premier issue of Verne Gagne's Pro Wrestling Report, *which became the official magazine and souvenir program for fans attending Minnesota matches beginning in 1984*

The acquisition of Mad Dog Vachon by the WWF, though considered a coup, in reality wasn't as important as it seemed. Vachon's only motivation was the money, as he was nearing the end of his active wrestling career and needed the extra cash. The WWF never did much with Vachon in any of their East Coast territories, using him mainly on cards in AWA country in an effort to lure AWA fans to their shows.

market as firmly as Vince McMahon would have liked. Nonetheless, when the WWF was in town, crowds were close to 15,000 for each card.

On July 22 the WWF appeared at the Met Center in Bloomington with a stiff challenger for Hulk Hogan: George "the Animal" Steele, who was pushed as a top contender for Hulk's gold. Another highlight was a Battle of the Giants as Andre the Giant met Big John Studd. Jesse "the Body" Ventura, lured away from the AWA by dollar signs and bright lights, defeated an unknown by the name of Salvatore Bellomo.

Jesse's old AWA partner Adrian Adonis was teamed with Dick Murdoch in a victory over Rocky Johnson and "Special Delivery" Jones. Popular Mil Mascaras and Bob Backlund were also on the card in singles matches against the Moondogs, Spot and Rex. But the real surprise for AWA followers was that former champion Mad Dog Vachon had officially made the jump to the WWF too.

For their August 26 card, the WWF again had Hogan face George Steele, but this time each had a partner. Hogan's was none other than popular announcer "Mean Gene" Okerlund, who was now in the ring as opposed to reporting on

An exclusive photo of the superstars who appeared in the AWA in 1979

it. Film clips of Hogan training Gene and getting him ready for the match appeared for several weeks prior to the big match to draw Twin Cities fans into the drama. Steele's partner was Japan's Mr. Fuji, who succumbed to a pin fall by Okerlund after Hulk had battered him around for a while.

Jesse Ventura faced Ivan Putski and came out on top, and Adonis and Murdoch successfully defended their WWF World Tag Team Championship to Afa and Sika, the Wild Samoans. The card also featured Bob Orton, Jr., Rocky Johnson, Brian Blair, Paul Orndorff, and Ken Patera.

When the WWF returned to Bloomington on September 23, the main event had AWA appeal written all over it. Hulk Hogan was back, of course, and this time teamed with Mad Dog Vachon to battle nemesis George Steele and his latest partner, Big John Studd. In the latter's corner was none other than Bobby "the Brain" Heenan. Others on hand for the show were David Shults, Tito Santana, Bob Orton, the Junkyard Dog, the Freebirds, and Pat Patterson.

During an All-Star Wrestling *TV match, the masked Doctor X was held by "Luscious" Lars Anderson while his partner, "Pretty Boy" Larry Hennig, brought on the assault. Several other wrestlers entered the ring to break up the sneak attack on the popular masked man.*

From the 1950s through the mid-1970s, Twin Cities fans watched *All-Star Wrestling* on Saturday nights from 6:00 PM to 7:30 PM on WTCN Channel 11. In the late 1970s, the program was moved to various other times, until it was finally settling into a Sunday morning time slot on KMSP Channel 9 in the early 1980s. ★ When the WWF invaded the AWA and the Twin Cities, their program was carried by WTCN Channel 11 on Saturday evenings at 6:00 PM—the same slot that *All-Star Wrestling* once had.

Although the newspaper-style *Verne Gagne's Pro Wrestling Report* was a professional-looking publication, it paled in comparison to the glossy, all-color *WWF Program*. In content, however, like the old AWA *Wrestling News* magazine, the *WWF Program*'s articles were generic and not specific to the territory.

To combat the WWF's attack on the AWA, Verne Gagne joined forces with Jim Crockett of the NWA to form Pro Wrestling USA, a joint promotional organization that allowed the two promotions to use talent from both companies and present "Super" cards, not only in Minnesota but in every town the two companies promoted. It also let them do what the WWF had done so successfully: step over territorial lines. Now fans on the East Coast who had always been under the promotional umbrella of the WWF could enjoy cards featuring the best grapplers from the AWA *and* the NWA collectively. ★ The arrangement between the AWA

The WWF came back on October 28 with Hulk Hogan winning by disqualification over John Studd. Andre the Giant beat Kamala the Ugandan Giant, George Steele lost his match with Junkyard Dog when he was counted out of the ring by the referee for fighting with Junkyard Dog's second, Mad Dog Vachon, and David Shults battled to a no-contest with Ivan Putski. Others on this card were Rene Goulet, the Iron Sheik, Jerry Valiant, and the Spoiler, also known as Don Jardine, who had been the original Super Destroyer in the AWA.

Like the AWA, the WWF presented a big Thanksgiving card, held Sunday November 25 at the Met Center. The main event was a Cage Battle Royale which they dubbed a Turkey Tournament. The loser of the Battle Royale would be the "turkey" of the night. Sixteen wrestlers battled for the prize of $10,000. The winner was Jimmy "Super Fly" Snuka, who had appeared in the AWA in 1972 under the name Lani Keoloha. The other entrants were Greg Valentine, Kamala, Jay Strongbow, Moondog Rex, David Shults, Ken Patera, Ivan Putski, S.D. Jones, Moondog Spot, Angelo Mosca, Bob Orton, Tony Atlas, Tito Santana, John Studd, and Bobby Heenan. Studd and Heenan were the two turkeys, as they were the co-losers of the night. In the special challenge main event Mad Dog Vachon defeated George Steele, and there were seven additional matches on the card.

On the final WWF card for 1984, Hulk Hogan made quick work of the Iron Sheik in a title defense in the main event. In another top match, Andre the Giant was teamed with Black Jack Mulligan, and they fought to a no-contest against John Studd and Ken Patera. Others rounding out the card were Shults, Atlas, Snuka Orton, and Brett Hart.

★ 1985 ★

For their first program of 1985, the AWA offered popular Rick Martel successfully defending the world title to cocky and arrogant "Gorgeous" Jimmy Garvin. Also on the card was a six-man tag team war that had the Crusher join forces with the Fabulous Ones to overcome the Road Warriors, Animal and Hawk, and their loudmouth manager Paul Ellering. In another tag contest, Bockwinkel and Mr. Saito won by disqualification over the much-loved father and son team of Larry and Curt Hennig. Still another tag team match featured High Flyers Greg Gagne and Jim Brunzell getting by Sheik Kaissey and his newest ally in crime, the Masked Superstar. For those who liked one-on-one confrontations, Jerry Blackwell was able to squeak by his rival "King Kong" Brody when the latter was counted out of the ring.

The joint AWA-NWA promotion Pro Wrestling USA presented its first Twin Cities taping session at the Roy Wilkins Auditorium on February 1. Over 6,000 fans paid normal ticket prices to be in the audience. They weren't disappointed. Matches and results: Jim Brunzell fought to a no-contest with Masked Superstar; Jerry Blackwell and Sgt. Slaughter defeated Nick Bockwinkel and jobber Tom Stone; the Road Warriors again won over the popular father-son Hennig team; former NWA World Champion Terry Funk defeated Steve Olsonoski; AWA America's Champion Larry Zbyszko kept his title by disqualification against former WWF champion Bob Backlund; Jimmy Garvin outlasted the Clawmaster, Baron Von Raschke; Masked Superstar and King Tonga defeated Brad Rheingans and jobber Rick Gantner; Greg Gagne won by disqualification over former AWA champion Nick Bockwinkel; Masked Superstar and King Tonga battled to a no-contest against Jerry Blackwell and Sgt. Slaughter; and Greg Gagne, Jim Brunzell, and Curt Hennig, in a six-man tag bout, wrestled to a time-limit draw with Bockwinkel, Steve Regal, and Terry Funk.

Live action returned to the Civic Center in St. Paul on February 22, with six outstanding matches on tap. The Road Warriors defended the AWA World Tag Team Championship to Blackwell and Slaughter. Rick Martel, the AWA world champ, was tested in a scientific match-up against former WWF champ Bob Backlund in the other feature bout.

The AWA also presented spectacular cards on March 24 in St. Paul, May 12 in Minneapolis, June 9 in St. Paul (a card that saw Bockwinkel and Ray Stevens back together), August 11 in St. Paul, September 29 in St. Paul, October 27 in St. Paul, and the annual Thanksgiving card on November 28 in St. Paul, when Scott Hall won the $100,000 cash prize, a special AWA monster truck courtesy of Jay Kline Chevrolet in Minneapolis, and a future world title shot.

To round off the year, the big Christmas Day card featured the first title defense between champion Rick Martel and challenger Stan Hansen, the wild man from Borger, Texas, who had been on a reign of terror leading up to the match. Martel held onto his belt when Hansen was disqualified, but four nights later in East Rutherford, New Jersey—WWF country—Martel dropped the AWA World Championship to Hansen after absorbing a tremendous amount of carnage.

With name stars like Stan Hansen and Scott Hall and familiar faces like Bockwinkel, Slaughter, Crusher, and others, the AWA had managed to stay in the game with the WWF. Things would only get tougher in the next year, as fans began choosing sides between the two wrestling companies.

1985 IN THE WWF

The WWF countered the AWA with an equally strong showing for 1985. Their first card was at the Met Center in Bloomington on January 29. Attendance was down because Hulk Hogan wasn't on the card, as fans in the Twin Cities market first and foremost wanted the Hulkster. Attendance was reported to be around 6,500, but was closer to half that, if not less.

Even without their big gun, though, the WWF had a decent lineup on tap. The main event featured Andre the Giant and Black Jack Mulligan trouncing John Studd and Ken Patera. Other bouts featured familiar names like Rene Goulet, Ivan Putski, Tito Santana, and Don Muraco.

and NWA also carried over to their television matches. Minneapolis, longtime home of *All-Star Wrestling*, was one of several cites to feature Pro Wrestling USA tapings that highlighted the biggest and best wrestlers from both organizations. One major difference from past *All-Star Wrestling* tapings, which were free to the fans, was that Pro Wrestling USA shows were treated as a regular card and the public paid to get in. ★ Pro Wrestling USA eliminated the "squash" matches that TV viewers had been conditioned to expect on *All-Star Wrestling*. A squash match was the pitting of a name wrestler against a "jobber"—men like Kenny Jay and a host of others whose "job" was to lose to the bigger name star. Matches between name wrestlers were only presented at live shows. On the new Pro Wrestling USA cards, fans were treated to main-event style matches formerly seen only at house shows, presented in the studio and later aired on *All-Star Wrestling*. This bold move by the AWA was another way to counter the WWF, which showed name versus name matches on TV. ★ Twin Cities fans also now had two great hours and times to view *All-Star Wrestling*. The show aired on KMSP Channel 9 on Saturday and Sunday mornings from 11:00 AM to noon.

The WWF scored big with their next card, held on March 17 in Blooming-ton. Not only was Hulk Hogan back in town, but he faced off with longtime ri-val Jesse "the Body" Ventura. Fans had been teased with the possibility of this confrontation back when both grapplers were still working for the AWA, and the fact that the WWF finally brought them together made it a major coup for the rival group. Aside from this much-anticipated match, the rest of the card was average at best.

Hulk lost to Jesse when he was counted out of the ring, so the two were scheduled for a rematch on April 20. This time Jesse lost his big chance to beat Hogan for the WWF title when he was disqualified.

Realizing that Hogan was the biggest draw they had, the WWF staged an-other title match on June 1. This time the challenger was Don "Magnificent" Muraco, who was more aggressive and bulked up since AWA fans last saw him

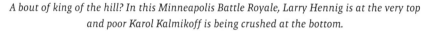

A bout of king of the hill? In this Minneapolis Battle Royale, Larry Hennig is at the very top and poor Karol Kalmikoff is being crushed at the bottom.

in the early 1970s. When he fouled Hulk during the match, Hogan lost his temper and was disqualified. Muraco won the match, but not the title.

For the September 15 card, the WWF brought in former AWA stars Jesse Ventura, Bobby Heenan, Mad Dog Vachon, Black Jack Mulligan, King Kong Bundy (formerly Jerry Blackwell's partner in the AWA), Bob Orton, Jr., and fourteen other grapplers to entice fans to the arena.

The WWF presented two more cards in Bloomington, on October 13 and November 28. The stars included Andre the Giant, Muraco, Bundy, Tito Santana, Ricky Steamboat (who had begun his career as rookie Dick Blood in the AWA), Mr. Fuji, John Studd, Vachon, Bobby Heenan's new protégé the Missing Link, Tony Atlas, Ventura, Putski, and the AWA's Jim Brunzell, who was the latest wrestler to defect to the WWF.

The WWF expansion took a toll on every major wrestling territory in the country. Often the night of a match would present a different lineup from the advertized card thanks to last-minute defections. Vince McMahon continually had his pocketbook open and stole other territories' top talent at an astonishing pace. To the credit of the business though, literally hundreds of excellent and talented wrestlers stepped in to replace the grapplers who walked out on their bookings.

★ 1986 ★

In 1986, Minnesota still drew some of the best wrestlers in the business. The year started off presenting huge names like the Mongolian Stomper (Archie Goldie), the Road Warriors, Stan Hansen, Sgt. Slaughter (whom Twin City fans had forgotten was previously Super Destroyer Mark II), the Long Riders (Scott and Bill Irwin), Big Scott Hall, and a pair of young energetic newcomers named Shawn Michaels and Marty Janetty, who called themselves the Midnight Rockers.

To compete with the WWF's hugely successful *WrestleMania,* Verne Gagne decided to put together a super card of his own. The extravaganza, called Wrestle Rock '86, was held in the biggest venue in the Twin Cities: the Hubert H. Humphrey Metrodome. The event boasted the most impressive lineup of matches and stars ever to appear in the Twin Cities.

In addition to the wrestling lineup, Gagne reluctantly took a page from McMahon's playbook and added country music legend Waylon Jennings to Wrestle Rock '86, offering fans both a concert and a wrestling card. Jennings was a superstar known as an outlaw in the country music field, and no one could dispute that he was a good match for a wrestling show. Gagne still believed that wrestling was what the fans paid to see, but if he had to add music to his show, it would be country music, not rock and roll.

To rent the Metrodome and pay all the wrestlers and musicians, Verne

The really big WWF event of 1985 was a new show called *WrestleMania,* a pay-per-view extravaganza that allowed fans to watch top-flight matches at home. The idea was conceived by Vince McMahon. He believed that with the right talent and the right matches he could broadcast mega wrestling shows that would far outdo live performances. *WrestleMania* was his first venture and was nothing short of spectacular. Hollywood celebrities and music icons were brought into the fold for the first time. The great pianist Liberace, rocker Cyndi Lauper, and TV's Mr. T were among the featured stars at the big event. ★ Over the next couple of years, the new pay-per-view venue would spell the end of the house shows and territories. Vince McMahon would achieve what no other promoter ever had before: control over the entire wrestling business. ★ *WrestleMania* became an annual event, and each show surpassed the last. In 1987, the event drew the largest indoor crowd ever for a professional wrestling match: 91,000 fans filed into the Pontiac Silver Dome in Michigan to witness Hulk Hogan not only defend his title to Andre the Giant, but also pick him up and body slam him to the canvas. This feat had reputedly never been accomplished before, and it officially passed the torch from Andre to Hogan as the top attraction in all of professional wrestling.

Gagne had to dig into his own pockets. He hoped this would convince Minnesota fans that "his" AWA, despite what Vince McMahon was saying, still offered the best wrestling in the world, and that he was willing to fight for that title.

To add to the glamour and prestige of Wrestle Rock '86, Governor Rudy Perpich declared April 20, 1986, Verne Gagne Day in Minnesota. Gagne came out of retirement for the show to avenge the broken ribs he'd acquired in Chicago courtesy of Sheik Kaissey. In order to get his showdown with the Sheik, Greg Gagne and Jimmy Snuka were required to defeat Kaissey's tag team of "King Kong" Brody and John "the Barbarian" Nord. They did, and Verne got his match.

Ringside tickets for Wrestle Rock '86 cost an astronomical $100, but they still sold out mere hours after the card was announced. The cheapest seat available was $25. The Metrodome can seat around 40,000 people for baseball games, and close to 50,000 for football. By adding seats on the playing field, Wrestle Rock '86 could accommodate as many as 60,000 fans. Promoters expected their all-star lineup of wrestlers and musicians to draw a full house.

Gagne reported that attendance was only around 44,000, and even that number was probably double the actual count. For a wrestling card to pull in 20,000 fans was still respectable, but hardly the blockbuster event Gagne had been hoping for. In hindsight, the high ticket prices, although necessary to cover the costs, prevented many fans from attending. Considering that wrestling tickets were still priced in the $10 to $20 range in most cities, tickets to Wrestle Rock '86 would have been a huge expense to most fans.

All this said, though, the card was without question the most impressive lineup of live professional wrestling matches ever presented in the Twin Cities.

Wrestle Rock '86 could have been more of a financial success than it was, but the rules had changed. Vince McMahon had broadened the scope of wrestling and the mindset of wrestling fans. They could now be treated to big cards and bigger names in the comfort of their own living rooms by tuning in to Vince's pay-per-view shows. His empire began with WrestleMania, but soon included others like the Thanksgiving Survivor series cards, the Royal Rumble, and in time, many, many more.

RESULTS FROM WRESTLE ROCK '86, APRIL 20, 1986:

★ Brad Rheingans over Boris Zhukov

★ Giant Baba over "Bulldog" Bob Brown

★ Tiger Mask (from Japan) over Buck Zumhofe

★ "Playboy" Buddy Rose and "Pretty Boy" Doug Somers over Marty Janetty and Shawn Michaels

★ Wahoo McDaniel disqualification over Col. DeBeers

★ Boxer Scott LeDoux over Larry Zbyszko (five rounds of boxing)

★ Mike Rotundo and Barry Windham over the Fabulous Ones, Stan Lane and Steve Keirn

★ Rick Martel no-contest with Harley Race

★ Sgt. Slaughter holds America's Title, over Kamala

★ Curt Hennig and Scott Hall keep AWA World Tag Team Title over the Long Riders

★ The Road Warriors over "Gorgeous" Jimmy Garvin and "Freebird" Michael Hayes, cage match

★ Stan Hansen keeps AWA World Title when disqualified against former champion Nick Bockwinkel

★ Greg Gagne and Jimmy "Superfly" Snuka over "King Kong" Brody and John "the Barbarian" Nord, cage match

★ Verne Gagne (out of retirement) over Sheik Adnan El Kaissey, cage match

The last four years of the AWA were difficult. House shows in the Twin Cities became far and few between, and when they did occur, they drew only the most loyal fans. With ticket sales barely enough to meet expenses, and sometimes not even that, wrestling associations in Minneapolis, St. Paul, and big cities all over the country were forced to shut their doors.

In 1988, Verne Gagne began a working relationship with Memphis-based promoters Jerry Jarrett and Jerry Lawler that allowed them all to benefit by sharing each others' talent. AWA fans were already familiar with Jerry "the King" Lawler, who had appeared on some early 1980s cards. Lawler was easily the most popular wrestler in Memphis, and had been the southern champion on many occasions. Lawler was even given the AWA world title when he defeated Curt Hennig on May 9, 1988. Hennig had held the championship for slightly over a year, having defeated Bockwinkel for the honors on May 2, 1987. The AWA handed over the title to Lawler for two main reasons: the AWA got additional credibility by having a highly recognized name like Jerry as the champ, and, more importantly, Hennig had given his notice to Gagne and was headed to the World Championship Wrestling.

Hennig made a big splash for Vince McMahon as "Mr. Perfect," and went on to enjoy several years in the limelight both with the WWF and then, in the late 1990s, with World Championship Wrestling.

The Gagne-Jarrett-Lawler partnership was riddled with distrust, as was common when promoters from different companies worked together. The relationship finally came to an end in January 1989 shortly after the three of them, along with Fritz Von Erich's Dallas-based WCCW, made an unsuccessful attempt to put together their own pay-per-view show. Major squabbles about payoffs and contracts sank the program and made any future relationship impossible. Gagne and the AWA announced that Lawler had been stripped of the title and that a tournament would be held to name a new champion.

At the St. Paul Civic Center on February 7, 1989, before a dismal crowd of barely 3,000 fans, Larry Zbyszko was given the title when he was the last man standing in a Battle Royale. As champion, Larry's biggest claim to fame was losing the belt to Mr. Saito in Tokyo in front of a record crowd of nearly 60,000 fans. Zbyszko took the title back from Saito in a rematch in St. Paul on April 8, 1990.

On paper, the American Wrestling Association quit promoting matches at the end of 1990. Larry Zbyszko was the last officially recognized AWA World Champion. He won the title for a second time on December 12, 1990, again from Mr. Saito. By the end of the month the AWA announced that he had been stripped of the championship. What they didn't announce was that Larry had left the AWA and jumped to rival World Championship Wrestling (WCW). This was the final announcement from the AWA. When 1991 rolled around, the AWA was officially out of business.

★ ★ ★

Trained by the legendary Bruno Sammartino, Larry Zbyszko came to the AWA to prove he was the best. He lived up to his boasting when he became AWA World Champion in February 1989.

Without their beloved AWA to present big auditorium shows, hardcore wrestling fans had to get their fix from the independent promotions, usually small cards promoted in bars and school gyms by former wrestler Eddie Sharkey, where the wrestling business had begun decades earlier.

By the 1990s the business had changed so much it barely resembled what it had been at its peak. Most of the name wrestlers of previous decades either were retired or had passed away. Fans who loved and lived professional wrestling in the days before loud music and meaningless fireworks turned it into mere entertainment are left with nothing but memories of four lights and a ring, back in the days when wrestling was real.

★ **SIX** ★

THE GOOD, THE BAD,

AND THE UGLY

Who was the all-time greatest wrestler in Minnesota? Many outstanding wrestlers would make the list. During wrestling's Golden Age, any wrestler who was a star of any magnitude eventually appeared in the state. From the late 1940s to 1990, Minnesota was always considered one of *the* places that a wrestler had to appear to make his name.

This meant that Minnesota fans were always the winners. The list of superstars who came to Minnesota is a who's who of the wrestling world: Tiny Mills, "Texas" Bob Geigel, Dr. Bill Miller, Gene Kiniski, "Killer" Kowalski, Johnny Powers, Mitsu Arakawa, Kinji Shibuya, Ivan Koloff, "Superstar" Billy Graham, Dusty Rhodes, "Mighty" Igor Vodik, "Black Jack" Lanza, Edouard Carpentier, Paul Diamond, Wilbur Snyder, Johnny Valentine, Billy "Red" Lyons, Pepper Gomez, "Crazy" Luke Graham, Tex McKenzie, Stan Pulaski, Harley Race, Leo Nomellini, Len Montana, Rocky Hamilton, Hercules Cortez, Bobo Brazil, Pedro Morales, Don Jardine, Dutch Savage, Pampero Firpo, Rene Goulet, Rick Martel, Stan Hansen, "King Kong" Brody, "Cowboy" Bob Ellis, Bearcat Wright, Pat Patterson, Terry Funk, "Bulldog" Bob Brown, Jerry Lawler, Skull Murphy, Lu Kim the Sailor, "Dirty" Dick Raines, Abe Kashey, George "Catalina" Drake, Jim Hady, "Ripper" Roy Collins, Jerry Blackwell, and Wahoo McDaniel are just some of the grapplers who come to mind.

Certain wrestlers, however, were Minnesota wrestlers first and foremost. They had such an impact on the local scene that whenever top talents are discussed, their names will invariably come up. Here are some of the classy and, yes, not-so-classy grapplers who are fondly remembered whenever fans talk about Minnesota wrestling.

★ HARD BOILED HAGGERTY ★

Don Stansauk first showed an interest in professional wrestling while he was attending the University of Denver, where he was trained by his idol Danny Loos. After graduating, Don was drafted by the Detroit Lions football team, who traded him after one season to the Green Bay Packers. During the off-season he wrestled under his real name.

Stansauk went to Chicago, where promoter Karl Pojello billed him as Don Sparrow, because he thought Don moved like a bird in the ring. Soon Don was making such good money wrestling he decided to quit football.

Stansauk was booked into the Minneapolis territory with little fanfare. Minneapolis promoter Wally Karbo came up with the idea of calling him Hard Boiled Haggerty, and convinced co-promoter Tony Stecher to add the newcomer in a bonus match against Kostas Devalis on Stecher's August 5, 1952, card, which Haggerty won. Haggerty was such a hit with the crowd that for the first time, the Minneapolis office promoted all summer instead of taking time off as they usually did.

Hard Boiled Haggerty turned out to be one of the hottest and most suc-

From the 1950s through the 1970s, Hard Boiled Haggerty, the self-proclaimed "king of the wrestlers," drew record crowds whenever he appeared on a wrestling card. Following his wrestling career, he turned to Hollywood and appeared in over one hundred movies and many television shows.

When John F. Kennedy visited Minnesota in 1961, he was greeted by Hard Boiled Haggerty, who offered the president some tips on how to run the country.

cessful draws in Twin Cities wrestling history. Most often he played the heel role, but when he occasionally tangled with a more hated adversary, the fans were 100 percent behind him. But Haggerty was always at his best as a heel. And as a heel, it was only natural that he would feud with Minnesota's own Verne Gagne. Their matches—and there were many—are still talked about by fans.

During this era, a wrestler could lose a match and still retain his "heat"— fans would still come back day after day, even if only to see him get his block knocked off again. The intense rivalry and hatred between Haggerty and Gagne—within the ring—always had the fans buying tickets. Haggerty's arrogance in the ring and overbearing cockiness on TV brought them back again and again, just to see him get his butt handed to him.

Haggerty garnered many titles during his ring career, among them the coveted NWA U.S. Championship in Hawaii. As a tag team competitor, he held the AWA World Tag Team Title three different times, with Len Montana, Gene Kiniski, and Bob Geigel. On the West Coast, he won the World Wrestling Alliance (WWA) World Tag Team Title several times with the Destroyer (Dick Beyer), with El Shereef (Jerry Woods), and with Wild Bill Savage. In Hawaii, he won the state title with Paul "Butcher" Vachon as a partner. He also had successful tag team runs with Kinji Shibuya, Dutch Savage, and Harley Race.

While in the Minneapolis territory during the 1950s, Haggerty was a constant challenger to the NWA World Champions of the era—including such wrestlers as Lou Thesz, Pat O'Connor, Billy Watson, and Dick Hutton—and then for the AWA world title in the early 1960s against Verne Gagne. In Montreal during the 1950s when Edouard Carpentier was the recognized champion, Haggerty often challenged him too. He had legendary battles with roughnecks like "Killer" Kowalski, Tiny Mills, "Dirty" Dick Raines, Gene Kiniski, and Bill

HARD BOILED HAGGERTY VERSUS VERNE GAGNE:

★ September 23, 1952, Minneapolis: Gagne defeats Haggerty

★ October 21, 1952, Minneapolis: Haggerty loses by disqualification against Gagne

★ November 27, 1952, Rochester: Gagne teams with Killer Kowalski to win over Haggerty and Bob Orton

★ February 17, 1953, Minneapolis: Haggerty loses by disqualification to Gagne

★ July 21, 1953, Minneapolis: Gagne teams with Pat O'Connor and defeats Haggerty and Kinji Shibuya

★ July 20, 1954, Minneapolis: Gagne, joined by O'Connor, wins over Haggerty and Fritz Von Erich

★ December 28, 1954, Minneapolis: Gagne and O'Connor defeat Haggerty and Hans Hermann

★ February 5, 1955, St. Paul: Haggerty, joined by Fred Atkins, loses by disqualification to Gagne and O'Connor

★ July 18, 1955, Minneapolis: Verne Gagne and Haggerty team on this rare occasion, losing to Kinji Shibuya and Fred Atkins when Haggerty walks out on Gagne, who is then double-teamed by opponents

★ November 26, 1957, Minneapolis: Haggerty loses by disqualification to Gagne

★ December 3, 1957, Minneapolis: Haggerty and Gagne battle to a no-contest decision

★ December 13, 1957, Winnipeg: Haggerty loses by disqualification to Gagne

★ January 6, 1958, Minneapolis: Haggerty teams with Joe Pazandak and battles to a draw against Gagne and Bronko Nagurski

★ February 7, 1958, St. Paul: Haggerty and Reggie Lisowski lose to Gagne and Nagurski

★ February 24, 1958, Minneapolis: Haggerty and Joe Pazandak win by disqualification over Gagne and Nagurski

★ October 14, 1960, Winnipeg: Haggerty teams with Gene Kiniski and loses by disqualification to Gagne and "Whipper" Billy Watson

★ November 29, 1960, Minneapolis: Haggerty and Len Montana defeat Gagne and Joe Scarpello

★ December 27, 1960, Minneapolis: Haggerty, Len Montana, and Gene Kiniski lose a six-man tag team match to Gagne, Wilbur Snyder, and Joe Scarpello

★ January 17, 1961, St. Paul: Gagne with Bob Rasmussen (for the start of the match) and Wilbur Snyder (for the third fall of the match) win over Haggerty and Len Montana

★ January 25, 1961, Minneapolis: Haggerty and Montana defeat Gagne and Snyder

★ February 15, 1961, Rochester: Haggerty loses by disqualification to Gagne

★ February 28, 1961, St. Paul: Haggerty, Len Montana, and Gene Kiniski lose in a six-man tag team match to Gagne, Wilbur Snyder, and Yukon Eric

★ March 21, 1961, Minneapolis: Haggerty wins over Gagne, who is disqualified by the referee

★ March 29, 1961, Minneapolis: Haggerty loses to Gagne

★ May 11, 1961, Duluth: Haggerty and Gene Kiniski defeat Gagne and Wilbur Snyder

★ May 24, 1961, Duluth: Haggerty and Kiniski lose to Gagne and Snyder

★ August 16, 1961, Minneapolis: Haggerty loses by disqualification to Gagne

★ September 15, 1961, Winnipeg: Haggerty and Kiniski defeat Gagne and Karl Krauser (Karl Gotch)

★ December 8, 1967, Minneapolis: Haggerty and Harley Race battle to a no-contest decision with Gagne and Cowboy Bill Watts

★ January 13, 1968, Minneapolis: Haggerty loses by disqualification to Gagne

★ February 24, 1968, Minneapolis: Haggerty loses by disqualification to Gagne

★ March 9, 1968, Mound, Minnesota: Haggerty and Dutch Savage lose to Gagne and Cowboy Bill Watts

Miller, and against babyfaces Butch Levy, Paul Baillargeon, Yukon Eric, Wilbur Snyder, and Leo Nomellini, to name just a few.

In 1969, AWA promoters brought the Hard Boiled one back to the Twin Cities to wrestle against the masked Doctor X. Fans hoped Haggerty would be the one to finally reveal the masked man's face. What the fans didn't know was that underneath the mask was Haggerty's old California partner the Destroyer (Dick Beyer). Their matches were donnybrooks, but in the end, X was always able to keep his mask on. Whether as rivals or partners, Haggerty and Dick Beyer were always magic for promoters, and a fan's delight on a wrestling card.

CHAMPIONSHIPS HELD BY HARD BOILED HAGGERTY:

★ NWA World Team Title (San Francisco): April 4, 1950, with Ray Eckert, defeated Ronnie Etchison and Larry Moquin

★ Pacific Coast Tag Team Title (Santa Rosa): January 29, 1954, with Tom Rice, defeated Enrique Torres and Ronnie Etchinson

★ NWA World Tag Team Title (Minneapolis): April 22, 1958, with Kinji Shibuya, defeated Mike and Doc Gallagher

★ Hawaiian Tag Team Title (Honolulu): January 27, 1960, with "Wild" Bill Savage, defeated Lord James Blears and Jerry Gordet

★ Hawaiian Tag Team Title (Honolulu): April 13, 1960, with Paul "Butcher" Vachon, defeated Herb Freeman and Lord James Blears

★ AWA World Tag Team Title (Minneapolis): October 4, 1960, with Len Montana, defeated Tiny Mills and Stan "Krusher" Kowalski

★ AWA World Tag Team Title (Minneapolis): March 18, 1961, with Gene Kiniski, awarded the championship when his regular partner Len Montana suffered a broken leg in a match with Verne Gagne

★ AWA World Tag Team Title (Minneapolis): July 19, 1961, with Gene Kiniski, defeated Wilbur Snyder and Leo Nomellini

★ AWA World Tag Team Title (Minneapolis): September 26, 1961, defeated Gene Kiniski in a singles match; chose "Texas" Bob Geigel as his new partner to retain the championship

★ Pacific Coast Tag Team Title (Vancouver): March 26, 1962, with Gene Kiniski, defeated "Whipper" Billy Watson and Mr. Kleen (Ernie Bemus)

★ Pacific Coast Tag Team Title (Vancouver): August 7, 1962, with Gene Kiniski, defeated Bearcat Wright and "Whipper" Billy Watson

★ Hawaii State Title (Honolulu): February 6, 1964, defeated Neff Maivia

★ WWA World Tag Team Title (Los Angeles): July 30, 1964, with the Destroyer (Dick Beyer), defeated Ramon and Alberto Torres

★ WWA World Tag Team Title (Los Angeles): October 27, 1964, with the Destroyer, defeated Fred Blassie and Mister Moto

★ United States North American Championship (Honolulu): February 24, 1965, defeated Enrique Torres

★ WWA World Tag Team Title (Los Angeles): October 28, 1965, with El Shereef (Jerry Woods), defeated Pedro Morales and Luis Hernandez

★ WWA World Tag Team Title (Los Angeles): December 10, 1965, with El Shereef; defeated Mark Lewin and Pedro Morales

By this time in his career, though, H.B. Haggerty—as he had now begun to call himself—had curtailed his wrestling career and turned his talents to Hollywood. He appeared in his biggest movie role alongside legendary actor Lee Marvin in the 1969 movie musical *Paint Your Wagon*. H.B. even sang in the movie. For mat fans, it was a treat to see the number-one ring bully bellowing out a tune—while holding a baby, no less. He went on to appear in many television shows during the 1970s, and was almost a regular on Redd Foxx's short-lived variety series.

In the 1974 movie *Earthquake,* starring Charlton Heston and George Kennedy, H.B. portrayed a pool player. In Verne Gagne's 1974 film *The Wrestler,* Haggerty played a bartender who attempts to break up a fight instigated by wrestling great Tosh Togo (real name Harold Sakata, who also played Oddjob in the James Bond movie *Goldfinger).* Haggerty played wrestler "Mr. Clean" in the 1977 made-for-TV movie *Mad Bull,* starring football great Alex Karas.

Hard Boiled made one of his last appearances in a Minnesota wrestling ring on August 28, 1973, when he was the special referee for a tag team match between AWA World Tag Team Champions Nick Bockwinkel and Ray Stevens against the Texas Outlaws, Dusty Rhodes and Dick Murdoch. Haggerty's old partner Len Montana was also a special referee for this show. Montana had similarly made the leap to movies, playing Luca Brasi in *The Godfather.*

Don Stansauk made his final appearance in Minneapolis on February 4, 1988. He was the special guest referee for a match between Dick the Bruiser and Sheik Adnan El Kaissey. This was also the last wrestling card ever staged in the Minneapolis Auditorium, which was demolished shortly after. It was also the last time that Dick the Bruiser ever appeared in Minneapolis.

Hard Boiled Haggerty suffered a broken neck in an automobile accident in 2003, and passed away in 2004.

★ THE CRUSHER ★

He was born Reggie Lisowski, but that name eventually became a distant memory even to those in the wrestling business.

Lisowski's professional career started in 1949 in Milwaukee. For many years, Reggie wrestled at night while working as a factory laborer and a bricklayer during the day. His big break came when he caught the eye of then–Chicago promoter Fred Kohler, who moved Lisowski from obscurity and put him on the road as a full-time wrestler. This move propelled Lisowski into the limelight as one of America's premiere wrestlers and top box office attractions.

Reggie Lisowski originally worked as a dark-haired babyface, wearing a red, white, and blue star-spangled jacket. Shortly after his debut, though, the all-American boy was transformed into a beefy, bleached-blonde, rule-breaking heel promoters knew they could count on to pack the house. He was heavily influenced by rugged Art Neilson, and together they became a tag team that wrestling fans still talk about. He and Neilson were widely recognized for close to three years as one of wrestling's best tag teams, and were often billed as world champions.

After Reggie's stint with Neilson ended, Lisowski hooked up in a "brother" tandem with equally tough bleached-blonde Stan Holek, and as Reggie and

In 1962, Crusher Lisowski burst onto the Minnesota and AWA scene as a hated bully. But before long he won fans' hearts and became the most beloved of all wrestlers by beating every ring ruffian promoters threw at him.

There's something of the blond Adonis in Reggie Lisowski, whose 250 pounds give him youth and power rising from a pair of shoulders the proverbial mile in width. He became interested in physical culture as a youngster and never tired of it. His one driving aim has been to build that body, and he still spends five to six hours a day in the gym.

On the weights, he can clean and jerk 300 pounds. It comes in mighty handy against some of the giants he faces in the ring.

The Full Nelson is the best Lisowski weapon, but he's liable to come up with an expert toe hold or scissors when he's pressed enough during a bout.

He has a growing public back home in Milwaukee that figures on Reggie one day supplanting Lou Thesz as king of all matmen.

— *Sports Facts,* March 26, 1957

Stan Lisowski they picked up right where Reggie and Neilson left off. The Lisowski Brothers were in demand in cities like Minneapolis, Milwaukee, and Chicago, and even worked the East Coast territory. They held a number of tag team belts. Fans wanted to see the arrogant Lisowskis beat, and all promoters had to do to fill the house was sign local favorites to oppose them.

As the 1950s came to a close, so did Reggie's desire to be a full-time tag team wrestler. He abandoned his "brother" Stan, and also lost his punk attitude. Gone, too, was his long blonde hair. Now sporting a crew cut, Reggie adopted a bully, tough-guy image, and changed his ring name to what became his immortal moniker: "Crusher" Lisowski. He immediately carved out a reputation for himself in Canada, in Texas, and on the East Coast. But Lisowski always seemed to find his way back to the Midwest, and it was here that he became a legend to his followers.

Crusher's ring tactics made fans so irate that riots broke out after many of his matches. He would kick, stomp, and scratch his opponents, doing anything necessary to have his hand raised in victory, and leaving a broken and beaten fan favorite lying in the ring. Promoters knew they were on to something special. Other wrestlers begged to be booked against Lisowski, because wrestling against him meant a big payday and recognition for them, too.

By 1963, Crusher Lisowski was known as "the Crusher" or simply "Crusher." His primary enemy in the ring was then–AWA World Champion Verne Gagne. The Crusher became the leading challenger for Gagne's title, and on three occasions defeated Gagne for the belt.

The Crusher didn't even need to wear the title belt in order to draw a crowd. His all-out brawling style was enough to keep him in main events. As a heel, the Crusher battled the likes of Doug Gilbert, Hercules Cortez, Moose Evans, Rene Goulet, Yukon Eric, and Verne Gagne, to name a few. The more Crusher won, the more the fans lined up to see him defeated.

Crusher teamed with Larry Hennig in the AWA in early 1963, but by August, the Crusher forged his most memorable tag team partnership, with fellow ruffian Dick the Bruiser. Promoters billed them as "cousins" due to their close resemblance. In their first match together in the AWA, they won the World Tag Team Championship from the equally hated Russian brothers Ivan and Karol Kalmikoff. Promoters billed the meeting as a Battle of the Butchers, and all four grapplers were covered in blood by the match's end.

THE CRUSHER'S AWA WORLD HEAVYWEIGHT CHAMPIONSHIPS:

★ February 15, 1963, Omaha: defeated Verne Gagne to win Nebraska version of AWA title

★ July 9, 1963, Minneapolis: defeated Gagne for AWA title

★ July 20, 1963, Minneapolis: lost title back to Gagne (Omaha and Minneapolis titles thereafter merged)

★ November 28, 1963, St. Paul: defeated Gagne

★ December 14, 1963, Minneapolis: lost title back to Gagne

★ August 21, 1965, St. Paul: defeated Mad Dog Vachon

★ November 12, 1965, Denver: lost title back to Vachon

The Novas, a Twin Cities rock group, had a small hit with their song "The Crusher." It got play on both KDWB (630 AM) and WDGY (1130 AM), both Top 40 rock stations from the 1950s into the 1970s. The song began with the famous Crusher roar, and the lyrics included the names of some of the Crusher's favorite wrestling holds, such as the eye gouge. The song was released between the summer of 1964, when the Crusher left the AWA as its top heel, and January 1965, when he returned as a babyface. The record is highly sought after by collectors of professional wrestling memorabilia.

Despite their ruthless and unruly tactics, the Crusher and Dick the Bruiser got cheers from the fans for the way they soundly pounded their opponents into defeat in match after match. Their most famous feud, with "Pretty Boy" Larry Hennig and "Handsome" Harley Race in the mid-1960s, sold out auditoriums for several years all over the AWA.

On August 21, 1965, Crusher won the AWA World Heavyweight Championship as a babyface fan favorite, beating the hated Mad Dog Vachon. The feud between the Crusher and the Mad Dog raged throughout the AWA well into the 1970s, and their matches were always popular with fans. They tangled in countless "specialty" matches—Algerian death matches, cage matches, saloon matches—and probably spilled more blood than any other two wrestlers in the history of Minnesota wrestling.

In the 1970s, the Crusher and Mad Dog Vachon finally buried the hatchet and even worked as a tag team on occasion, especially against pairs of villains that both Crusher and Mad Dog hated. Fans were kept guessing about whether Crusher could trust Mad Dog, and vice versa. The team was a promoter's dream.

By the early 1970s, the Crusher became so popular that he could outdraw even the great Verne Gagne. This didn't always sit well with Gagne, who often tried to promote his territory without having the Crusher on the cards. Attendance nosedived without him, though, so Gagne would eventually have to swallow his pride to boost the gate. The Crusher would reappear in some angle that brought him back to headline against the territory's top heels.

Over the years, anytime a bad boy in the AWA was running amok, the Crusher was the guy fans wanted to see take him down. Promoters were always eager to sign the Crusher against the likes of "Superstar" Billy Graham, Dusty Rhodes (in his heel days), Black Jack Lanza, Ray Stevens, Nick Bockwinkel, Ivan Koloff, Larry Hennig, Harley Race, and many others. None managed to take over Crusher Country.

In 1971, Crusher was partnered with Red Bastien for the AWA Tag Team Championship after title holder Hercules Cortez died in a car accident. Together, Bastien and Crusher continued on as AWA World Tag Team Champions for the next six months before dropping the belts to Ray Stevens and Nick Bockwinkel in Denver on January 20, 1972.

After losing the belts, Bastien left the AWA to work the Texas territory, while the Crusher continued to battle Stevens and Bockwinkel in both singles and tag matches with various partners. In 1974, Crusher again got a run at the tag team title, this time with popular English sensation Billy Robinson. In 1975, the Crusher and the Bruiser held the AWA belts together for the last time.

The Crusher won the tag team championship one final time. To counter the loss of their superstar Hulk Hogan to the rival World Wrestling Federation (WWF), the AWA brought Crusher back in 1984. Even though he was almost sixty years old, Lisowski, along with reformed heel Baron Von Raschke, beat the hated combination of Jerry Blackwell and Ken Patera.

Shortly thereafter the Crusher retired. He passed away in October 2005. He will always be remembered as one among the most popular and recognizable grapplers in Minnesota wrestling history.

★ DOCTOR X ★

Of the many gimmicks in wrestling, a mask is one of the simplest, but also one of the most successful. For Dick Beyer, donning a mask was what made his career, though he began as just himself.

Beyer started as an amateur wrestling champion and football star at Syracuse University. He earned an MA in education and was a football coach in the early 1950s. On April 3, 1952, Beyer scored a mild upset in the National AAU Wrestling Championships when he defeated Robert Maidegen, a member of the 1948 Olympic team. Beyer finished third in the finals after dropping his last two matches.

In 1954, Dick turned to pro wrestling and worked under his own name. He became closely associated with fellow wrestler Billy Red Lyons. Over the years they would be in the ring together many times—sometimes as opponents, sometimes as partners. Beyer and Lyons were actually brothers-in-law in real life: Dick was married to Billy's sister.

Between 1959 and 1961, Beyer and Lyons often joined forces as babyfaces in attempts to rid the area of teams like Chris and John Tolos, Mike and Doc Gallagher, Mister Moto and Mister Hito (Kinji Shibuya), Duke and Sato Keomukoa (Sato was another name used by Shibuya), and Ivan and Karol Kalmikoff. They had legions of fans behind them in every match.

In 1962, popular babyface Dick Beyer disappeared from the wrestling business forever, and in his place appeared a new wrestler calling himself the Destroyer. From April 27 to June 16, 1962, the Destroyer racked up forty consecu-

In 1959, Dick, along with Lyons and mutual friend and fellow wrestler Ilio DiPaolo, bought the Rochester, New York, promotion from Pedro Martinez. They got a local TV station to broadcast the wrestling, and Dick Beyer did play-by-play, commentary, and interviews for the show. Their top heel at the time was Fritz Von Erich. Dick also worked for Martinez putting tags on his Cleveland and Toledo tapes. Dick would record an opening, closing, and promo for the town's shows. This microphone experience proved invaluable in Beyer's career.

He sat in the TV audience of All-Star Wrestling *and asked for a match. Ignored for several weeks, the masked man leaped into the ring and attacked champion Verne Gagne. Immediately, every wrestler in the territory wanted a piece of Doctor X, who became the best-known masked wrestler to appear in the AWA.*

During this period, the Destroyer also wrestled extensively in Japan. He allied himself with Shohei "Giant" Baba, who was the promoter and top Japanese wrestler for the Pacific Wrestling Federation (PWF). The Destroyer was the only American wrestler to be received by Japanese fans with cheers—American wrestlers always played the heel role in Japan. He was also the only American wrestler to work against *other* American wrestlers when they toured Japan at this time.

tive victories before going to a time-limit draw with Sandor Szabo on June 18 in Las Vegas.

For the next five years, the Destroyer boasted not only that he was the greatest masked wrestler of all time, but also that he would never be unmasked. And although dozens of top wrestlers tried, none succeeded.

Once Beyer became the Destroyer, Billy Red Lyons became one of his biggest challengers and attempted to unmask him on multiple occasions. But even when Beyer was wearing the mask, the two would still occasionally team up. In 1965 in California, they formed a formidable tag team combination—this time as heels—and even won the World Wrestling Alliance (WWA) Tag

Before assuming the identity of Doctor X, he was Dick Beyer of Syracuse University. Earning too little money wrestling as himself, he donned a mask and became one of wrestling's most hated ring villains.

Team Championship from Don Manoukian and Ray Stevens. They also captured the Japan Wrestling Alliance Asian tag team title from "Giant" Baba and Toyonobori.

In October 1965, both the Destroyer and Billy Red Lyons began working in the Texas territory—but this time on opposite sides of the ring. The Destroyer came in as a heel, while Lyons was one of Texas's most popular good guys. They had many hard-fought matches while in this territory, with the fans pulling for Lyons to unmask the unruly masked man. Their legendary battles thrilled fans until mid-1967, when the Destroyer left Texas.

For a short time during 1967, the Destroyer worked the Indianapolis territory (co-owned and promoted by Dick the Bruiser and Wilbur Snyder, a fact not known to fans) and feuded with the Bruiser for the WWA world title. Indianapolis shared talent with the Chicago branch of the AWA, and it was in Chicago that the Destroyer first encountered Verne Gagne. It would prove to be a fateful meeting. Just as Dick Beyer had disappeared in 1962 to become the Destroyer, the Destroyer now faded from the scene. In his place appeared a new super-secret masked man: Doctor X.

In August 1967, a masked man in a suit began appearing in the audience of TV's *All-Star Wrestling*. During a few shows he made his way over to the interview area and politely interrupted announcer Marty O'Neill, saying that he wanted to have a match with one of the TV wrestlers. With each attempt, promoter Wally Karbo came out and told the unknown man that he had to return to his seat or he would be escorted from the studio by security. This went on for several weeks.

The masked man finally took matters into his own hands during an August 19 match that featured then-champion Verne Gagne wrestling against veteran Jack Pesek. Fans were stunned when the masked man leaped from his ringside seat and climbed to the top rope of the wrestling ring. He jumped Verne Gagne and clamped a figure-four leg lock on him, refusing to release the hold until the champion submitted.

As the defeated Gagne was helped from the ring by other wrestlers, the masked man went to the interview area and told Marty O'Neill that he was tired of being ignored. He had repeatedly asked in a gentlemanly way for a chance to wrestle, he said, and the local promotion wasn't giving him a chance. He boasted that not only had he proven that he was a wrestler, but that he could go up against the best the AWA had to offer. Promoter Wally Karbo entered the fray and said that if it was a match the masked man wanted, then he would grant that wish. Wally shocked the audience when he announced that on August 27, 1967, in St. Paul, the masked man would face his first opponent: the Crusher. At this time, no one was more popular than the Crusher, and fans felt certain that no one was more likely to defeat the masked man.

In a subsequent interview, Marty O'Neill asked the masked man what his name was. The reply: "You can just call me Doctor X." He claimed that he hid his identity because if other wrestlers knew who he was, they would refuse to face him, as they had in the past. So to get the top matches with the opponents he felt he deserved, he decided to hide his identity from his fellow wrestlers and promoters. Doctor X also stated that he would only reveal his true identity and unmask if he was pinned or forced to submit in two submission falls. And as an added incentive, he declared that he would give $5,000 to the wrestler who unmasked him.

As was the case with the Destroyer, the masked Doctor X proved to be one of the hottest wrestlers in AWA and Minnesota history. He proceeded to win his first match against the seemingly invincible Crusher, and had many more battles with him all over AWA territory for the next three years.

Doctor X headlined cards in Minneapolis, Winnipeg, Chicago, Denver—

Why did Beyer change from being the Destroyer to Doctor X? Here's what he said in a 2002 interview with me. ★ "The Indianapolis and Minneapolis offices were co-promoting Chicago. I was working Indianapolis as the Destroyer, but didn't start wrestling as Doctor X until 1967. Verne Gagne was the boss in Minneapolis and called all the shots. He was a real egomaniac. Wally Karbo was the front man. Wally only had a piece of Minneapolis, but he worked the book, took care of all the headaches, and called all the shit. Gagne was the guy that just stirred the shit up. ★ "Anyway, after a match in Chicago, Gagne sent one of the policemen, who took me to and from the ring, to my dressing room with a note. He wanted to talk with me and asked me to meet him at the Playboy Club in downtown Chicago. We had a hell of a match against each other that evening. Gagne was a hell of a wrestler. Obviously, he liked the match we had, and liked my style. He asked me to come to Minneapolis, but said he didn't want the Destroyer. When I asked him why, he said that it had been reported in a couple of magazines that I was Dick Beyer. I told him that was a bunch of bullshit! But, he stood his ground and said that he wanted

virtually every city that the AWA promoted in. Like the Destroyer, Doctor X was challenged by the best wrestlers in the business. None managed to take the required two pin falls or two submission falls from the good Doctor and reveal his face to the fans.

On March 30, 1968, Doctor X finally got an AWA world title match with Verne Gagne in what *Sports Facts* billed as "The Biggest Mat Card in Twin Cities History." The match ultimately ended with X disqualified. When the chance to meet Gagne again came on August 17, 1968, in Bloomington, the result was different: Doctor X defeated the longtime champion and won the AWA world title.

Gagne had a rematch clause in his contract, and that match was signed for August 31 in Minneapolis. On that fateful night, however, before the auditorium match, Doctor X lost to a newcomer to the AWA: Billy Red Lyons. When X subsequently lost the rematch and the title that same night to Gagne, he angrily shouted that it was all Lyons's fault. The ensuing X versus Lyons feud lasted a year and a half, and thrilled fans all over the AWA.

During his AWA stay, Doctor X also had several runs with various partners in tag team bouts. Among those to join him were Mad Dog Vachon and Harley Race, and for six-man tags, he often hooked up with either Mad Dog and Butcher Vachon or Larry Hennig and Harley Race.

me to come in, but under a different mask and name. And so I went into Minneapolis with an all-black outfit. The Doctor X mask hid my nose. I did everything opposite of what the Destroyer did. When I finally went into Chicago again as Doctor X and not the Destroyer, not one person noticed the difference." ★ Beyer also said that Gagne eventually wanted Doctor X to unmask, and Beyer made it clear that he was never going to do that for him or any other promoter. His success at the gate allowed Beyer to enforce his stand.

RECORD FAVORS LYONS

If rugged Red Lyons carries a broom with him into his corner tonight before the big bout with Dr. X, don't be alarmed . . . it will just be his way of showing fans that he plans on a "clean sweep."

Lyons has battled Dr. X twice in one-fall bouts, and has emerged victorious both times, using the near paralyzing figure-four leg lock to gain the fall in each of the two bouts.

That in itself isn't so unusual except that's also the hold Dr. X has been using here for months to wipe out the opposition.

In fact, Dr. X has claimed he'll pay $5,000 to any man who can break away from HIS figure-four. Now, instead of concentrating on applying that hold to his opponents, Dr. X has to be on the defensive against the very same maneuver which carried him to the top.

So, conducting a little "world series" of his own, Lyons goes after a 3–0 margin tonight, and with the match scheduled for two of three falls, the Toronto wizard could also be the first to officially unmask Dr. X.

The masked man's contract very specifically states that he'll take off the cover if anyone beats him twice within a single bout . . . but both falls MUST be via the submission route. Lyons can't help but display some confidence as the big battle nears.

"I know better than to get too confident," he told *Sports Facts.* "But still, you have to consider that two falls over that guy in two different matches . . . and both with the figure-four hold, prove that I'm capable. The fans around here want to know who this masked fellow is. I plan to show 'em."

Lyons has been the talk of the town since he came to town with no advance notice. Fans didn't really perk up until he toppled Dr. X with that leg lock. When he did it two times in succession, it was like calling your shot on the roulette wheel.

— *Sports Facts,* October 12, 1968

In May of 1970, Doctor X showed up with another masked wrestler he called Double X. Now the fans had two mystery men they wanted to see defeated. The X partners battled, among others, the teams of Crusher and Edouard Carpentier and Pepper Gomez and Carpentier. Even Verne Gagne got into the action against the masked men when he took Paul Diamond along to beat them in a match in Minneapolis on June 30, 1970.

By this time, though, Minneapolis promoter Wally Karbo and St. Paul pro-

If one mask is good, then two must be better. When Doctor X needed a super secret partner, he brought in Double X. Together the X-men were quite a team, often confusing referees with their identical outfits, builds, and masks.

I asked Beyer how Jim Osborne entered the picture as Double X. Here is how Dick says it came about. ★ "That was my idea, because they didn't know how to use Jim Osborne. So I told them to give him to me as a partner. I'd call him Double X. Wearing the same ring outfit, and having similar builds, I thought it was a natural. We did pretty well together."

The *Minneapolis Tribune* sports desk told a mysterious telephone caller that yes, indeed, we'd like to know the identity of Doctor X.

Doctor X, in case you haven't watched him work during the past two years, is a masked meanie who stalks this corner of the pro wrestling world, wiping out foe after foe, keeping his identity hidden and his billfold bulging.

His most recent outing, last weekend, appeared to be his final one. But a last-minute switch with his super-secret partner, Double X, meant that the wrong masked man was defrocked, to be identified as Jim "Red" Osborne.

The week turned out to be a bonanza for grappling fans when the local wrestling promoter's informant called in the results to the *Tribune*.

" . . . And the winner of the next bout was Big Bill Miller. Oops. I mean Mister M."

Sure enough, the cards promotion boasted "the return of the mysterious Mister M." The promotion neglected to say that three years ago, when Mister M terrorized the local wrestling scene, he was eventually unmasked as Big Bill Miller.

So that knocked off two of the local scene's three mysterious masked men, leaving only Doctor X.

The anonymous caller claimed to be a former wrestling promoter, traveling through the area. And he backed up his claim by describing some misadventures of masked wrestlers while he was promoting.

"Wrestling fans," he said, "seem to think a masked wrestler appears in the ring then vanishes into thin air until his next bout. They stand by the dressing room door, but they're waiting to see a guy come out in a suit still wearing the mask.

"One time a card was short of wrestlers, so the masked man took off his mask and wrestled under his real name in a preliminary. Then he put the mask on and wrestled in the feature . . .

"Time," we told the caller, "is running out. Even now, Doctor X is threatened with suspension from wrestling. He faces Mister M tonight, and it might be his finish. Who is he?"

"Sure, they threaten him with suspension," the caller said. "How else is he going to get a vacation? That's the best way to handle it when a guy wears out the mask thing.

"If you do unmask a masked marvel, it's really pretty dull. I mean, you got 6,000 people standing there breathlessly, and you show 'em some guy they've never seen before . . . a stranger. And all the people say to themselves, 'So this is what I've been coming here for the last thirty-two months to find out?'"

The subconscious tension music was building to a crescendo as we pleaded, "OKAY, we don't care who you are. But who, sir, is Doctor X?"

"Doctor X is really," he said, pausing to let the full effect through the phone lines . . . "Dick Byers!"

Two thoughts occurred. One was: "Why didn't we figure that out?" The second was: "Who the heck is Dick Byers?"

"Byers was a legitimate college and AAU wrestler," the caller said. "He went to Los Angeles and called himself the Destroyer. He wore a mask, was undefeated for five years, sold Destroyer masks on the side and even Destroyer cigarette lighters.

"He was always rated No. 1, 2, or 3 in the country by the wrestling magazines, but the Destroyer thing finally wore out. So suddenly the Destroyer drops to No. 27 in the ratings and Doctor X comes from out of nowhere to be No. 1.

"Oh, he's Byers all right. But if you asked promoter Wally Karbo if Byers was really Doctor X, he'd never tell you if you lived to be 110. And if any wrestler spouts off, he just won't get any more work."

So that's it! Wow! Big Bill Miller, Red Osborne, and Dick Byers . . . all in one fabulous week!

"Well," the caller said, finally, "I've got to get going. I'm pretty busy these days."

Hmmmm . . . And what, Mr. Mysterious Caller, keeps you so busy?

"I travel around the country," he said, "checking up on Unidentified Flying Objects."

— John Gilbert, *Minneapolis Tribune*, June 1970

moter Eddie Williams announced to the fans that they had finally had enough of Doctor X, and that they had a surprise opponent for him. When X's opponent was revealed, it was a shock to the fans: *another* man with his face hidden by a mask, calling himself Mister M. But this time, promoters were eager to reveal the real name of the masked man. He was the famous Bill Miller, who, as Mister M, had been the AWA's first masked wrestler in the early 1960s. Mister M was the most successful masked wrestler in the AWA before Doctor X, and was AWA World Champion in 1962. Miller said he was returning as Mister M to end the new masked man's reign of terror.

Mister M met Doctor X in St. Paul on July 18, 1970, and when the match ended, fans saw X unmasked—or so they thought. When the confusion ended, it turned out that Double X had been unmasked, not Doctor X. He and X had switched places when the referee was knocked down, and Mister M had tossed Doctor X out of the ring onto the arena floor. Double X quickly rolled out from under the ring and replaced him. M proved too much for Double X, though, and quickly defeated him and stripped off his mask. Fans immediately recognized the face of Jim Osborne. Of course, a rematch was arranged for M and X, and this time, as usual, Doctor X remained masked, and sent Bill Miller to the showers with a loss.

In August 1970, X began teaming with fellow heel Black Jack Lanza against Red Bastien and Pepper Gomez, but after a disagreement in a TV match, X and

THE NEWS

WILL "DOCTOR X" UNMASK?

The biggest question in professional wrestling will be answered tonight when Doctor X walks down the St. Paul Auditorium aisle to the ring.

Will he be carrying his mask or be wearing it is something that even promoter Eddie Williams could not answer three hours before ring time.

Doctor X has said getting Black Jack Lanza in the ring is more important to him than his mask or winning Verne Gagne's championship.

He has publicly said that if necessary to get the rematch with Lanza he would take off the mask. But he could change his mind and there is nothing Lanza, Williams, or the American Wrestling Alliance can do to force a decision until he makes it.

The possibility of Doctor X revealing his own identity had the fans and members of the professional wrestling fraternity buzzing.

Some matmen speculated that Doctor X was forced to make a secret agreement with Lanza to unmask to obtain the rematch. But Williams scoffed at that possibility.

"In no way could Lanza force Doctor X to unmask to get the rematch," said Eddie. "For Lanza it was either sign to meet Doctor X again or be dropped out of the running for a title shot at Gagne. It was as simple as that."

The masked man stated, "I am ready for anything and everything. It'll be a war when the bell rings and I walk out to meet Lanza. I am determined to destroy him and his gabby manager Bobby Heenan. I took my licking, now we'll find out how much punishment he can absorb and still stay on his feet. They hauled me out a bloody mess the last time. This time Lanza goes out on the stretcher."

— *Wrestling Facts,* August 29, 1970

Lanza began fighting each other instead of their opponents. The planned tag match for that night was changed to a singles bout between the two would-be partners, and it was a blood fest. As expected, the overzealous Bobby Heenan got into the action, and he and Lanza relentlessly attacked Doctor X. They were victorious—maybe even *too* victorious. They were able to partly tear off X's mask, but his face was so covered in blood it was almost impossible to identify him. Fans were left wondering: who was the man under the mask? And would he return to the ring?

Doctor X not only returned; he demanded, in no uncertain terms, another showdown with Lanza. He called promoter Wally Karbo out, and begged to be signed against Black Jack. He told Karbo that he wanted the match so bad, he would even take off his mask and reveal his identity *before* the match, just to get a shot at Lanza. The fans supported Doctor X's demands, hoping to finally find out who he was, but also hoping to witness an end to Lanza and Heenan's reign.

The St. Paul Auditorium hosted the highly anticipated showdown. When ring announcer Marty O'Neill entered the ring, St. Paul promoter Eddie Williams was with him. As silence fell upon the crowd, a masked Doctor X made his way to the ring. As the masked man stood with his arms folded, O'Neill began to tell the audience about the man of mystery.

He revealed that he was a former football player at Syracuse University, and that he coached there for nine years. As Marty finished speaking, X lifted off the mask that he'd worn for three years in the AWA and handed it to promoter Eddie Williams. O'Neill said, "Ladies and Gentlemen, let's hear and have a big round of applause for DICK BEYER!"

Beyer got a standing ovation. The fans could finally see the face of the man under the mask, and now they were solidly behind him. The crowd's cheers quickly turned to jeers when into the ring came Black Jack Lanza and his equally hated manager Bobby Heenan. The formerly masked man proved that he could whip Lanza, but Heenan made the match uneven. Doctor X lost to

THE NEWS

DOCTOR X DISAPPEARS

Doctor X is as much of a mystery now as he was the first time he appeared on the Twin Cities wrestling horizon more than two years ago.

The masked man took off his mask before facing Jack Lanza and then, after losing the match, vanished into thin air.

He's gone and his whereabouts remain a mystery. Whether he will return to gain revenge on Lanza and gain his goal of meeting champion Verne Gagne is a question only he can answer.

— *Wrestling Facts,* September 26, 1970

Lanza that hot summer night. Just as suddenly as he had appeared on the AWA scene, Doctor X now disappeared.

Immediately after the Lanza matches, Dick Beyer once again donned his famous Destroyer mask and was off with his family for a tour around the world. He headed to Honolulu, where he quickly won that territory's North American championship from Pedro Morales on September 30, 1970. For the next three months, as the Destroyer, he defended the title until dropping it to England's Billy Robinson on December 16, 1970.

Just when Minnesota and AWA fans figured they would never see Doctor X again, the masked man was back. He returned to the AWA scene in October 1971. Upon his re-entry, it appeared that he would once again adopt his heel persona, as he joined fellow bad guy Larry "Pretty Boy" Hennig for some tag team matches. But fans' expectations turned out to be wrong, as X entered the ring in a white mask and costume instead of his former black. During the match itself, he also wrestled with the scientific style of a babyface, instead of the roughhouse style of a heel.

Needless to say, this new ring approach for Doctor X did not sit well with the always aggressive Larry Hennig. Words were exchanged between the two, and then the "Pretty Boy" decked the masked man. To add insult to injury, he was assisted in his efforts by his regular tag team partner "Luscious" Lars Anderson. Several wrestlers entered the ring in an attempt to assist Doctor X, who was doing his best to battle two men at once. After the donnybrook, Doctor X claimed that he was determined to wrestle clean from then on, as he wanted to set a positive example for his young son.

With his new ring style, and fans backing him 100 percent, Doctor X became one of the most popular wrestlers in the AWA. He got some revenge on Hennig and Anderson in both singles matches and tag team bouts, where he was joined by such greats as Billy Robinson, Red Bastien, Dick the Bruiser, Wahoo McDaniel, and even his old foe the Crusher.

Beyer's babyface run in the AWA as Doctor X came to a close in 1972. Records show that he lost his last two AWA matches, against Ray Stevens in Rockford, Illinois, on November 4, 1972, and Dusty Rhodes in Fargo, North Dakota, on November 22, 1972.

For the next six years, Dick Beyer returned to being the Destroyer, and wrestled primarily in Japan for his good friend and sometime partner Shohei "Giant" Baba. For a September 20, 1975, card in Chicago, Doctor X returned to team with Dusty Rhodes—now a fan favorite himself—against AWA champions Ray Stevens and Nick Bockwinkel. This match, which X and Rhodes lost, was a one-night stand, and X returned to Japan immediately after.

Another AWA appearance came two years later in Denver on March 25, 1977, when Denver promoter Gene Reed brought Beyer in, as Doctor X, to put over the new masked man on the AWA scene: the Super Destroyer. This was a customary move for promoters during this era: bring in a former big-name star to face the *new* top star of the territory. Doctor X did his job and lost the match.

In another one-night stand, Doctor X was joined by the Crusher in a tag team bout against the Super Destroyer and his partner Angelo Mosca on September 17, 1977, on Crusher's hometown turf in Milwaukee. The 5,800 fans in attendance saw their heroes lose the match.

Doctor X's final match in the AWA took place in Minneapolis on August 26, 1979. He put over yet another masked man, the Super Destroyer Mark II. Though he wasn't the first wrestler to use the mask gimmick, and he certainly wasn't the last, Doctor X is still remembered as the greatest of the masked wrestlers in AWA history.

DICK BEYER (AS THE DESTROYER AND DOCTOR X) CHAMPIONSHIP HISTORY:

★ WWA Title (Los Angeles): July 27, 1962, defeated Fred Blassie; July 22, 1964, defeated Dick the Bruiser; November 13, 1964, defeated Cowboy Bob Ellis

★ International TV Tag Team Title (Los Angeles): December 19, 1962, with Don Manoukian, defeated Abe Jacobs and Haystack Calhoun

★ NWA Pacific Northwest Tag Team Title (Salem): September 25, 1963, with Art Mahalik, defeated Danny Hodge and Shag Thomas; January 22, 1964, with Art Mahalik, defeated Nick Kozak and Nick Bockwinkel

★ NWA Pacific Northwest Title (Portland): January 3, 1964, defeated Mad Dog Vachon; April 20, 1964, defeated Tony Borne

★ WWA World Tag Team Title (Los Angeles): July 30, 1964, with Hard Boiled Haggerty, defeated Ramon and Alberto Torres; October 27, 1964, with Hard Boiled Haggerty, defeated Fred Blassie and Mister Moto

★ NWA World Tag Team Title (San Francisco): March 27, 1965, with Billy Red Lyons, defeated Ray Stevens and Don Manoukian

★ Japan Wrestling Association (JWA) Asian Tag Team Title (Tokyo): June 3, 1965, with Billy Red Lyons, defeated Shohei Baba and Toyonobori

★ World Class Tag Team Title (Dallas): February 8, 1966, with the Golden Terror (Clyde Steeves), defeated Antonio Inoki and Duke Keomuka

★ American Wrestling Alliance (AWA) World Title (Minneapolis): August 17, 1968, defeated Verne Gagne

★ NWA North American Title (Hawaii): September 30, 1970, defeated Pedro Morales

★ Pacific Wrestling Federation (PWF) United States Title (Tokyo): September 30, 1970, defeated Pedro Morales; December 3, 1975, defeated Abdullah the Butcher; September 11, 1978, defeated Mil Mascaras

★ Pacific Wrestling Alliance (PWA) World Masked Man Title (Tokyo): January 5, 1985, awarded to the Destroyer

On August 9, 1993, in Tokyo's Budokan Hall, the Destroyer retired after thirty-nine years in the wrestling business. Dick Beyer, who had turned sixty-three years old just three weeks before, was joined for a six-man tag team match by his son Kurt Beyer and "Giant" Baba in a winning effort against Masao Inoue, Haruka Eigen, and Masa Fuchi. The end came when the Destroyer clamped his famous figure-four leg lock on Inoue, while at the same time Baba had Fuchi in an abdominal stretch and Kurt Beyer also had Eigen in a figure-four leg lock. The Destroyer's retirement from the ring was major news in Japan, and covered on Nippon TV's nightly world news program.

After the match Beyer held a press conference and removed his mask before the camera. He handed the mask to his son Kurt, and announced that when Kurt returned to Japan in the future, he would be the Destroyer, Jr. It was a touching moment and a monumental end to a spectacular career.

In the United States, Dick Beyer had done what he set out to do in 1962: he had never been unmasked, nor removed his mask in the ring, as the Destroyer. He continued to wear his mask to the annual Cauliflower Alley Club reunions. At the 2002 meeting, Larry Hennig ribbed the Destroyer, saying, "Dick, it's over! Take it off." Though Larry's comment brought laughter from those in attendance, there wasn't a single person who would have wanted Beyer to remove his mask. Without it, he would never be recognized. With it, he is and always will be the greatest masked wrestler in history. No one can dispute Beyer's claim.

★ LARRY HENNIG ★

Larry Hennig! Just say his name, and fans of television's *All-Star Wrestling* know exactly who you're talking about. One of Minnesota's finest wrestlers, Larry began as a state wrestling champion at Robbinsdale High School in Minnesota.

Hennig came into professional ranks as a protégé of the legendary Verne Gagne. In fact, Larry was the first of dozens of wrestlers who got their early training from Gagne. In his early years, Larry worked preliminary matches, traveling with the ring to various small towns, and also served as a referee, for which he was highly regarded.

Soon, though, Larry began making more and more appearances as a wrestler. He acquired a legion of fans who appreciated his rugged yet gentlemanly approach to his matches. Hennig was often a last-minute substitute for wrestlers like Tiny Mills, Black Jack Daniels, Ray Gordon, and others who, for whatever reason, were unable to make their scheduled bouts. These matches helped Larry gain experience, and by 1961, Larry had been in the ring with some of the top wrestlers of the day: Gene Kiniski, Jim Hady, Frank Townsend, Roy McClarty, Thor Hagen, Bob Rasmusson, Wilbur Snyder, Tony Baillargeon, and even Hard Boiled Haggerty. These greats, and many others, were quick to sing Hennig's praises.

The year 1962 was a big one for Larry Hennig. After a successful series of matches with AWA World Champion Mister M in late 1961, Larry had proved himself a force to be reckoned with on the local scene. On January 15 in St. Paul, Hennig joined forces with Duke Hoffman for a one-night tag team tournament to determine the new AWA World Tag Team Champions. Because of their youth, Hennig and Hoffman were not favorites, but to the fans' surprise they came up on top of three of the roughest teams the AWA could toss at them. For the next month, Hennig and Hoffman toured around the AWA, celebrating and defending their prized title.

The end of their championship reign came on February 13, 1962, in Minneapolis, when "Texas" Bob Geigel and Stan "Krusher" Kowalski finally took their title away. But Larry Hennig had tasted success, and losing the tag team championship wasn't going to stop him.

In April 1962, Hennig and Hoffman were offered the opportunity to show their stuff in Japan. They jumped at the chance. With them on the tour were such outstanding American wrestlers as Dick Hutton, Arnold Skoaland, Buddy "Killer" Austin, Mike Sharpe, Fred Blassie, and the great Lou Thesz.

Hennig's time in Japan was a turning point for the young wrestler. When he returned to the Twin Cities, promoters and fans immediately noticed a change in his wrestling. Hennig no longer bothered to follow the rules in his drive to win, and his new ring style was extremely aggressive. Larry claimed that he was tired of being fouled during matches, and that now he was going to be the one to throw the first punch. He started to hang around with other bad boys of the AWA like Stan Kowalski, Rocky Hamilton, and the biggest

Left to right:

A very young Larry Hennig shortly after he joined the pro ranks

In the 1970s, after a successful tour of the East Coast, Larry Hennig returned to the AWA reborn as "the Axe." Leaving behind his villainous ways, he began battling the wrestlers fans hated.

It will be a Civil War, Robbinsdale style, tonight when Larry Hennig and Verne Gagne meet in the main event for the world's title.

A feud between the two has been simmering for the past two months. Gagne has accused Hennig of lowering his standards and becoming a dirty, brawling type of wrestler.

Gagne took special interest in the Hennig switch because it was actually Gagne who taught Hennig much of his wrestling when the red-haired Larry first started the pro wars.

Gagne, intending for Hennig to follow his scientific style, was shocked upon seeing Hennig wrestle on the latter's return from the West Coast this year. Hennig has turned into a "crusher type" and Gagne was quick to show his disapproval.

Tonight's match stems from a fracas on TV June 17, 1963. Gagne was wrestling Red Gruppe, who bopped Hennig (the referee) when he wasn't looking. Hennig accused Gagne of the act and promptly disqualified him.

Gagne showed his displeasure by slugging Hennig and demanding tonight's match which, by the way, was signed right in front of the huge viewing audience.

The affair served to heighten Gagne's anger at the refereeing job Hennig has been doing in the past month or so. Gagne claims that Hennig should be taken off Wally Karbo's referee list because he is prejudiced and incapable of doing a satisfactory job.

Gagne indicated after the signing that he would probably abandon his scientific style for the most part and give Hennig a taste of his own medicine.

"I want to show him that I am still in the driver's seat and that he is far away from winning the world's title," said Gagne.

Tonight's match is a one-fall one-hour limit bout.

— *Sports Facts,* June 25, 1963

heel of them all, Crusher Lisowski. Hennig became more uncontrollable with every match. He was often disqualified, and it wasn't long before the fans no longer supported him and his bullish tactics. They now loudly cheered anyone who faced him.

Someone else took offense at Larry's newfound bully style in the ring: his old tutor Verne Gagne. Gagne claimed Hennig was taking the easy way out because he couldn't win matches using the scientific wrestling style he was taught. Hennig retaliated on *All-Star Wrestling,* shouting, "That Gagne was just

Larry Hennig lashed out against Verne Gagne last week, leveling a barrage of blasts and insults at the popular champion. Following are a few choice samplings:

"I was Robbinsdale's best wrestler and football player. If Gagne played when I did he would have been sitting on the bench."

"Compared to me Gagne is puny. I weigh over 270 pounds and am a tower of strength. Compare this to Gagne's 220 pounds and pot belly."

"I wrestle rough because I don't want to look like Gagne when I am old like he is. Did you ever notice how beat up he looks after his matches, while I hardly show any strain?"

— *Sports Facts,* June 25, 1963

jealous of my success." This verbal war eventually led to a showdown between the teacher and his former pupil. This was wrestling at its finest.

This first showdown between Hennig and Gagne ended with Larry being disqualified. They continued to blast each other verbally at any opportunity, and fans eagerly anticipated another confrontation.

In the 1960s professional wrestling had twenty-five to thirty strong promotional territories, and any wrestler who wanted to make his mark in the business had to travel. Hennig didn't like to travel, so the feud with Verne Gagne was to his benefit. Any time the local promoters needed a main event they knew would draw, all they had to do was rekindle the feud between Gagne and Hennig, and the fans responded at the gate.

Larry Hennig did have a couple of successful stints outside of AWA territory. In addition to his trip to Japan, he made short ventures to Amarillo, Texas, in mid-1964 and again in early 1968. He worked the East Coast WWWF territory in 1974 for about six months, and spent a couple of months in Florida in 1975.

GAGNE SAYS HE PITIES HENNIG

Besides being angry at Larry Hennig, Verne Gagne also has pity for him. "He is only hurting himself," stated Gagne. "He wasn't a bad wrestler when he got out of high school, but since then he hasn't progressed at all. In fact, he may be going downhill."

Gagne added that Hennig is still acting like a child, re-fusing to do what is best for him. "He'll never get anywhere acting and wrestling like he does," said Gagne. "But try telling something to a child. It can't be done," said Verne.

"I pity him and hope he wakes up in time to realize he is making a big mistake," Gagne concluded.

— *Sports Facts,* June 25, 1963

It was during the 1964 Amarillo trip that—according to the storyline—Hennig met his new partner, Harley Race. During the summer of 1966, Hennig and Race took a short break from the AWA to wrestle in Australia. The duo became the first tag team champions recognized by the International Wrestling Alliance (IWA) in Australia.

Race and Hennig battled Verne Gagne in many team confrontations. Regardless of who Gagne partnered with, Twin Cities promoters made the most of the rivalry between the two hometown wrestlers. Gagne even hooked up with his longtime foe the Crusher for some especially exciting matches.

On November 1, 1967, in Winnipeg, the feud between Hennig and Gagne reached its bitterest point. In this match, Gagne accidently put him on the shelf for over six months. Because Hennig was unable to defend the AWA World Tag Team Championship that he held with Harley Race, he was forced to forfeit his half of the tag title. The AWA allowed Race to take Chris Markoff for a partner, but they lost the championship to Wilbur Snyder and Pat O'Connor.

GAGNE VS. HENNIG

"I'll take him over my knee, like the fat boy he is, and spank him until he learns some manners!"

With these words, world champion Verne Gagne let everybody know just what he thought of Larry Hennig's ever pressing campaign of constant harassment to get another shot at the champ's title.

Hennig, on the other hand, has not beat around the bush regarding his attitude toward Gagne. "He'll probably find some last-minute excuse not to meet me, just like he's done for the past two months," Hennig told *Sports Facts* during a recent interview. "He knows that on any given day I get him in the ring I'll be able to use all of my fantastic natural wrestling ability to kick him from pillar to post and right through these ring ropes into next week."

Gagne doesn't see the match in quite the same light. "Hennig is a crybaby," the champion told a TV audience last week, "in addition he's a quitter . . . a quitter when the going gets rough. He's got a big head now because he's come out on top with a few so-so matches, but it certainly doesn't seem like a record to warrant him a title match . . .

Larry Hennig's humility, or the obvious lack of it, is of no apparent concern to Hennig himself. "I try to be humble," the Robbinsdale native confides to the world, "But when you're as great an all-around athlete as I am . . . well it's just hard to keep from telling the truth to the fans, not only here in the Upper Midwest, but all over the country, who love me for the great wrestler that I am . . . just imagine," Hennig mused, "How much more they'll love me and idolize me after I whip Verne Gagne and become the champ."

Hennig's confidence is only exceeded slightly by his brass as evidenced by the rumor that he has already urged the city fathers of his hometown of Robbinsdale to plan a big celebration in honor of his capturing of the wrestling crown and champion's belt. According to what *Sports Facts* editors have been able to find out there is, as of press time, no apparent sign of a civic celebration in the offing. This is probably explained by the fact that most Robbinsdale natives seem more inclined to claim Verne Gagne as a favorite son rather than Larry Hennig.

— *Sports Facts,* November 9, 1963

In 1965, Verne Gagne had proudly introduced his latest protégé: Larry Heiniemi. After his rookie year in the business, Heiniemi left the Twin Cities and the AWA. He changed his name to Lars Anderson, traveled to the South, and for the next three years honed his heel skills with fellow Minnesotan and Gagne pupil Gene Anderson. ★ Lars boasted that he changed his name from Heiniemi to Anderson because many of the big names in wrestling would otherwise be scared off by him and his sound amateur background.

The loss of the tag team title fueled Hennig's demands for revenge on Gagne. When Larry finally returned to local ring action in early March 1968, he and Harley Race re-formed their partnership, but they never got another chance at the championship that had made them famous. When Race departed the AWA in late 1969 and started his legendary climb to eight NWA World Championships, Larry was paired with Lars Anderson. The partnership seemed like a natural because Lars, like Larry, was a former Gagne pupil.

The team's first Minneapolis appearance was on *All-Star Wrestling* on December 27, 1969. Hennig now had another Gagne pupil with him who claimed that Gagne's scientific style of wrestling was not for him. The pair soundly defeated opponents Kenny Jay and Bruce Kirk (later known as Frank Monte). At the house show later that evening in the Minneapolis Auditorium, fans saw the new combination live. "Pretty Boy" Larry Hennig and "Luscious" Lars Anderson were joined by Harley Race and lost a six-man tag team contest against Red Bastien, Billy Red Lyons, and Pepper Gomez.

The pair never gained the AWA World Tag Team Title, but they were constant title contenders against champions Mad Dog and Butcher Vachon, meeting them in classic heel versus heel battles in AWA cities including Minneapolis. The team stayed together until March of 1972, when the AWA suspended Lars Anderson for injuring Pepper Gomez during a TV match. It was announced that this was the last draw for Lars, and that the AWA wasn't going to tolerate his unruly tactics any longer. The angle explained Lars leaving the AWA, as he was going to wrestle in California.

Larry Hennig was put into another combination, this time with "Dirty" Dusty Rhodes. Rhodes was a young bully at this time, and had just come out of a tag team partnership with his fellow Texan, "Dirty" Dick Murdoch. Billed as "the Texas Outlaws," Rhodes and Murdoch were champions in the Detroit territory. When he joined Hennig, Rhodes began calling Larry "Lawrence Henry Hennig" during their TV interviews. As a team, Larry and Dusty were popular heels with the fans, and they did very well in the AWA until October of 1972. Dick Murdoch then ventured to the AWA, and was reunited with his old pal Dusty Rhodes.

Left without a partner, Larry Hennig announced that he was going to concentrate on a singles wrestling campaign, and that Verne Gagne was his target. Larry said it was time someone retired "the bald-headed, spindly-legged champion," and boasted that he was the one to do it. Though they faced each other several times, Larry fell short of his goal. He was never able to defeat Gagne in a title match and take the AWA World Championship.

In early 1974, Larry Hennig left the AWA for a short time to work for the WWWF on the East Coast. There he battled champion Bruno Sammartino and other WWWF superstars. When he returned to the AWA, he had grown a full red beard, and now called himself Larry "the Axe" Hennig. Along with his new look, he had a new goal: Hennig boasted that he was going to end the career of Verne Gagne's son, Greg, who had entered the pro ranks in 1973. Greg Gagne had formed a popular team with "Jumping" Jim Brunzell of White Bear Lake, Minnesota. Both Greg and Jim had come out of the Verne Gagne training camp, and had been trained by Gagne and the English wrestler Billy Robinson.

The feud with the younger Gagne was in full swing in 1974, and Larry battled him all over the AWA. Then, in mid-1974, Hennig began acting strangely. First, he joined up with former partner Lars Anderson, who had returned to the AWA under his real name of Larry Heiniemi. Larry had formed a tag team with "cousin" Les "Buddy" Wolff, and for six-man matches, Hennig was their third partner. During a match in Minneapolis on July 13, 1974, Hennig seemed to have a little trouble communicating with his partners—just before he "accidentally" dropped an elbow onto Heiniemi, breaking his arm. Heiniemi and Wolff cried foul, and claimed that Hennig had done it because he was jealous of their success.

That was just the beginning. On August 24, while Greg Gagne and Jim Brunzell were wrestling on TV against former tag team champions Nick Bockwinkel and Ray Stevens, a brawl erupted. Bockwinkel and Stevens and their manager Bobby "the Brain" Heenan began manhandling the young combination.

Several wrestlers came to Gagne and Brunzell's aid, and were quickly tossed out of the ring by Heenan's men.

Then, to the audience's shock, huge Larry "the Axe" Hennig came into the ring. At first it seemed as though he would join forces with Bockwinkel, Stevens, and Heenan—but when the melee ended, Larry carried the fallen Greg Gagne out of the ring. He went to the interview area of the TV studio and said that although he had his own battles with Greg and his father, he could not stand by and watch the brutal attack on Greg, which could have ended his career. Larry stated that someday his own son would be in the pro ranks, too, and he would not want someone to try to end his career, either.

The result: Larry "the Axe" Hennig became an instant fan favorite. He began battling with his former friend Heiniemi, and was joined by his new allies, the Gagnes and Jim Brunzell. Larry also teamed with former enemy the Crusher, and with former partner Dusty Rhodes, who was now also a very popular babyface. Hennig became one of the most popular grapplers on the AWA circuit.

In the fall of 1975, Larry hooked up with huge Canadian Joe LeDuc, and billed as the "Lumberjacks," they battled Jimmy and Johnny Valiant, Mad Dog Vachon and Baron Von Raschke, and the champions Nick Bockwinkel and Ray Stevens. Their team ended when LeDuc left the AWA. After his departure, Hennig resumed singles wrestling. He had notable matches with foes like Bockwinkel, Lanza, and Angelo "King Kong" Mosca.

As the 1970s came to a close, Larry eventually retired from the ring. He did return briefly in the early 1980s when his son Curt joined the professional ranks. They even teamed together in Seattle and Portland, and became the first father-son tag team to win the Pacific Northwest Tag Team Championship, on April 27, 1982. They won the belts from Rip Oliver and Matt Borne, and held the championship until the rematch on May 1.

When Curt returned to the AWA, Larry also worked some tag team bouts with him until early 1983, when the Axe retired for good.

★ KENNY "SODBUSTER" JAY ★

Kenny Jay was a loser! Perhaps only in professional wrestling can an athlete lose in virtually every game he plays and still be highly regarded by fans and fellow athletes. When fans talk about wrestling's glory days, names like Verne Gagne, the Crusher, Mad Dog Vachon, Red Bastien, Nick Bockwinkel, Larry Hennig, and Harley Race come up—and every now and then, so will Kenny Jay. Back in the old days in the AWA, Kenny Jay was a big a name among his fellow wrestlers. Even though he hardly ever won a match, Kenny Jay was acknowledged as one of the best.

Kenny Jay was a "jobber." That meant that Kenny seldom, if ever, won matches—but that wasn't what he was paid to do. Kenny Jay was paid to lose.

When he went up against the likes of Bastien, Bockwinkel, or any of the other "pushed" wrestlers, Kenny's primary objective in the match was to give them an impressive victory. Those who worked in the Golden Age will all tell you, "Kenny Jay was the guy that helped put us over."

Doctor X (Dick Beyer) probably wrestled against Kenny Jay in the AWA more than any other opponent. Kenny was the loser in every one of their matches. In each match, however, fans always believed, if only for a couple of minutes, that Kenny Jay might get lucky and pull an upset over the masked man. Outside of the ring, Beyer and Jay were the best of friends with nothing but the utmost respect for each other.

Jay was always introduced as "the very capable Kenny Jay," and he was exactly that: capable. Kenny Jay did his job well. He put other wrestlers over. The jobbers of the wrestling business came and went, but Kenny Jay was always willing and able to give the promoters a decent match. And the wrestlers themselves knew that wrestling Jay would give them a nice workout and a chance to look good.

In real life, Kenny Jay was Kenny John Benkowski. When he started wrestling in Milwaukee, his sister suggested he use his middle initial and call himself "Kenny Jay." Kenny liked the idea, and he never used any other name.

Kenny didn't follow wrestling as a kid. His family lived in the country and never had a TV. He had never seen wrestling until he moved to Milwaukee after he graduated from high school in 1955. Kenny started working at the Bucyrus-Erie machine shop in Milwaukee, and he bought his parents their first TV as a Christmas present after he started working.

After about a year, Kenny was laid off. He happened to see an advertisement in a Milwaukee newspaper for a professional wrestling training school. Kenny remembers thinking, "I don't have anything else to do, so I'll answer the ad."

The owner of the school was a guy named Bob Hukinson. After attending the school for about three months, Kenny and his instructor, Joe Armstrong, took off for Minnesota, where they wrestled in carnivals for a short time, taking on all comers. They did this for three weeks, and then Kenny started wrestling in professional bouts. His first pro match was at Southside Armory in Milwaukee, and he wrestled on the card for nothing. He was just trying to get his foot in the door. He showed up every Thursday, and after a few weeks began getting paid.

Kenny wrestled two or three times a week for a promoter in Chicago and around Gary, Indiana. Then the tag team combination of Johnny Gilbert and Billy Goelz took Kenny Jay under their wing and brought him to the old Marigold Arena in Chicago. Kenny was hooked up with the Sheik (Ed Farhat) and signed to face the champions. However, the draft board called, and Kenny never had his championship match.

While on leave from the army, Kenny worked wrestling matches in Omaha and Minneapolis for promoters Joe Dusek and Wally Karbo. Kenny also got to wrestle in Barcelona, Spain. After the army, Kenny continued working for

Karbo, and Jay was always there for him. If they needed somebody in Omaha, Wally would call and say, "Gosh, Kenny, can you make it?" Kenny would pack up and leave within the hour.

When TV matches in either Omaha or Minneapolis were taped, more often than not Kenny Jay wrestled more than once per evening. Whether it was against a heel like Mad Dog Vachon or a babyface like Red Bastien, Kenny gave a credible and professional account of himself. Fans could believe that Kenny had a fighting chance, and many times they pulled for him and cheered him on.

One of Kenny's biggest thrills was when he had the chance to wrestle boxer Muhammad Ali in 1976 as a prelude to the Ali versus Antonio Inoki closed-circuit television match in Chicago's International Amphitheatre. Kenny got a call from Wally Karbo, who said, "Can you go to Chicago and wrestle Muhammad Ali?" The wrestling office flew Kenny to Chicago for the match, and flew him back to Minneapolis once it was over. Kenny lost, of course.

Another highlight for Kenny came in the summer of 1965, when Verne Gagne and the Crusher chose him to be their third partner for a six-man tag match against the unholy threesome of Larry Hennig, Harley Race, and Chris Markoff. The trio boasted during TV interviews that they were going to make an example of Kenny Jay, and give him the worst beating of his professional career for agreeing to be Gagne and Crusher's partner.

But Hennig and company were shocked when Kenny Jay turned the tables on them. After the match was even at a fall apiece, it was the "very capable" Kenny Jay who scored the winning fall by pinning Harley Race.

Kenny Jay was honored in April 2005 by his peers in Las Vegas at the annual Cauliflower Alley Club reunion. Dick "the Destroyer" Beyer and I presented "the Sodbuster" with his award. He received a standing ovation.

★ BARON VON RASCHKE ★

The Baron Von Raschke fans knew from TV interviews was a mean, snarly German who claimed to have been born behind the Berlin Wall, a man who hated everything American. But that was his wrestling character. The real Baron, Jim Raschke, was a quiet, humble, and mild-mannered man born in 1940 in Omaha, Nebraska.

Raschke went to Omaha North High School where he played football, wrestled, and ran for the track team. He excelled at wrestling, and he was the state champion at Omaha North High School in 1958. He went on to the University of Nebraska, where he was the Big Eight Conference Champion in the heavyweight division in 1962 and a two-time All-American. He played football for two years and earned a degree in zoology, graduating in 1963.

He was then drafted, but the army allowed him to continue wrestling and he trained at the New York Athletic Club in Manhattan. His roommate was a submariner named Tom Cunningham, a big professional wrestling fan. Tom took Raschke to the local Omaha TV station every Saturday where a weekly pro wrestling program was filmed.

When Raschke got out of the army in 1965, he got a job teaching school in Omaha, but realized fast that he wasn't making much money. So he contacted Omaha promoter Joe Dusek, who introduced him to Verne Gagne. Verne said that if Raschke ever came to Minneapolis, he could train with him.

Raschke credits Gagne with teaching him the difference between amateur and professional wrestling, but says that he was never actually let in on the inner workings of the business. He remembers picking up most of that from the back seats of cars while traveling. He'd listen to other wrestlers discuss their matches and absorb everything he heard.

Raschke's first professional match was in Milwaukee on September 16, 1966, against a rugged veteran named Johnny Kace. Raschke won! He gives a lot of credit to Kace for working with him, to make him look good in his first match.

Raschke credits guys like Killer Kowalski, Johnny Valentine, Mad Dog Vachon, Gagne, Snyder, Jay York (the Alaskan), Stan Kowalski, and Tiny Mills for sharing tips on the psychology of working a match and a crowd. He says they were all good teachers, each in their own way. He learned early on that

The dreaded and popular Baron Von Raschke gestures his feared claw hold to ringside fans.

in pro wrestling, you borrow from everyone, but create your own character and style.

Mad Dog Vachon advised him to be more aggressive in the ring and thought he would make a good German heel. Mad Dog wanted to call him "Baron Von Pumpkin." This led to his professional name.

In May 1967, Mad Dog convinced Raschke to join him in Montreal. Together they forged a now-legendary tag team that fans remember fondly. Canadian promoters billed Baron as Baron Fritz Von Raschke, but in St. Louis he was just Von Raschke. Raschke smiles when he remembers and says, "In St. Louis, I was demoted."

Promoters everywhere clamored for the Baron's services as an evil German menace, and soon he was headlining cards instead of working the preliminaries. He worked night after night with men like Rene Goulet, Edouard Carpentier, Johnny Rougeau, Gino Britto, Dan Miller, Mark Lewin, Bobo Brazil, and countless other ring legends.

Raschke enjoyed an extensive run on the East Coast and battled champion Bruno Sammartino. He formed a successful tag team with fellow German Hans Schmidt (in reality a Canadian)—after all, if one despicable German brought in fans, two would be even better.

During his storied career, Raschke worked most of the major territories in the United States, and along the way racked up numerous wins and championships. In the early 1980s, the Baron had a change of heart and joined the good guy camp, holding the AWA tag team title with Crusher Lisowski. He retired from wrestling in February 1995. In 2007, the History Theatre in St. Paul produced a play featuring the Baron and his career.

CHAMPIONSHIPS HELD BY BARON VON RASCHKE:

★ AWA World Title (Montreal version): 1967, as Baron Fritz Von Raschke; won championship from Edouard Carpentier

★ WWA World Title (Indianapolis): March 7, 1970, defeated Dick the Bruiser; October 14, 1970, defeated Dick the Bruiser; June 2, 1972, defeated Billy Red Cloud (Bill Wright)

★ American Title (Texas): July 1970, defeated Fritz Von Erich

★ WWA World Tag Team Title (Indianapolis): February 24, 1973, with Ernie "the Cat" Ladd, defeated Crusher Lisowski and Dick the Bruiser

★ NWA North American/Central States Tag Team Title (Kansas City): September 30, 1976, with Mad Dog Vachon, defeated Black Gordman and Goliath

★ NWA Mid-Atlantic TV Title (Charlotte): December 1977, defeated Ricky Steamboat (Dick Blood)

★ NWA World Tag Team Title (Charlotte): 1978, with Greg "the Hammer" Valentine; 1979 with Paul Jones

★ NWA Georgia Title (Atlanta): June 8, 1980, defeated Austin Idol (Mike McCord)

★ NWA Florida TV Title (Hollywood, Florida): November 26, 1980, defeated Barry Windham

★ AWA World Tag Team Title (Minneapolis): May 6, 1984, with Crusher Lisowski, defeated Ken Patera and Jerry Blackwell in Green Bay, Wisconsin

★ Pro Wrestling America (PWA) Tag Team Title (Minnesota): December 29, 1991, with Ken Patera, defeated the Punishers, Sledge and Hammer; January 25, 1992, with Ken Patera, defeated the Punishers, Sledge and Hammer

★ NICK BOCKWINKEL ★

Nick Bockwinkel's greatest achievement in the ring took place in St. Paul on November 8, 1975, when he won the AWA World Heavyweight Championship from the legendary Verne Gagne. Bockwinkel reigned as champion until Gagne regained the title almost five years later, on July 18, 1980, in Chicago. The crafty Bockwinkel held the title three more times in his illustrious career. He also shared the AWA World Tag Team Championship with Ray Stevens on three different occasions between January 1972 and October 1974.

Nick was a second-generation wrestler, the son of Warren Bockwinkel. Because his dad wrestled around the country, Nick attended high school in "four different schools, six times," he recalls. He played football at Jefferson High School in San Francisco and went on to the University of Oklahoma on a football scholarship, but lost his scholarship when both his knees were broken. He moved to southern California and started wrestling professionally in 1955.

Nick didn't have an extensive amateur wrestling background, but he grew up around the wrestling business with his dad. Friendly wrestlers grabbed him and put holds on him, and Nick picked up the moves. He recalls hating to see his dad getting beat up in the ring, but his dad always assured him that he was okay after the matches ended.

Nick's early training came from the best in the business, with guys like Lou Thesz, Wilbur Snyder, Gene Kiniski, Lord James Blears, and of course his father tutoring him. He trained most often with Wilbur Snyder. Warren Bockwinkel had trained Snyder when he first entered the business. Nick's dad never told him about the inner workings of wrestling. He learned how it was all done by osmosis, just from being in the dressing rooms.

During his earliest matches, Nick was billed as "Young Nicky Bockwinkel, the old ladies' favorite." He also wrestled as "the Phantom" for a short time in Omaha, working in a mask with Dr. Bill Miller, the villainous Dr. X. In Buffalo, New York, Pedro Martinez billed Nick as "Roy Diamond." Nick remembers that when Martinez asked him to change his name, Nick said, "You can call me 'asshole' just as long as you pay me." When he was in the army stationed at Fort Ord he wrestled as Dick Warren and Nick Warren because the military forbade men from wrestling in their off time.

In the 1960s Bockwinkel traveled across the United States and enjoyed moderate success. In the Oregon territory with promoter Don Owen his career started to click. He became one of the most popular wrestlers on the circuit. He was given the Pacific Northwest championship two different times, in 1963 and 1964.

Nick also combined with Texas favorite Nick Kozak to win the Pacific Northwest Tag Team Championship two times and once with Buddy Moreno. During the 1960s Nick also won titles in California, Hawaii, and Georgia wrestling against guys like Ray Stevens, Ciclon Negro, Art and Stan Neilson, Curtis

Nick played football at Jefferson High in San Francisco as a fullback. The tackle in front of Nick was a big 6' 4" 235-pound guy by the name of John Madden, who carved out a legendary career of his own.

Iaukea, Dick the Bruiser, Buddy "Killer" Austin, Tony Borne, Art Mahalik, Pat Patterson, Don Manoukian, and Johnny Barend.

In 1966 he toured Australia and battled the likes of Waldo Von Erich, Pampero Firpo, Bobby Graham, and Killer Kowalski. In November 1969, Nick went to Georgia, and for the first time in his career he played a heel. It remained his ring persona from then on. Unlike other ring heels, Nick didn't rant and rave during interviews. Instead he displayed a very calm, collected demeanor, but also came across as confident and arrogant. It worked, and fans took to booing and hating him.

Bockwinkel headlined matches with NWA World Champion Dory Funk, Jr., three different times in 1970, going to a one-hour draw with the champion on April 10 in Atlanta, losing a close match on June 19, and then another one-hour draw on August 14, again in Atlanta. Nick also captured the Georgia state title during this run.

In December 1970 Nick disappeared from Georgia and showed up in Minneapolis. Announcer Marty O'Neill interviewed Nick on *All-Star Wrestling,* then broadcast on WTCN-TV (Channel 11) from the Calhoun Beach Hotel. When Marty asked him why he'd come to the AWA, Nick said that he had been chasing the champion Verne Gagne for years, but that Gagne would not agree to meet him. "So," Nick said smugly, "I've decided to come to the champ's hometown and challenge him here." He looked directly into the TV camera and said, "Verne Gagne, in Hawaii where I was the state champion, when someone is leaving, we say 'Aloha.'" After a short pause, he concluded with, "Aloha, Verne Gagne," and walked away.

These comments positioned Bockwinkel as a force to be reckoned with, but as with all challengers, Nick would have to prove himself. He started by defeating fan favorites like Paul Diamond, Billy Red Cloud, Edouard Carpentier, Red Bastien, Bull Bullinski, and even the Crusher. After seven months of racking up victories, Nick still hadn't gotten a shot at Gagne's title. But there was another undefeated grappler in the AWA too, by the name of Hercules Cortez. A match between the two superstars was arranged, with the stipulation that the winner would be in line for a championship match.

The showdown was scheduled for July 24, 1971, in Minneapolis. But in the early morning hours of that day, while driving back from Winnipeg, Hercules fell asleep at the wheel of his car and died in a crash. Though the wrestling world was shocked and saddened by Cortez's death, a card had been set in the Minneapolis Auditorium for later that night, so with 6,000 fans filling the arena, Verne Gagne agreed to substitute for the fallen Hercules, with the stipulation that his title would not be on the line.

Nick finally got his chance to face the champion in the ring and prove himself a worthy contender. All went well until midway into the bout, when Gagne clamped his famous sleeper hold on Bockwinkel, and it looked like Nick would lose the match. Ray Stevens jumped up on the ring apron to protest the hold.

A wrestler named Ray Stevens made his Minneapolis debut on the July 24 card. Ray came from California with a solid reputation and had title aspirations of his own. He announced that he would sit at ringside to scout both Gagne and Bockwinkel during the match.

Gagne released the hold on Bockwinkel and punched Stevens to the ring floor. Quickly, Nick hit the champ from behind, fell on him for the pin—and defeated the world champion. Though the title was not at stake, Nick boasted to everyone that he had beaten the champion, and it was just a matter of time until he did it again with the title on the line.

Nick and Ray Stevens decided to form a tag team to gun for the World Tag Team Championship as well. Together they lifted the crown from champions Red Bastien and the Crusher in Denver in January 1972. For the rest of the year, the new champs defended their title belts to many combinations that included Bill Watts, Wahoo McDaniel, Dr. X, the Crusher, Red Bastien, and others. They had a firm grip on the belts, and showed no signs of dropping them. At the end of 1972, the hated duo finally lost the belts for a week to old nemeses Verne Gagne and Billy Robinson, but quickly regained them the first week of January 1973.

For the next two years, Nick Bockwinkel put his aspirations of becoming world champion on hold as he and Ray Stevens successfully defended their tag team belts hundreds of times to some of the top combinations promoters could throw at them. In July 1974, Nick and Ray finally lost the championship to the team of the Crusher and Billy Robinson. The storyline was that they were bitter about the loss and felt that they were given a raw deal by the referee. They vowed that they would regain the championship, and to further assure it would happen, they acquired the services of Bobby "the Brain" Heenan as their manager.

Their plan worked, and in October 1974 they took back the championship belts. The unpopular duo and their cocky manager continued their winning streak until August 1975, when they were finally stopped again by the Crusher, this time teamed with his "cousin" Dick the Bruiser.

After losing the belt, Nick announced that it was his time to prove to Verne Gagne once and for all that he was a worthy contender, and that with Bobby Heenan at his side, there was no way he could miss. His prognostication came true in November 1975 in St. Paul. Nick defeated Gagne, this time with the title at stake, and Bockwinkel became the new AWA World Champion.

For the next five years, Nick proved night after night in town after town that he was the champion by defeating everyone promoters challenged him with. His list of opponents is a who's who of the wrestling business. One opponent Nick refused to wrestle, though, was the former champ, Verne Gagne. For five years, Nick said that Verne wasn't a worthy contender, and that because Gagne made him wait so long for a match, he was going to make Gagne wait too.

Gagne finally got the match on July 18, 1980, in Chicago. The wily veteran made the best of his chance—and won back the title. Nick cried foul as usual, but to no avail. By this time Gagne was thinking of retiring from wrestling, as the victories weren't coming as easily as they once did. Promoter Wally Karbo signed Gagne to defend his title to Bockwinkel in what was billed as Gagne's final match, on May 10, 1981.

Nick vowed that he was going to embarrass Gagne in his last showing, and prevent him from retiring as world champion. On that night, though, the 17,000 plus fans in the St. Paul Civic Center rallied behind their longtime hero Verne Gagne and saw him get the nod over his arrogant challenger. Then true to his word, Gagne retired from wrestling.

With Verne retired, the AWA needed a new world champion, and they awarded the title to Nick Bockwinkel. The decision of course didn't set well with the fans, and now Bockwinkel was more hated than ever. Over the course of the next few years, Nick was challenged by wrestling's best, and he proved as he had in the past that he was champion for a reason.

Nick decided to end his career in 1987. When he left the ring for good, wres-

CHAMPIONSHIPS HELD BY NICK BOCKWINKEL:

★ NWA World Tag Team Title (San Francisco): April 28, 1958, as Dick Warren with Ramon Torres, defeated Hans Hermann and Art Neilson

★ NWA World Tag Team Title (San Francisco): July 14, 1958, as Dick Warren with Ramon Torres, defeated Tiny Mills and Hombre Montana

★ NWA World Tag Team Title (San Francisco): November 10, 1962, with Wilbur Snyder, defeated Mitsu Arakawa and Kinji Shibuya

★ United States Title (Hawaii): 1962; Nick was the first recognized champion

★ Pacific Northwest Title (Salem): October 30, 1963, defeated Tony Borne

★ Pacific Northwest Tag Team Title (Oregon): March 22, 1964, with Nick Kozak, defeated the Destroyer (Dick Beyer) and Don Manoukian; Kozak was injured and replaced during the match by Buddy Moreno, aka Omar Atlas

★ Pacific Northwest Title (Portland): May 22, 1964, defeated the Destroyer (Dick Beyer)

★ Hawaiian Title (Honolulu): November 25, 1964, from Johnny Barend

★ World Tag Team Title (Amarillo): April 25, 1968, with Ricky Romero, defeated Kurt and Karl Von Brauner

★ Hawaiian Tag Team Title (Honolulu): March 12, 1969, with Bobby Shane, defeated "Crazy" Luke Graham and "Ripper" Roy Collins

★ Georgia State Title (Atlanta) April 1970

★ Georgia State Title (Atlanta): July 24, 1970, defeated Paul DeMarco

★ AWA World Tag Team Title (Denver): January 20, 1972, with Ray Stevens, defeated Red Bastien and Crusher Lisowski

★ NWA Florida Tag Team Title (Tampa): July 20, 1972, with Ray Stevens, defeated Tim Woods and Hiro Matsuda

★ AWA World Tag Team Title (St. Paul): January 6, 1973, with Ray Stevens, defeated Verne Gagne and Billy Robinson

★ AWA World Tag Team Title (Winnipeg): October 24, 1974, with Ray Stevens, defeated Crusher Lisowski and Billy Robinson

★ AWA World Title (St. Paul): November 8, 1975, defeated Verne Gagne

★ AWA World Title (Minnesota): May 19, 1981, awarded the championship when Verne Gagne retired with the belt

★ AWA World Title (Chicago): October 9, 1982, defeated Otto Wanz

★ Southern Title (Memphis): October 11, 1982, defeated Jerry "the King" Lawler

★ AWA World Title (Denver): June 29, 1986, awarded the championship when Stan Hansen refused to defend the title

tling fans, promoters, and fellow wrestlers realized that they were seeing the end of an era. Nick was admired by all who watched him wrestle and by the men he wrestled with. He set out to prove that he was the best and he did prove it. Nick Bockwinkel was inducted into the professional wrestling hall of fame in New York and in Waterloo, Iowa. When Minnesota wrestling legends are remembered, Bockwinkel is foremost among them.

Nick Bockwinkel with arm-lock on Larry Hennig

★ THE ANNOUNCERS ★

The wrestling announcer. The pitch man. Wrestlers may have been the main event, but the announcer was the show. Any fan who ever watched *All-Star Wrestling* in the Twin Cities remembers the voices of Marty O'Neill and Gene Okerlund. Week in and week out, they told the fans why they shouldn't miss the card, and where to get their tickets.

Between the 1950s and the early 1980s, Marty O'Neill was that little guy with the sunglasses who calmly carried out interviews that excited or irritated fans, but above all, got them to tune in. When Marty was unable to cross union picket lines in the late 1970s, Verne Gagne, desperate to get his show on the air, asked a marketing executive named Gene Okerlund if he could open the show and do the interviews. Gene did, and became the second-most-recognized personality on *All-Star Wrestling*.

Wrestling on television in Minneapolis and St. Paul was originally aired over WTCN Channel 4 beginning in 1950. In 1952, Channel 4 changed its call letters to WCCO, and a new WTCN appeared on Channel 11 in 1953. During those early years, the wrestling program was called *Schmidt's Minneapolis Wrestling* and was shown every Tuesday night at 8:30. In reader polls, the show was voted the best sports show of 1951 and 1952.

Marty O'Neill hosted the show from the very beginning, and continued when it became *All-Star Wrestling* in 1960. In those days it was live from the KMSP Channel 9 studios, and hit living rooms around the Twin Cities every Saturday night at 7:00. Reruns were shown on Wednesdays at the same time. The show moved to WTCN Channel 11 on September 29, 1961. In November the intro of the show was: "Verne Gagne and his All-Stars, live and direct from the studios of WTCN-TV." It aired at 6:30 on Saturday nights. In December the intro changed to "Verne Gagne's All-Stars, the best grapplers in the country, from the studios of WTCN."

In the 1960s, the show opened with this announcement, with "The Golden Gate March" playing underneath: "Live and pre-recorded from the WTCN-TV studios in the Calhoun Beach Hotel, it's *All-Star Wrestling* . . . and now, let's go to the ring and Marty O'Neill." Wrestling fans still get goose bumps when they hear this intro.

In 1974, the theme music was changed to a drum rhythm, with Rodger Kent's voice saying, "*All-Star Wrestling* . . . featuring the greatest professional wrestlers from the United States, Germany, Japan, England, Canada, Russia, Australia . . . the greatest professional wrestlers from around the world. Now, let's go to the ring." This opening was used until 1990, when *All-Star Wrestling* left the airwaves.

During the forty years of the show, Marty and Gene were the big names, but they were far from the only ones on the program. Jack Horner, Butch Levy, Rodger Kent, Rod Trongard, Al DeRusha, Ken Resnick, Doug McLeod, Ralph Strangis, Lee Marshall, Larry Nelson, and Dick Jonkowski all at one time or other lent their voices and personalities to *All-Star Wrestling*. Without each and every one of them, the wrestling that kept us glued to our screens would not have been possible. As Marty so often said, "Run, don't walk, to the box office to get your tickets!"

★ MASKED MEN ★

One of the most successful angles presented in professional wrestling was as simple as putting a mask on a wrestler and billing him from Parts Unknown. Promotions would claim no knowledge of who was under the hood, and then send the best wrestlers in the territory out to try to unmask him. Over the years and throughout the territories, masked men packed auditoriums large and small with fans who hoped that this might be the night the mystery wrestler was pinned and his mask removed.

Even if a masked wrestler was revealed, however, fans would often have no idea who he was. In the days before cable television and the Internet, wrestling fans were generally unaware of happenings outside their territory. This made things easy for promoters, because it allowed them to claim that when the un-masking occurred, it was exclusive to their territory, in front of their fans.

Often the mask gimmick was used by wrestlers with limited talent or charisma who were trying to kick their careers into high gear. Sometimes, though, talented wrestlers simply decided to create a new persona and wrestle under a mask. The masked men were usually unruly and demanding and, generally speaking, heels. They commonly claimed to be so good that the big names refused to face them, so they were forced to hide their identity to get the matches they deserved.

A mask could also provide an opportunity for a wrestler to move to a different territory and start fresh. Sometimes a wrestler could work two territories at the same time: one with the mask, and the other without it. Fans usually had no idea that their masked wrestler was a jobber or maybe even a big name in a neighboring territory.

Once he'd put on a mask, a wrestler needed a name to go with his new hidden identity—names like Assassin, Professional, Spoiler, Grappler, or Avenger seemed appropriate. Sometimes, two wrestlers would join together as masked tag teams, making for twice the mystery. Promoters claimed to know nothing about the mystery men who appeared on their cards. They often proclaimed that they didn't know where the masked man came from or if he could even wrestle.

Minnesota and the AWA saw a fair number of masked wrestlers in the Golden Age. Two of the most successful were Mister M (Bill Miller) in the early 1960s and Doctor X (Dick Beyer) in the late 1960s and early 1970s. The two grapplers were hugely popular. But they weren't the only wrestlers to don a mask in the AWA. Over the decades, many appeared under a hood. Their escapades may not have been as memorable as those of Mister M and Doctor X, but they still brought their fair share of excitement to the territory's rings.

MASKED MAN

This guy was truly original. Tony Nero, a journeyman wrestler in the early years of the AWA, worked under a mask on some cards billed simply as "Masked Man." Basically, he was used as an extra wrestler to fill out a card. On some cards he would actually wrestle twice: once as Tony Nero, and then later on the card as Masked Man. There was no storyline attached to the hooded wrestler. He was never given any sort of push and eventually disappeared from the AWA. Perhaps his biggest claim to fame came when Harley Race was out with an injury in 1965 and Larry Hennig had Masked Man as his partner for a couple of spot show cards (wrestling cards held in small towns). Race was recuperating after being stabbed during a scuffle outside the ring. Tony Nero filled Harley's spot with Hennig, with no fanfare as to who he was and no explanation of why he wore the mask.

EL ROJO CARA

This wrestler made only one appearance in the AWA under a mask. On January 15, 1962, he teamed up with the also-masked Mister M in an eight-team tournament in St. Paul to determine the new AWA World Tag Team Champions. El Rojo Cara under the mask was Dan Miller, the younger brother of big Dr. Bill Miller—the man under the Mister M mask. M needed a partner to enter the tournament, and the AWA decided to bring in his younger brother, but only for this one night. Dan Miller had an outstanding career in other territories, held many titles, and in fact often teamed with Bill without a mask. Dan Miller worked several preliminary matches in the AWA under the name Harry Simpson in 1961.

DOUBLE X

Though he had a longer stint under the mask than El Rojo Cara, Double X is not well known by fans. He came on the scene during the reign of another masked man, Doctor X, near the end of X's first run in 1970. There was never a serious attempt to hide the identity of the man under the XX mask. He was journeyman veteran Jim Osborne, and that was the name he used in AWA rings in the summer of 1970. He worked some preliminary matches in the Twin Cities and other AWA towns—and then Osborne disappeared. Suddenly, the masked Doctor X, the most hated heel in AWA history, had a new partner: Double X. He looked almost exactly the same as Doctor X, and the masked men used their carbon-copy appearances to their advantage. Double X first joined Doctor X in a tag match in Minneapolis on May 2, 1970, when they downed the team of veterans Joe Scarpello and Kenny Jay. The masked men continued to trounce the local favorites for many long weeks, but on July 18 their reign came to an end. In that fateful match in St. Paul, Double X was unmasked by the AWA's original masked marauder: Mister M (Bill Miller).

As with Double X, promoters made no effort to keep the identity of Mister M a secret. He was brought in to try to end the reign of Doctor X, who was now in his third straight year of pummeling opponents from beneath a mask. Bill Miller returned to the AWA for this one match, donning his M mask for the first time in nearly eight years, with his mission clear: unmask Doctor X.

After several minutes of battling Mister M, Doctor X slipped out of the ring while the referee was knocked out, and traded places with his lookalike partner Double X. It was an attempt to give Doctor X a rest, but the plan backfired when M was able to not only defeat Double X, but also unmask him. Thus the face of Jim Osborne was revealed, and the fans had to wait for another day to see Doctor X lose his mask.

After being unmasked, Jim Osborne continued to work some Twin Cities and AWA cards, still billed as Double X even though he did not wear his mask. When Osborne finally left the AWA, his career took off in the Oklahoma and mid-South territory, where he wrestled as Doctor X. Because he resembled Dick Beyer, the AWA Doctor X, many fans thought that he actually was Beyer under the hood. Osborne went on to win the NWA Junior Heavyweight Championship from Ramon Torres, and continued to work for many years as Doctor X.

THE SUPER DESTROYER

The man under the Super Destroyer mask was actually one of the most talented and respected wrestlers in the business. Unbeknownst to fans, he had worked in the AWA earlier in his career without a mask. In 1962, he appeared on many wrestling cards under the name Sonny Cooper. During that stint, he

In the tradition of great masked wrestlers, the Super Destroyer, aka Don Jardine, was not popular with fans.

was usually booked in the opening matches. He would win some, lose some, or reach a draw with his opponent. In other territories, he worked under his real name, Don Jardine. He had tremendous success while teamed with Dutch Savage, and sometimes worked with Mad Dog Vachon in the Pacific Northwest territory.

In the mid-1960s, Jardine decided on a masked career, and was one of the very few wrestlers to gain fame under two different masks and names. First, and most famously, he was the Spoiler. As the Spoiler, Jardine was a huge box-office draw in Texas and Oklahoma, and held several individual and tag team championships. In tag teams, he was often joined by another "Spoiler," usually billed as Spoiler No. 2. Under the masks his partners were equally big names like Les "Buddy" Wolfe and Don "Smasher" Sloan. The Spoiler often had his manager "Playboy" Gary Hart at ringside with him, and more often than not, Hart would assist the Spoiler in winning a match and retaining his mask.

Jardine also wrestled under a different mask and outfit, calling himself the Super Destroyer. It was under this name that he invaded the Minneapolis-based AWA territory. He was billed as coming from Singapore, and his manager and sometime tag team partner was Lord Alfred Hayes. Jardine also often teamed with Angelo "King Kong" Mosca, of Canadian football fame, for tag bouts.

The Super Destroyer's stint was short lived. He hit the AWA in 1977, but by the end of the year he was gone. His disappearance was explained with the story that he was unmasked in Denver by Crusher Lisowski; however, no name was given for the man under the mask, and no record of an actual unmasking in Denver by the Crusher can be found.

After leaving the AWA, Jardine continued on as the Super Destroyer in the mid-Atlantic and Florida territories. In the early 1970s, while in the WWWF, Jardine also worked as the Spoiler, but without a mask. This was because the New York State Athletic Commission had a law that no wrestler could wrestle under a mask. Jardine is also remembered for his ability to actually walk on the top ring rope and jump off onto an opponent.

THE SUPER DESTROYER MARK II

Immediately after Don Jardine left the AWA, manager Lord Alfred Hayes appeared on the scene with a wrestler he referred to as "a bigger, stronger, and better Super Destroyer." This was Super Destroyer Mark II, who was said to be from Gibraltar—as in the Rock of. Unlike Super Destroyer I, who was a big name under the mask, the man under the SD II hood was a young wrestler trained by Verne Gagne for the pro ranks. He was Bob Remus, but fans did not recognize him with his mask and black tights, trunks, and boots. During SD Mark II's run in the AWA, Hayes sold his contract to the other top AWA manager at the time, Bobby Heenan. As part of the Heenan family, SD Mark II was joined by Heenan and his other charge, AWA World Champion Nick Bockwinkel, in battling Hayes and still another Super Destroyer, this one Mark III. SD III was eventually unmasked, but his real name was not given. He was Neal Guay, who

I asked Nick Bockwinkel, AWA World Champion at the time, for the real story of Super Destroyer's supposed unmasking by the Crusher. He said, "Don Jardine did not feel that unmasking would have been any benefit to his career at the time. And so he left."

Jardine taught Mark Calaway, aka the Undertaker of WWF fame, his famous top rope technique. Calaway has had an outstanding career as one of most bizarre characters ever created by WWF (later WWE) owner Vince McMahon, Jr.

When the original Super Destroyer left the AWA, the bigger and stronger Super Destroyer Mark II, Bob Remus, took his place.

in other territories used the names of the Hangman and Jean Louie. Eventually, Super Destroyer Mark II was unmasked, and his name revealed as Matt Burns.

Many fans did not recognize Matt Burns as the rookie Bob Remus who had been wrestling just a few years earlier. The name itself was a joke; wrestlers often suffer "mat burns," similar to rug burns, from the canvas in the ring. After he left the AWA, Remus took on a new persona as a drill instructor, calling himself Sgt. Slaughter. As Slaughter, he had tremendous success in the mid-Atlantic territory of the WWWF. He returned to the AWA as Slaughter, again unrecognized by fans, and went on to hold the AWA America's title. Fans sometimes wonder whether Remus would have been the star he was if Don Jardine had not left the AWA. There is no doubt that Remus, as Super Destroyer Mark II, was in the right place at the right time.

THE MASKED SUPERSTAR

Bill Eadie had the ability and credentials to rival both Bill Miller and Dick Beyer for the title of Minnesota's greatest masked wrestler. Unfortunately, Eadie's tenure in the AWA as the Masked Superstar took place at the wrong time in wrestling history. He was brought into the territory in the mid-1980s, at a time when the AWA, and all the territories, were struggling for survival against the WWF.

Eadie entered the wrestling ranks in Pittsburgh in 1974 under the name of Bolo Mongol, as the new partner of his trainer Geeto Mongol. Shortly thereafter, he traveled to the Georgia territory, headquartered out of Atlanta. It was there that Bill Eadie disappeared forever from the wrestling scene. In his place was a new masked wrestler, appropriately dubbed the Masked Superstar.

Bill Eadie became a top wrestler everywhere he competed. When he came to the AWA as the Masked Superstar, he signed Sheik Adnan El Kaissey as his manager.

During his run in Atlanta, Eadie won the Georgia title four times, eventually unifying it with the NWA National Championship. In the WWWF in the late 1970s, Masked Superstar competed against many top wrestlers, including WWWF Champion Bob Backund.

As the Masked Superstar in the AWA, Eadie played the role of enforcer for Sheik Adnan El Kaissey, who also had King Tonga under his managerial wing. However, the AWA was experiencing low attendance and was losing talent, and Eadie eventually left the territory.

Bill had a second stint in the WWF in 1985 under a different hood, calling himself Super Machine, with partners Andre the Giant, who was Giant Machine, and Black Jack Mulligan, as Big Machine. The three-man Machine team was brought in to rival Bobby Heenan's massive duo of Big John Studd and King Kong Bundy.

In January 1987, Eadie dropped his Super Machine gig and was transformed into Ax, one-half of a tag team calling themselves Demolition. His partner was Barry Darsow, who called himself Smash. Darsow was a Minnesota wrestler who'd received his early ring training from wrestler-turned-promoter Eddie Sharkey.

Demolition was Vince McMahon's attempt to duplicate the success of Animal and Hawk, the Road Warriors, who had just finished a run with the AWA as its tag team champions and were now in the NWA, where they also held tag team belts.

On the microphone, Eadie was one of the best talkers of his era. In 2003, he was ranked as number 113 of the 500 best singles wrestlers by *Pro Wrestling Illustrated,* one of the main national newsstand wrestling magazines.

OTHER MINNESOTA GRAPPLERS WHO WORKED UNDER A MASK DURING THEIR CAREERS:

★ *Big Moose Evans* appeared in St. Louis as "Goliath" under a mask.

★ *Killer Kowalski* was one of the Executioners, who, along with John Studd, covered their faces on the East Coast. And in Florida, Kowalski wore a mask and called himself the Destroyer for a while in the early 1970s.

★ *"Tiger" Joe Tomasso* wrestled as the Bat, and later as one of the Assassins, with partner Guy Mitchell, the other Assassin. They were the first wrestlers ever managed by Bobby Heenan.

★ *Big Ike Eakins,* who appeared in the Twin Cities in the 1950s, put on a mask in some territories and became the Clawman. He carried the gimmick to the point of having his wife and their dog wear masks too.

★ *Reggie Parks* was famous in Minnesota for his iron stomach—one of his many feats of strength was allowing a Volkswagen van to drive over his abdomen. He worked a babyface mask as the Avenger in the mid-South and southern regions.

★ *Len Montana,* who battled alongside Hard Boiled Haggerty in the early 1960s, also worked under the hood at one time. He was simply called the Mask.

★ *H.B. Haggerty,* at one point in the early 1960s, worked as Mister M under a mask. This was right before Bill Miller became Mister M in the Twin Cities. Haggerty never appeared as Mister M in Minneapolis or St. Paul.

MINNESOTA MASKED WRESTLERS IN OTHER TERRITORIES

Other wrestling territories had their share of great masked men too, and many of them were well known to Minnesota wrestling fans.

Minnesota favorite Doug Gilbert wore a mask and enjoyed several years as "the Professional" in Atlanta during the late 1960s. First as a heel and then as a babyface, the Professional held the coveted NWA Georgia State Championship four different times. He also co-held the NWA Georgia Tag Team Title with partners Assassin #2 (Jody Hamilton) and El Mongol. Later, without the mask, Gilbert held the same tag team belts with Bobby Shane. Under another mask and yet another name, this time as Super Inferno, Doug also held the NWA Georgia Tag Team Championship with a wrestler named Don Smith, who was the other Super Inferno.

Putting a mask on any wrestler during the Golden Age almost always meant money in the bank for both the wrestler and the promotion. As for the fans, the intrigue and mystique—and especially the hope of being in the audience when an unknown grappler was unmasked—helped entice them to spring for a ticket. Even if it didn't happen on a particular night, the possibility was there, and the fans came back again the next week, and the week after that, hoping to find out the answer.

★ SEVEN ★

TAG TEAM COMBOS

One-on-one combat in the squared circle was always exciting for the fans, especially when it pitted Mom's apple pie white-hat good guys against dastardly evil black-hat bad guys. In the 1940s, promoters began giving fans double their pleasure when they paired up two popular fan favorites to do battle with two not-so-favorites. This kind of match was called an Australian tag team match, though whether the concept actually originated in Australia is unknown. As with singles matches, there was a specific set of rules, even though promoters knew that, to make it exciting, those rules would be—*had* to be—broken, to keep fans on the edge of their seats and coming back week after week.

The first match involving four wrestlers paired up and forming teams took place in Houston, Texas, on October 2, 1936. Tag team matches were held in the Pacific Northwest territory in 1937 and 1938, and soon they became a regular attraction on wrestling cards in territories around the country, most prominently in Ohio, Georgia, and Missouri.

In a tag team match, only two of the four wrestlers, one from each team, could be in the ring at the same time. The two teams were on opposite sides of the ring, and the wrestlers not involved in the match were supposed to hang on to the "tag rope" that was tied to a corner turnbuckle on the ring post. They had to stay outside the ring on the apron, and they weren't allowed back into the ring until their partner tagged their hand. In theory, it was a one-on-one battle, just like in a singles match.

The rules were meant to be broken, though, and more often than not both wrestlers from one team were in the ring double-teaming an opponent, and often all four wrestlers would end up in the ring.

There was no way one referee could handle four sweaty, out-of-control behemoths. But that was the point. The idea was to give them so much action and mayhem that they couldn't resist entering the ring themselves to restore law and order. To make things even more exciting, the referee often missed important tag in and tag outs, and more often than not, completely missed the bad guys breaking every rule in the book.

There was an art to putting a tag team together. Teams were normally two babyfaces against two heels, but in most cases the teammates had something in common with each other as well. Often two babyfaces joined together in an attempt to rid the wrestling business of two dastardly heels who had been running roughshod over all the other tag teams. The old adage "blood is thicker than water" also played well in tag team wrestling, and there were plenty of "brother" tag teams throughout the territories. Some of them were real-life brothers, but many times, two wrestlers who resembled each other were simply billed as brothers. Stories were created telling of their backgrounds and histories together to persuade fans to either love them or hate them.

Sometimes promoters paired a better-drawing wrestler with one who was less popular to generate attendance. This allowed the lesser talent to add to his credibility by association with the bigger-name star.

After World War II ended, many fans still held resentments against the Japanese, the Germans, the Russians, and other foreign wrestlers—or wrestlers who were billed as foreign. It wasn't uncommon for promoters to pit down-home U.S. wrestlers against the evil gents from other countries. Fans flocked to auditoriums around the country to see America's heroes rid the wrestling world of their enemies. From the late 1940s through the next several decades, it was as though World War II was being fought again and again, but this time in a ring.

Sometimes promoters signed matches between two heel teams who would battle it out for supremacy, forcing fans to choose a side. Which was the lesser of two evils? Fans could also hope that both teams would simply eliminate each other from the scene.

What about two babyface teams facing each other? That could happen, too, leaving the fans hard-pressed to decide which of the two teams they wanted to win. In these match-ups, one of the teams would usually become subtle heels, so that the fans could put their support behind the other team.

Often, tag team matches between two heel teams ended with the referee declaring a double disqualification or no-contest, while battles between babyface teams ended in a time-limit draw, usually after each team had won a fall in the match. No matter which tag team match-up the fans preferred, when four wrestlers entered the ring to do battle, the action was wild, fast, and furious.

Minnesota was a hotbed for tag team wrestling beginning in the 1950s. The trend continued on through the early 1980s with literally hundreds of colorful, scientific, and villainous combinations battling for not only local supremacy, but also the right to be called champions. Any attempt to rank one combination over another leads to heated discussions about which team was better and why. The wrestling promoters never officially put out any ranking, though they would often create fictional ratings if it served to build up a particular match between two teams.

What was the greatest tag team combination to appear in Minnesota? Longtime followers of wrestling remember when Ivan and Karol Kalmikoff ruled the roost, or perhaps the Japanese duo of Mitsu Arakawa and Kinji Shibuya. Or maybe a popular "brother" team like Joe and Guy Brunetti. But no matter who is compiling the list, five Minnesota teams are almost certain to be included.

★ IVAN AND KAROL KALMIKOFF ★

These Russian "brothers" were arguably the most successful tag team ever in all of wrestling. Together Ivan Kalmikoff, real name Edward Bruce, and Karol Kalmikoff, real name Karol Piwoworczyk, wrestled against an incredible 368 different tag team combinations.

The Kalmikoffs were mainstays in the Minneapolis territory during the

Perhaps the greatest tag team combination of all time, Ivan and Karol Kalmikoff were multiple-time champions and one of the most hated of the Russian teams that terrorized wrestling rings after World War II.

1950s, and also traveled extensively around the country, creating mayhem and demonstrating their brutality in many different territories.

Statistics alone justify the Kalmikoffs' top spot on any list of great teams, and quite possibly the number-one team of all time in not only Minneapolis, but the wrestling business as a whole. If you were a wrestling fan during the 1950s and 1960s and had the pleasure of seeing Ivan and Karol Kalmikoff together as a team, you were privileged to witness one of the all-time great wrestling tag teams.

Ivan and Karol's first match together was on October 28, 1953, in Amarillo, Texas, with a victory over George and Jack Curtis, and their last match together was October 5, 1963, in Minneapolis when they lost to Reggie "the Crusher" Lisowski and Dick "the Bruiser" Afflis. Ivan and Karol Kalmikoff teamed together for an amazing ten-year run. Prior to their team-up, the two had actually wrestled against each other on several occasions. Karol went by the name of Karol Krauser in those days. Wrestling great Karl Gotch was also originally named Krauser, and changed his name to avoid confusion with Karol.

After the Kalmikoffs' first victory in Amarillo in 1953, their first winning streak ran in Texas and New Mexico until March 1954. They headed to Canada, where fans in Montreal, Ottawa, Hamilton, and Toronto were treated to their brand of destruction. The Canadian tour also took them to Buffalo and Niagara Falls, New York.

On October 25, 1955, they appeared for the first time in what would eventually be their most successful territory: Minneapolis. On that date, they defeated the fans' darlings Paul and Adrian Baillargeon. Subsequent victories cemented their main event status in the Twin Cities. They met the hated Japanese team of Mitsu Arakawa and Kinji Shibuya on several occasions and managed to prove superior in those matches, too.

Karol's incredible physique was used as the model for Superman in the 1940s animated cartoons.

IVAN AND KAROL KALMIKOFF WIN/ LOSS RECORD—657 MATCHES:

★ Matches won: 335

★ Matches won by disqualification: 42

★ Total victories: 377

★ Matches lost: 95

★ Matches lost by disqualification: 42

★ Total losses: 137

★ Matches wrestled to a draw: 86

★ Matches ending in no-contest decisions: 57

CHAMPIONSHIPS HELD BY THE KALMIKOFFS:

★ Southwest Tag Team Title

★ Southern Tag Team Title

★ Canadian Open Tag Team Title (Toronto): March 17, 1955, from Tiny and Al Mills

★ NWA (Upper Midwest) Tag Team Title (Minneapolis): January 8, 1957, over Fritz Von Erich and Karl Von Schober; June 4, 1957, over Joe and Guy Brunetti; March 5, 1959, over equally hated Reggie and Stan Lisowski; June 1959,

awarded championship after Verne Gagne, who held the title with Butch Levy, failed to make a scheduled title defense

★ AWA World Tag Team Title (Minneapolis): January 1, 1963, from Doug "Mr. High" Gilbert and Dick "Mr. Low" Steinborn

★ Ivan and Nikita Kalmikoff held the Canadian Open Tag Team Title (Toronto): June 12, 1958, from "Whipper" Billy Watson and Bobo Brazil; October 9, 1958, from Watson and Bernard Vignal

An August 6, 1957, contest between the Kalmikoffs and Mitsu Arakawa and Kinji Shibuya in Minneapolis was a blood fest that saw Ivan and Karol leave the ring victorious, as usual. In a return match on August 13 in Minneapolis, the Russians' winning streak was halted by Arakawa and Shibuya, who also snatched the NWA Tag Team Championship with the win.

After dominating the tag team scene in the Twin Cities for nearly two years, Ivan and Karol left the Minneapolis territory following their title loss and began a new reign of terror back in their old stomping grounds in Canada and on the East Coast. They spent most of 1958 away from Minneapolis, re-

During their heyday in Minnesota between 1955 and 1959, many of the Kalmikoffs' tag team matches were filmed in Minneapolis and syndicated on television throughout the United States and Canada. Unfortunately, the tapes of these matches have disappeared over the years. A wrestling book published in the mid-1950s featured photographs of the Kalmikoffs demonstrating wrestling holds on each other. ★ Both Ivan and Karol were established wrestlers in their own right, having been in the business as far back as 1938. They were strong fundamental grapplers, but found their best roles as heels.

Eric Pomeroy was known under many names. As Stan Vachon, he played "brother" to the famous real-life brothers Maurice "Mad Dog" and Paul "Butcher" Vachon. Stan's successes as the third Vachon brother took place in the southern territories, where he and Butcher teamed against the famous Torres Brothers trio of Ramon, Alberto, and Enrique. When the three Torres Brothers hooked up for six-man tag team action, Stan and Paul would import their older brother Maurice Vachon to even things up. ★ While in Omaha—also AWA territory—Eric worked under the name of Stan Pulaski as a fan favorite. He often teamed with equally popular Reggie Parks to battle AWA World Tag Team Champions Mad Dog and Butcher Vachon. Of course, fans

turning with a vengeance to St. Paul on October 18 against huge Tex McKenzie and Bearcat Wright. After total bedlam erupted and the referee lost control of the match, he ruled the bout a no-contest.

For the next year and a half, the Russians would divide their ring time between the Twin Cities and New York, Cleveland, Oklahoma, and Canada. After another brief run with the NWA Tag Team Title in 1959, the Kalmikoffs left the territory in April 1959. They didn't return to the Twin Cities until December 29, 1962, when they defeated Jack Allen and Pepe Gonzales in Minneapolis. Then on January 1, 1963, they captured the coveted AWA World Tag Team Championship from fan favorites Doug Gilbert and Dick Steinborn. Ivan and Karol controlled the title until their defeat at the hands of Crusher and Bruiser in Minneapolis on August 20, 1963.

When Ivan and Karol weren't teamed with each other, they were sometimes teamed with their other "brothers," Nikita and Igor Kalmikoff. Ivan was joined in the AWA (Twin Cities) in the early 1960s for tag bouts with Nikita Mulkovitch, who became younger "brother" Nikita Kalmikoff while he worked the AWA territory. Nikita highlighted his AWA stay with a March 13, 1962, main event when he battled masked AWA World Champion Mister M.

Eric Pomeroy was a veteran journeyman wrestler who was consistently in main events in his native Canada and also in the United States. As Igor Kalmikoff, he and "brother" Karol Kalmikoff had their first match together on March 7, 1964, when they defeated Red McKim and Tom Manousos in Oklahoma City.

As a team, Karol and Igor Kalmikoff had twenty-one victories, and only five losses. The AWA planned to eventually reunite Karol with Ivan, but that was not to be. Their final match together was on July 2, 1964, in Wichita Falls, against opponents Bobby "Hercules" Graham and Jerry Kozak. Shortly after this match Karol Kalmikoff had a heart attack and passed away.

With Karol's untimely passing, the AWA decided on a different course for Ivan Kalmikoff. They came up with the angle of turning the long-hated Russian into a babyface and teaming him with "Mighty" Igor Vodik, a young Polish kid who wanted wrestling training.

To explain Ivan's turn from heel to hero, the AWA had Ivan come to the assistance of Igor Vodik, who allegedly couldn't speak English. Igor sat in the television audience for several weeks in street clothes, and indicated that he wanted to wrestle. Promoter Wally Karbo asked the veteran Ivan to translate for Igor, who played the role well. The story was that he spoke no English and had no previous wrestling experience. Actually Igor had wrestled for several years and had even won the title of Mr. Michigan in a body-building competition. His real name was Dick Garza, and when he removed his long trench coat, fans gaped in awe at his incredible physique.

Igor's strength became a big part of his persona. He would have Ivan Kalmikoff place a cement block on top of his head while he was seated in the middle of the ring, and then have Ivan take a sledgehammer and smash the cement block into pieces while Igor smiled and clapped his hands. He would also sit against a wall and hold back an automobile accelerating at sixty miles per hour.

During this time, Larry Hennig and Harley Race were an undefeated tag team and top heel challengers for the AWA World Tag Team Championship. Ivan and Igor became one of their early and regular opponents in the AWA. Ivan was portrayed as the rugged veteran who had held numerous tag team titles with his late "brother" Karol, and who was now interested in developing the ring skills of the supposedly inexperienced Igor.

When the Ivan and Igor combination lost a match, Ivan usually took the fall for the team, as he was nearing the end of his active career as a wrestler and could afford to appear weak. Then Igor would enter the ring to make the save and rescue his mentor. Igor would often lose his temper and be disqualified, due to his inability to understand the referee trying to hold him back.

Igor Vodik was one of Minnesota's most popular and successful wrestlers from late 1964 to 1968. When he left the AWA territory, he and then-retired Ivan Kalmikoff had a long stay in Michigan and Ohio, where Ivan worked as Igor's manager. Igor made a return to the AWA in 1977, now minus Ivan, but he only had a minor push on his second run in the territory. He continued to wrestle for smaller independent promotions through the mid-1980s.

★ TINY MILLS AND STAN "KRUSHER" KOWALSKI ★

When veteran Tiny Mills joined the ten-years-younger Stan Kowalski, the result was magic. Mills started his outstanding career on December 2, 1948, in Salt Lake City against the villainous Dave Ruhl. Tiny lost this match, but there was little doubt in promoters' and fans' minds that they were seeing a future superstar. Tiny spent the next two years of his rookie induction carving out his trademark brawler tactics. He was on the road to becoming one of wrestling's all-time great heels and one of the game's most respected workers.

Tiny Mills was from Camrose in Alberta, Canada. He boasted of working in the lumberjack camps and fighting bullies there, saying that he began working in professional wrestling so he could beat guys up and get paid for it. Mills actually followed his real-life brother Al Mills into the business. After Tiny started to earn main events, promoters hooked him up with Al, and together they held numerous tag team titles. In those days, Al Mills was considered the better wrestler of the two, but it was evident to promoters that Tiny would eventually surpass his brother and become a legend. The Mills brothers were together, off and on, from the early to mid-1950s, and held many championships together.

In 1958, while on tour in Hawaii, Tiny hooked up with a near-lookalike grappler named Stan Kowalski for a match on August 10, which ended in a stalemate draw. Both Tiny and Stan realized they had magic together. Soon they were being billed as Hawaiian Tag Team Champions, and held that honor until Novem-

weren't told that in other parts of the country, Pulaski was the third Vachon brother. ★ When Eric Pomeroy worked the Twin Cities market in 1966, he used the name Sergi Pulaski and was again billed as being from Russia. He worked many arena cards and TV matches, and faced then-former AWA World Champion Verne Gagne in a July 30, 1966, showdown in St. Paul, in a headline match to build Gagne up for a rematch with reigning AWA World Champion Mad Dog Vachon.

Billed as Murder Inc., Tiny Mills and Stan "Krusher" Kowalski were the first recognized AWA World Tag Team Champions.

ber 2, 1958. Mills and Kowalski were referred to as Murder Inc. because of their brutality in the ring. From Hawaii, they ventured to Australia, Japan, and India. After traveling more than 25,000 miles around the world, Tiny and Stan brought their mayhem to the Midwest, and the Minnesota territory in particular.

Murder Inc. hit the Twin Cities in 1959 billed as International Tag Team Champions. They immediately started headlining wrestling cards, and became one of the premiere teams in the area. Throughout the 1950s, Mills was one of the most hated heels in the Twin Cities, and built a reputation on his desire to destroy local hero Verne Gagne. Mills and Kowalski would fight many matches against Gagne, who teamed with other grapplers in an attempt to derail Murder Inc.

In August 1960, when the American Wrestling Alliance (AWA) was formed, Mills and Kowalski were declared the first AWA World Tag Team Champions because of their international reputation, and because they were already recognized as NWA International Tag Team Champions.

MILLS AND KOWALSKI WIN/LOSS RECORD—89 MATCHES:

★ Matches won: 40

★ Matches won by disqualification: 5

★ Total victories: 45

★ Matches lost: 31

★ Matches lost by disqualification: 5

★ Total losses: 36

★ Matches wrestled to a draw: 5

★ Matches ending in no-contest decisions: 3

TITLES HELD BY MILLS AND KOWALSKI:

★ NWA International Tag Team Title, reportedly won on a tour of Japan and Australia in 1959

★ NWA World Tag Team Title: declared champions on March 5, 1960, as plans were being made to form the rival AWA promotion, and again on July 19, 1960, from Verne Gagne and Leo Nomellini

★ Canadian Open Tag Team Title (Toronto): December 29, 1960, from Billy "Whipper" Watson and Ilio DiPaolo

★ AWA World Tag Team Title: declared the first champions upon formation of the American Wrestling Alliance due to their NWA title recognition

Note: Not included are matches while on tour of Australia, Japan, and India, where Mills and Kowalski reportedly gained the majority of their success before coming to Minnesota.

Even though Stan Kowalski met Tiny Mills in Hawaii, Stan was actually a hometown boy. Stan was from the Minneapolis suburb of Fridley, and he had a grudge to settle with Gagne, too. In fact, Stan disliked Verne both inside and outside the ring. For the rest of his career, Stan would feud with the popular Gagne, and their matches drew huge crowds whenever they hooked up. Due to his unruly tactics in the ring, Stan earned the nickname Krusher. He and Tiny worked the AWA as champions until they met fellow bad men Len Montana and Hard Boiled Haggerty in St. Paul on September 24, 1960, and were relieved of the title belts.

After winning and losing the title, what would the Mills and Kowalski duo do next? For promoters, the answer was simple: split up. So Tiny and Stan had a falling out, feuding with each other over who was the better man on the team.

Tiny claimed that Stan wasn't holding up his end, and that he had to do all the work in the ring while Stan rested on the apron. Stan claimed that Tiny was old and past his prime, and that he had to carry the old man in all their tag

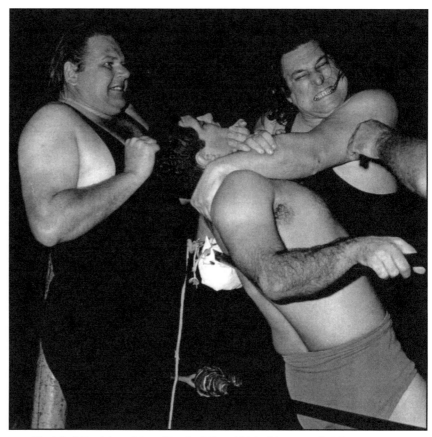

Black Jack Daniels and Stan "Krusher" Kowalski double-team a helpless opponent.

team matches. Their battles against each other were some of the wildest and most brutal encounters Twin Cities wrestling fans ever saw.

Though Tiny eventually became the favorite, he was winding down his in-ring career. Instead, he became one of the AWA's top referees, specializing in matches that needed someone who could control bouts that were expected to be donnybrooks.

Stan Kowalski's tag team title days didn't end when he and Tiny Mills split. He went on to hold the AWA World Tag Team Championship again, with rugged "Texas" Bob Geigel, and later in the mid-1960s formed a top-contending combination with the huge Alaskan Jay York. Together they had intense, hard-fought battles with Doug Gilbert and Reggie Parks and with the Crusher and Dick the Bruiser. Stan also teamed regularly with his longtime buddy "Black Jack" Daniels, and together they were Southern Tag Team Champions.

Kowalski also successfully teamed with and managed the career of the big Russian Bear, Ivan Koloff. Stan brought Koloff into the AWA to challenge champion Verne Gagne, and the two formed a strong tag team combination. Another of Stan's charges was Japan's Shozo "Strong" Kobayashi, who challenged and wrestled Gagne, and joined with Stan for tag team bouts.

In the early 1970s, Stan met Bruno Sammartino in a title match for the

Stan "Krusher" Kowalski and Black Jack Daniels held championship titles in the southern and Central States territories. Minnesota fans booed the two villains at every encounter.

WWWF championship. While on the East Coast, promoters billed Stan as "Krippler" Karl Kovacs to avoid confusion with their legendary heel Walter "Killer" Kowalski. The billing as Kovacs was a sore spot with Stan. He thought he could have retained the Kowalski name and either teamed or feuded with Killer.

Earlier in his career, Stan had endured another unwanted name change. In 1963, he had a series of battles with Reggie Lisowski, who wanted to use the name "Crusher" Lisowski—too close to Stan's "Krusher" Kowalski for comfort. Stan was eventually relegated to simply being billed as "the Big K." He felt that Verne Gagne was trying to demean his status as a fellow top wrestler from Minnesota. Though Stan worked with Verne professionally, they were not close outside the ring.

In 1974, as Stan was winding down his own wrestling career, he teamed with the young Kim Duk—also known as Tiger Tagouchi in some territories—in the mid-South region, eventually winning the area's tag belts.

Tiny Mills passed away in the early 1980s. Stan Kowalski retired from the wrestling business in the late 1970s and for the last thirty years has been involved with lodge work with the Veterans of Foreign Wars and as a volunteer and speaker for the United Way.

Young Kim Duk signed with veteran Stan Kowalski as his manager and tag team partner when they met in the AWA. The rugged pair became U.S. Tag Team Champions in the mid-South.

★ "PRETTY BOY" LARRY HENNIG AND "HANDSOME" HARLEY RACE ★

If asked who the most remembered, most hated, and most successful tag team in the AWA was, any longtime follower of Minnesota wrestling will almost certainly name the boastful combination of Larry Hennig and Harley Race.

Hennig and Race's journey together began on September 25, 1964, when they debuted on the Minneapolis *All-Star Wrestling* show against young Eddie Sharkey and K.O. Ken Yates. Hennig and Race proved from the onset that they would be tough to beat in the ring, and made it clear that their eventual goal was the World Tag Team Championship.

Hennig claimed that he met the young, blonde Harley Race while on a tour of Texas in late 1963 and early 1964. Larry boasted that he knew right away that their meeting was destiny, and that he and Harley watched the sunset in Texas one night, and proclaimed that together they would become the greatest tag team the wrestling world had ever known.

In their TV interviews, Race would proclaim, "We have bodies men fear and women crave," and boasted that he and Larry had "the minds of Einstein, the bodies of Hercules, and the faces of the Goddess of Love." Their arrogance and bragging earned them the fans' hatred, but they claimed that the fans and other teams were just jealous of their ability and good looks. Promoters billed them as "Pretty Boy" Larry Hennig and "Handsome" Harley Race to further incite the fans' rage.

Their record was completely lopsided with victories from the very beginning: from their September 1964 start as a team to December 21, they racked up forty-seven consecutive wins with no losses. During this time, Hennig and Race constantly demanded that promoters sign them to face the World Tag

"Pretty Boy" Larry Hennig and "Handsome" Harley Race became partners in 1964 and earned the AWA World Tag Team Championship three different times. Their matches against the Crusher and the Bruiser thrilled fans for more than three years in the AWA.

Team Champions. The champions at the time were the Crusher and Dick the Bruiser, but the problem, according to the promoters, was that they didn't know where the Crusher was. In July 1964 in St. Paul, Crusher had lost a "Loser Leave the AWA" match to Verne Gagne and hadn't been seen since. As for Dick the Bruiser, he wasn't active in the AWA at the time. This brought about one of the most intriguing and best-remembered storylines in AWA history.

HENNIG AND RACE WIN/LOSS RECORD—409 MATCHES:

★ Matches won: 281

★ Matches won by disqualification: 13

★ Total victories: 294

★ Matches lost: 56

★ Matches lost by disqualification: 27

★ Total losses: 83

★ Matches wrestled to a draw: 4

★ Matches ending in no-contest decisions: 9

★ Matches with result unknown: 19

CHAMPIONSHIPS HELD BY HENNIG AND RACE:

★ AWA World Tag Team Title (Minneapolis): January 30, 1965, from Crusher Lisowski and Dick the Bruiser

★ AWA World Tag Team Title (Minneapolis): August 7, 1965, from Verne Gagne and Crusher Lisowski

★ Australian IWA (International Wrestling Association) Tag Team Title: recognized as champions in January 1966

★ AWA World Tag Team Title (Chicago): January 6, 1967, from Crusher Lisowski and Dick the Bruiser

Hennig and Race had been feuding for several months with Verne Gagne, who was successfully teamed with Reggie Parks. During one of their battles, Wilbur Snyder, who was in town for some matches, decided to sit at ringside and lend support to his longtime friend Verne. As fans could have predicted, when the going got rough, and while Hennig and Race were double-teaming Gagne, Snyder got the attention of the referee and pointed out their rule breaking. Naturally, this did not sit well with Hennig and Race. The following week, they appeared on TV screaming that if Wilbur Snyder wanted to stick his nose into their business, they would find a third partner and Snyder could join Gagne and Parks.

Naturally, Minneapolis promoter Wally Karbo was quick to accept their offer, and Snyder was equally eager to join the Gagne and Parks combo. Hennig and Race's potential choices for their third partner became the talk of the Twin Cities wrestling community.

With fan anticipation at its peak only a week before the big showdown, Hennig and Race revealed their surprise teammate: none other than the man billed as "the world's most dangerous wrestler," Dick the Bruiser. Bruiser also held the World Tag Team Championship with his famous "cousin" the Crusher, so Hennig and Race boasted that they had pulled the upset of the decade by getting the Bruiser to join them. As Larry said in a TV interview, "Dick the

When Larry Hennig and Harley Race didn't like a referee's ruling, they took matters into their own hands. In this case, Hennig lifts the ref to drop him on Race's knee.

Bruiser is one-half of the World Tag Team Champions, so you know Harley and I have the best partner we could have on our side."

On the night of December 26, 1964, the big six-man tag showdown took place in the Minneapolis Auditorium before a huge sold-out crowd. The outcome of the donnybrook shocked fans: Hennig and Race monopolized the action, leaving the Bruiser on the sidelines, until he finally had enough and took out his own partners. To the fans' delight, it was the first time since their joining together as a team that "Pretty Boy" Larry and "Handsome" Harley had suffered a defeat.

The Hennig-Race-Bruiser feud quickly escalated, as Dick brought the Crusher back from disgrace and the two heel teams rattled their sabers. When they finally met for the first time, on January 17, 1965, not even special referee Tiny Mills could keep order. Verne Gagne himself finally entered the ring and delivered a knockout punch to Hennig, leaving Crusher and Bruiser the champions.

Dick the Bruiser and Wilbur Snyder were close personal friends outside the ring. Together they owned the Indiana-based World Wrestling Alliance (WWA) territory, which promoted wrestling from 1964 into the early 1980s.

In a rematch on January 30 in Minneapolis, however, Larry Hennig and Harley Race lived up to their boasts and became the AWA World Tag Team Champions. The loss of the belts didn't set well with the Crusher, and he was a constant thorn in the new champions' sides for the rest of their reign together.

For the next four years, "Pretty Boy" Larry Hennig and "Handsome" Harley Race were the team every fan wanted to see defeated. The AWA pitted them against countless combinations in hopes of seeing them lose the championship.

Ultimately, however, Hennig and Race did not lose the title in a match. Their title-holding days came to an abrupt halt when Larry Hennig accidentally broke a leg while wrestling Verne Gagne in an October 1967 singles match in Winnipeg.

Promoters had already signed title matches, so with Hennig unable to defend his belt, the AWA decided to allow Harley Race to choose a new partner to defend the title. Race's choice was longtime heel Chris Markoff, who had often joined the Hennig and Race duo in six-man tag team wars.

As it turned out, though, Race didn't have the chemistry with Markoff that he did with Hennig, and they lost the championship in their first defense of the title. They were defeated by the scientific tandem of old nemesis Wilbur Snyder and former NWA World Champion Pat O'Connor in Chicago on November 10, 1967.

The record books show that Larry Hennig and Harley Race never lost the AWA World Tag Team Championship in the ring. When Hennig's leg mended in mid-1968 he rejoined Race, but they were unable to gain a shot at the championship, and soon thereafter they decided to part company.

Hennig was hot on the trail of the man who put him out of action, Verne Gagne, and Race departed the AWA for the NWA. Harley Race went on to not only win the NWA World Heavyweight Championship, but hold it an unprecedented eight times between May 1973 and March 1984.

Hennig continued his feud with Gagne and also formed other formidable tag team combinations with partners like Lars Anderson, Dusty Rhodes, and Joe LeDuc, but he was never able to attain the success he shared with his best partner.

Hennig and Race remained good friends, and in contrast to their villainous ring image, were the nicest gentlemen you could ever meet, always willing to talk about the old days and sign autographs for the fans.

★ THE CRUSHER AND DICK THE BRUISER ★

Reggie Lisowski and Dick Afflis, better known as the Crusher and Dick the Bruiser, joined together for the first time as a tag team combination in October 1959 in Indianapolis, Indiana. At the time, this was simply the pairing of two of the roughest, toughest, and most respected brawlers in the wrestling business. They had signed for matches against two of the top-rated teams of the

From 1963 to 1985, no team in wrestling was more popular with fans and in demand from promoters than Crusher Lisowski and Dick the Bruiser. Billed as "cousins," the beer-drinking duo held the AWA World Tag Team Championship five times.

era: Roy and Ray Shire (Roy Shire and Ray Stevens) and Verne Gagne and Wilbur Snyder. They lost to the Shire Brothers twice in heel versus heel matches on October 11, 1959, and February 18, 1960, but won against Gagne and Snyder in Boston on October 24, 1959.

Few could have anticipated after these first three matches that Crusher and Bruiser would become one of the most dominant and in-demand tag teams ever, and stay that way for the next two decades.

It wasn't until August 20, 1963, in Minneapolis that Crusher and Bruiser hooked up again. In that first match back together, they defeated the highly regarded, highly successful, and deeply hated Russian brothers Ivan and Karol Kalmikoff to win the AWA World Tag Team Championship. The match was billed as a Battle of the Butchers. The fans were the winners, as the match was one of the wildest and most talked-about tag team matches in Twin Cities wrestling history, and remains so to this day. This championship would be the first of many title reigns for the Crusher and the Bruiser.

William Afflis was born June 27, 1929, and raised by his widowed mother. The boy who would become the Bruiser was known as a troublemaker in his hometown, Indianapolis. He was an All-State football player at Purdue. He lost a football scholarship while at Purdue when he decked a line coach with his football helmet, and eventually ended up at the University of Nevada in Reno, where he changed his name to Dick. During the off-season from football, he worked as a bouncer at the famed Harold's Club.

THE CRUSHER AND THE BRUISER WIN/LOSS RECORD—241 MATCHES:

★ Matches won: 143

★ Matches lost: 59

★ Matches ending in no-contest decisions or draws: 39

CHAMPIONSHIPS HELD BY CRUSHER AND BRUISER:

★ AWA World Tag Team Title (Minneapolis): August 20, 1963, from Ivan and Karol Kalmikoff

★ AWA World Tag Team Title (St. Paul): February 23, 1964, from Verne Gagne and Moose Evans

★ AWA World Tag Team Title (Minneapolis): May 28, 1966, from Larry Hennig and Harley Race

★ WWA World Tag Team Title (Indianapolis): January 21, 1967, from Angelo Poffo and Chris Markoff

★ WWA World Tag Team Title (Lafayette, Indiana): July 15, 1967, from Angelo Poffo and Chris Markoff

★ AWA World Tag Team Title (Chicago): December 28, 1968, from Mitsu Arakawa and Doctor Moto

★ WWA World Tag Team Title (Chicago): December 28, 1968, from Mitsu Arakawa and Doctor Moto

★ International Tag Team Title (Sapporo, Japan): August 11, 1969, from Shohei "Giant" Baba and Antonio Inoki

★ WWA World Tag Team Title (Chicago): December 2, 1972, from Black Jack Lanza and Black Jack Mulligan

★ AWA World Tag Team Title (Chicago): August 16, 1975, from Ray Stevens and Nick Bockwinkel

★ WWA World Tag Team Title (Indianapolis): September 20, 1975, from Sgt. Jacques Goulet (Rene Goulet) and Soldier Lebouef

★ WWA World Tag Team Title (Indianapolis): May 1, 1976, from Doug "Ox" Baker and "Big John" Studd

On December 28, 1968, both the AWA and WWA tag team titles were on the line. The Crusher and the Bruiser won both titles, and held the championships simultaneously.

From 1951 to 1954 Dick played for the Green Bay Packers, where he earned the nickname Bruiser. Dick entered the professional wrestling world in 1954, and quickly carved out a reputation as a bully in the ring. Known for his brute strength and an unmatched all-out style, Bruiser was barred from several territories. In New York in 1957, he was teamed with Dr. Jerry Graham against Edouard Carpentier and Antonino Rocca. The four grapplers caused a riot that received national attention from the media.

Promoters were assured of a packed house whenever Dick the Bruiser was signed to appear on their cards. He met and defeated virtually every major grappler from the 1950s through the 1980s in a career that earned him the billing "the world's most dangerous wrestler" by promoters, magazines, and fans.

Meanwhile, Reggie Lisowski was active as the Crusher for most of the 1950s as a top draw in the Midwest and on the East Coast. He became a tag team partner to rugged rule breaker Art Neilson in 1954, and they were quickly recognized as tag team champions by many promoters. After Reggie's stint with Neilson, he hooked up with fellow blonde Stan Holek, and they wrestled as "brothers" Reggie and Stan Lisowski for several years. They, too, were recognized as champions in most of the territories in which they competed, including Minnesota.

But when Reggie, as the Crusher, joined Dick the Bruiser and they billed themselves as "lookalike cousins," they became one of the most dominant and in-demand tag teams in wrestling history. Promoters sought to sign them for their cards. They wrestled together, off and on, from 1959 to 1985.

Together they stomped, punched, kicked, and mauled every team they met, and the fans loved every match. Their feuds with top-rated combinations like Ivan and Karol Kalmikoff, Larry Hennig and Harley Race, Mad Dog and Butcher Vachon, the Black Jacks (Lanza and Mulligan), and the Chain Gang (Jack and Frank Dillinger) are still remembered and talked about as some of the greatest and most legendary battles in wrestling.

Reggie Lisowski passed away in October 2005 at age 79, Dick Afflis in 1991 at 62. The Crusher and Dick the Bruiser, along with their legendary interviews and no-nonsense ring style, are remembered by wrestlers and the legions of fans that followed them for four decades in the business.

★ RAY STEVENS AND NICK BOCKWINKEL ★

The team of Ray Stevens and Nick Bockwinkel was generally considered by those in the know to be one of wrestling's most unlikely combinations. In the ring, they were as different as night and day, but perhaps for that very reason, they were extremely successful together.

Nick Bockwinkel had been on the Minnesota scene a year and a half before the villainous Ray Stevens came to the territory. Their collaboration was literally due to an accident. In the early morning of July 24, 1971, while driving back to the Cities from Winnipeg, tag team champions Red Bastien and Hercules Cortez had a serious accident when Hercules lost control of his car and crashed. The accident left Bastien with minor injuries, but cost Cortez his life.

The irony of the accident is that the next night Hercules Cortez, who was undefeated in Minnesota and the AWA at the time, was signed to meet the also-undefeated Nick Bockwinkel in a Minneapolis main event match. The winner of this high-profile bout was to receive a title shot at AWA World Champion Verne Gagne. At the top of every wrestling program were the words "Program Subject to Change," and never were those words so prophetic as they were that night. Nick Bockwinkel was now without an opponent, with thousands of fans anticipating his battle with Cortez.

Minneapolis promoter Wally Karbo quickly announced that Verne Gagne himself would face Bockwinkel in a non-title match. Despite the circumstances,

Nick Bockwinkel and Ray Stevens first won the AWA World Tag Team Championship in January 1972 and then took Bobby "the Brain" Heenan as their manager in 1974 to win it again. This California duo held the belt three different times.

the match was a great opportunity for Bockwinkel, as he had been chasing down the Gagne match since his arrival in the Twin Cities in December 1970.

It was on this night that Bockwinkel and Stevens met. Their paths had crossed many times in years past, but only as opponents. Early in his career, Nick had been a popular babyface, while Stevens was at his best in the heel role. Ray was making his Twin Cities and AWA debut on this card, and in fact was scheduled to meet Hercules's partner, Red Bastien. Before entering the AWA, Ray Stevens had been the number-one wrestler in San Francisco all through the 1960s—selling out the world-famous Cow Palace on numerous occasions—but he was unable to lay claim to a world title. So he moved to the AWA hoping to fulfill that goal by getting Verne Gagne in the ring.

When the Bockwinkel versus Gagne match was ready to begin, Stevens came to ringside to, as he claimed, "scout out the champion." As the match went on, Stevens sat attentively in a chair at ringside, minding his own business. After about twenty minutes of torrid action, Gagne finally clamped his dreaded sleeper hold on Bockwinkel, and the match seemed to be in the champion's grasp. Suddenly, Stevens jumped up on the ring apron to inform referee Aldo Bogni—a great wrestler in his own right—that he thought Gagne was choking Bockwinkel. Gagne, distracted by Stevens's accusations, released Nick from the sleeper and punched the blonde bomber from California. While Gagne was distracted, Bockwinkel delivered a dropkick and won the match.

STEVENS AND BOCKWINKEL WIN/LOSS RECORD—159 MATCHES:

★ Matches won: 83
★ Matches won by disqualification: 12
★ Total victories: 95
★ Matches lost: 36
★ Matches lost by disqualification: 13

★ Total losses: 49
★ Matches wrestled to a draw: 3
★ Matches ending in no-contest decisions: 12

Note: Six-man tag team matches where Stevens and Bockwinkel were joined by other partners are not included in these statistics.

CHAMPIONSHIPS HELD BY STEVENS AND BOCKWINKEL:

★ AWA World Tag Team Title (Denver): January 20, 1972, from Red Bastien and Crusher Lisowski
★ AWA World Tag Team Title (St. Paul): January 6, 1973, from Verne Gagne and Billy Robinson

★ AWA World Tag Team Title (Winnipeg): October 24, 1974, from Billy Robinson and Crusher Lisowski
★ NWA Florida Tag Team Title (Tampa): July 20, 1972, from Hiro Matsuda and Tim Woods.

Though Ray Stevens claimed that he did not care who won the match, and that he only jumped up on the apron to bring Gagne's "choke" hold to the referee's attention, it quickly became apparent that he and Bockwinkel were destined to go forward together. They both wanted not only the singles championship, but the tag team belts too.

Stevens and Bockwinkel did indeed join forces, and immediately became the leading contenders for the AWA World Tag Team Championship. After the untimely death of Hercules Cortez, Red Bastien was allowed to choose a new partner and retain the title. His choice was none other than the one, the only, the Crusher! Together, Bastien and Crusher held back teams like Hans Schmidt and Baron Von Raschke, Larry Hennig and Lars Anderson, and Stevens and Bockwinkel. Bastien and Crusher's luck finally ran out on January 20, 1972, in Denver, when they were upset by Ray Stevens and Nick Bockwinkel for the championship.

The new champions carved out a reputation as one of the most hated, yet respected, tag teams in history. They went on to hold the championship a total of three times until finally dropping it for the last time on August 15, 1975, in Chicago to the Crusher and Dick the Bruiser.

These five teams, arguably the top five all-time best-remembered combinations, are far from the only tag teams longtime Minnesota wrestling fans remember well. Here are a few others that garner fond memories.

★ RED BASTIEN AND BILLY RED LYONS ★

Red Bastien, a Minneapolis native, began his career wrestling in local carnivals, taking on all comers. When he broke into the professional ranks, it was evident to his peers that he was going to be a star for years to come.

During the mid- to late 1950s, Red worked preliminary matches on Twin Cities wrestling cards and was a real favorite of the ladies for his high-flying ac-

Put two redheaded wrestlers with similar ring styles together and the result is the high-flying combination of Red Bastien and Billy Red Lyons. Here the boys are being interviewed by TV announcer Marty O'Neill on All-Star Wrestling.

robatic style in the ring. Bastien made dropkicks and flying head scissors look easy, and he made many opponents look silly trying to avoid his onslaught.

In the 1960s, Bastien took to the road and worked many of wrestling's leading territories around the country. He made a tremendous splash in the early years of the decade with his half-brother Lou Klein. Lou took the Bastien name, and he and Red carved out an immensely successful ring record on the East Coast.

Red and Lou Bastien had one of the most original gimmicks ever for a tag team. They would come into the ring carrying a treasure chest filled with silver dollars. They claimed that each silver dollar represented one of their victories as a team. After each match, Red and Lou would toss yet another silver dollar into the chest. During a brutal feud with Eddie and Jerry Graham, the Grahams managed to get hold of the coveted chest after one match, and dumped the coins all over the ring and the floor of the arena. The Graham-Bastien confrontations drew some of the highest-grossing crowds on the East Coast to the world-famous Madison Square Garden.

After leaving Lou Klein, Red went on to become one of the most sought-after wrestlers in the business thanks to his flashy high-flying style. He had long winning streaks and huge pushes in Australia and on the West Coast, among other territories. When the AWA asked him to return home, he jumped at the chance, and the wheels were put in motion to hook him up with fellow redhead Billy "Red" Lyons.

Lyons had joined the AWA ranks in August 1968, and was not only a fan favorite, but also considered one of the leading challengers for Verne Gagne's AWA World Heavyweight Championship. He'd had some initial success with Frankie Laine, but his real fame came when he joined Bastien.

To make the teaming seem even more natural, fans were told that the two were longtime friends and former partners up and down the West Coast. This was only hype to make their match-up seem like a reunion. False history or no, they really did mesh well together, and their solid teamwork had fans buzzing about the possibility of them challenging AWA champions Mad Dog and Butcher Vachon.

Fans were not disappointed. Not only did the Redheads become persistent challengers to the Vachon Brothers, they gained many victories over them. But each time the Vachons found a way to keep their belts: usually they were disqualified or the matches ended in no-contest decisions, with all four wrestlers throwing out the rule book.

On December 27, 1969, Bastien and Lyons joined together with fiery superstar Pepper Gomez, and they were able to pull out a victory over the threesome of Larry Hennig, Harley Race, and Lars Anderson. From this match, the AWA christened them the AWA World Six-Man Tag Team Champions. The title was never mentioned again after this match, and was apparently forgotten by the AWA. Shortly thereafter, Billy "Red" Lyons was reportedly injured by Black Jack Lanza.

The Bastien brothers were half-brothers in real life. After behind-the-scenes squabbles, they dissolved their partnership and tried wrestling in singles matches and with other wrestlers.

In fact, Billy had decided to leave Minnesota and move his base of operations to the mid-South territory promoted by Leroy McGuirk. As usual in those days, fans were unaware that the injury story was an angle designed to give a push to Black Jack Lanza. Lyons was often teamed with his old AWA partner Cowboy Bill Watts in the mid-South territory. They had some memorable battles with the German team of Waldo Von Erich and Karl Von Brauner, and with the "Hollywood Blondes," Jerry Roberts and Buddy Roberts.

RED BASTIEN AND BILLY "RED" LYONS WIN/LOSS RECORD—96 MATCHES:

★ Matches won: 56

★ Matches won by disqualification: 14

★ Total victories: 70

★ Matches lost: 18

★ Matches lost by disqualification: 3

★ Total losses: 21

★ Matches wrestled to a draw: 2

★ Matches ending in no-contest decisions: 3

CHAMPIONSHIPS HELD BY BASTIEN AND LYONS:

★ AWA Six-Man Tag Team Title (Minneapolis): December 27, 1969, with Pepper Gomez, defeating Larry Hennig, Harley Race, and Lars Anderson

★ Texas Tag Team Title (Dallas): June 6, 1972, from Mike York and Frank Monte (who wrestled as "the Alaskans")

Billy became one of the leading challengers for the American championship recognized in the mid-South. He later formed a tag team with popular black wrestler Tom Jones, and they defeated the masked Spoilers (Don Jardine and Buddy Wolfe) for the U.S. Tag Team Championship on May 31, 1971, in Shreveport, Louisiana. The duo defended the belts for close to a year before losing them to Lorenzo Parente and Bobby Hart on March 21, 1972, in Shreveport.

When Lyons left the mid-South in 1972, he returned to his old stomping grounds in Texas, where he was reunited with Red Bastien. They became one of Texas's most popular tag teams and were pushed all the way to the championship. Still later in his career, Billy donned a mask along with Dewey Robertson and they became "the Crusaders" in Canadian rings.

After Lyons's departure from the AWA, Bastien was joined by Pepper Gomez and they teamed together for many months, becoming new fan favorites until Pepper was "injured" on TV in January 1970 by Larry Hennig and Lars Anderson. Huge Spanish grappler Hercules Cortez came to the aid of the fallen Gomez, and he and Red Bastien then took up where Bastien and Gomez left off.

Although the AWA World Tag Team Championship had eluded the fiery Bastien with previous partners Billy "Red" Lyons and Pepper Gomez, luck was finally on his side in May of 1971 when he and the giant Hercules defeated the Vachon Brothers in Milwaukee to win the belts. Fate stepped in, though. Hercules Cortez's tragic death in a car accident on July 23, 1971, left Bastien again without a partner.

The AWA and its fans were in mourning. Red Bastien, who suffered minor injuries in the accident, was allowed to take some time off from the ring, and when he returned to action, he would choose a new teammate and retain the championship. Before the popular redhead returned full-time to the AWA, he participated in matches in Japan, and was joined by journeyman wrestler Billy Howard for tag team matches.

Upon Red's anticipated return to the AWA, he announced that his new partner was none other than the AWA's undisputedly most popular wrestler, the Crusher. Together Red and Crusher went on to defend the AWA World Tag Team Championship until January 20, 1972, when they were upset in Denver by the California duo of Ray Stevens and Nick Bockwinkel.

After losing the belts, Red Bastien left the AWA for a year to compete in the Texas territory, and the Crusher feuded with the new champions with other partners and worked singles matches. The Crusher was able to gain back the AWA World Tag Team Title two times from Bockwinkel and Stevens: once on July 21, 1974, in Green Bay, Wisconsin, with Billy Robinson as a partner, and then again in Chicago on August 16, 1975, with his old buddy Dick the Bruiser.

Before retiring, Lyons formed a successful tag combination with Dewey Robertson in Detroit and Toronto, and later became a TV wrestling commentator.

★ GENE, LARS, AND OLE ANDERSON ★

The three Anderson Brothers never actually wrestled in Minnesota as a tag team combination, but all three were from Minnesota and began their individual wrestling careers in the state. The three grapplers attained great success both as individual wrestlers and in various team combinations, but they were all Minnesotans first and foremost—although they weren't actually brothers. Gene Anderson was the only "real" Anderson. His "brothers" were Larry Heiniemi, who was Lars, and Allen Rogowski, who was Ole.

Verne Gagne trained each of them for the pro ranks, and each went on to attain legendary status in the grunt and groan game.

Gene Anderson was born on October 4, 1939, in South St. Paul. He was a state wrestling champion in high school, and wrestled professionally in Calgary, Canada, for a short time before returning to Minnesota and joining the AWA in 1961. For the next four years, Gene was a fixture on local cards and in TV studio matches. He was respected by his peers and fans alike. He'd win some, and lose some, but one thing was always certain: he gave a good account of himself, no matter who his opponent was. Gene was excellent at working a crowd and generating heat. The fans hated him, and that was his objective.

Larry Heiniemi (Lars) was a native of Grand Rapids, Minnesota, and was born the same year as Gene Anderson. Lars's AWA debut was in September

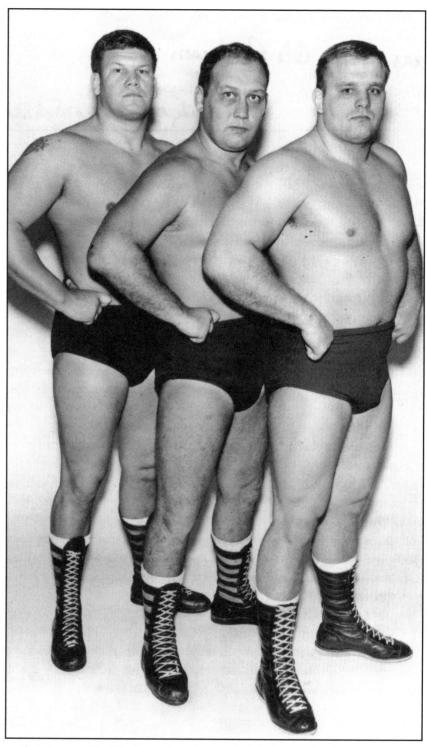

The Minnesota Wrecking Crew—Lars, Gene, and Ole Anderson—together and as single wrestlers put more opponents out of action than perhaps any other "brother" team in history. Each was trained by Verne Gagne but traded his scientific ring style for all-out brawling tactics to win their matches.

1965. He came to wrestling in a strange way. He was working on his master's degree in psychology at St. Cloud University when it dawned on him that, with his high school and college wrestling background and his knowledge of the psychology behind working a crowd, joining the pro ranks might be a viable option.

He sought out AWA owner Verne Gagne and started his pro training. With him was Gene Anderson, who was in his rookie years and assisted Gagne in coaching young hopefuls for the business.

There was nothing flashy about Gene and Lars Anderson. No outlandish tights or trunks, just plain roughhouse-style wrestling. Together Gene and Lars started a legendary dynasty in the southern territories of Tennessee, Georgia, Florida, and most of the mid-Atlantic area of the country.

When Gene and Lars first worked together in September 1966, they got off to a slow start. But booker Leo Garibaldi in Georgia realized their potential as a tag team and they were given a run with the Georgia version of the NWA world title.

In 1968, Gene and Lars brought a third "brother" into the territory to work with them in six-man matches. Allen "Rock" Rogowski was a friend of Larry Heiniemi's from college. Rogowski was born in 1942, attended high school in Minneapolis, and landed at St. Cloud University, where he met Heiniemi. Rogowski, like his "brothers," was trained by Verne Gagne. When he began wrestling, he was first said to be related to the famous wrestling "cousins" Crusher Lisowski and Dick the Bruiser, because of his resemblance to them. Rogowski had some early success in the AWA as a tag partner of Cowboy Bill Watts, and also became a regular main headliner in the Omaha and Central States territory. Then Rock hit the mid-Atlantic territory as Ole Anderson in 1968.

Soon after Ole joined the team, Lars returned home to Minnesota to form a formidable pairing with "Pretty Boy" Larry Hennig, whose regular teammate Harley Race had left the AWA to pursue NWA laurels.

After Lars left, Ole continued to team with Gene, and for close to twenty years they were *the* team to beat in the South. Because of this, the Gene and Ole version of the Andersons is probably the best remembered. They had memorable and now-classic matches against Paul Jones and Wahoo McDaniel. Fans fondly recall the two teams simply beating the hell out of each other, and they drew record crowds for their efforts.

The Andersons all had a great ability to project their nastiness over the microphone. And like the best wrestlers in those days, they were believable in the ring. They could make fans hate them within seconds of entering a ring. And the more they were hated, the more money they made.

Gene was always considered the captain of the Minnesota Wrecking Crew. When he retired from professional wrestling, he left behind a legacy. Never had a "brother" combination been so successful for so long.

With oldest brother Gene out of the sport, Ole reentered the ring with yet another Anderson and another Minnesota-born grappler. His name was

Verne Gagne sent his trainees to different territories after their initial debut in the AWA. This gave them additional experience by working with other wrestlers and wrestling styles. Some of the trainees eventually returned to the AWA, but Gene and Ole did not. Lars came back for a successful run in the late 1960s and early 1970s.

Marty Lunde, but when he hooked up with Ole, he became Arn Anderson. During various storylines over the next decade, Arn was billed as Ole's brother, nephew, and cousin. It is unclear why Arn's relationship to Ole kept fluctuating, but it certainly must be said that Ole and Arn Anderson were a top-notch tandem. They, like the original version of Andersons, were called the Minnesota Wrecking Crew.

In 1986, the team's history was again rewritten. During a TV interview, with limited time remaining, the production crew put Ole and Arn together with Tully Blanchard (son of wrestler Joe Blanchard) and Ric Flair. It was during this interview that Arn commented, "To see this much havoc wreaked by so few people, you need to go all the way back to the Four Horsemen of the Apocalypse!" With that statement was born the first four-man tag team combination: The Four Horsemen. Ole Anderson served as the leader of the group, and then later they added a manager, James J. Dillon, who had been an accomplished wrestler in his own right.

"Brother" Lars Anderson, after a couple of years teaming with Larry Hennig, eventually headed to San Francisco, where he joined Paul DeMarco to win the NWA World Tag Team Title. When Lars again returned to Minnesota in 1974, he declared that he was going back to his rightful name of Larry Heiniemi, and then brought in his "new" partner, "Beautiful" Buddy Wolfe. Heiniemi and Wolfe were college roommates and longtime friends. Now they boasted that

Ole Anderson is also remembered as one of the sport's great bookers. Ole always had an abrasive personality. He could be very hard to get along with, and was sometimes described as bullheaded. With Ole, you either liked him, or you didn't—there wasn't really a middle ground.

GENE, LARS, OLE, AND ARN ANDERSON CHAMPIONSHIPS:

★ NWA Southern Tag Team Title (Atlanta office): February 1967, Gene and Lars defeated Ramon and Enrique Torres in Atlanta; May 1967, Gene and Lars defeated Ramon and Enrique Torres in Atlanta

★ AWA Midwest Tag Team Title (Omaha office): March 3, 1971, Rock Rogowski (Ole) teamed with Doug "Ox" Baker defeated Reggie Parks and Stan Pulaski in Omaha

★ NWA World Tag Team Title (San Francisco office): May 13, 1972, Lars teamed with Paul DeMarco defeated Pepper Gomez and Rocky Johnson in San Francisco

★ NWA Georgia Tag Team Title (Atlanta office): May 29, 1974, Gene and Ole defeated Robert Fuller and Mr. Wrestling II (Johnny Walker) in Columbus; September 13, 1974, Gene and Ole defeated Mr. Wrestling I (Tim Woods) and Mr. Wrestling II in Atlanta; October 22, 1976, Gene and Ole defeated Tom Jones and Pork Chop Cash in Atlanta; March 1977, Gene and Ole defeated Mr. Wrestling I and Mr. Wrestling II

in Atlanta; June 1977, Gene and Ole defeated Clyde "Thunderbolt" Patterson and Mr. Wrestling I in Atlanta; November 1977, Gene and Ole defeated Tommy "Wildfire" Rich and Tony "Mr. USA" Atlas in Atlanta; March 1978, Lars and Ole defeated Tony Atlas and Mr. Wrestling II in Atlanta

★ NWA Florida Title (Florida office): 1977, Lars defeated Dusty Rhodes in St. Petersburg

★ NWA Georgia TV (National) Title (Atlanta office): April 1978, Ole defeated Abdullah the Butcher in Atlanta; 1978, Gene defeated Thunderbolt Patterson in Atlanta; March 2, 1979, Ole defeated Thunderbolt Patterson in Atlanta

★ NWA National Tag Team Title (Atlanta office): April 28, 1985, Ole and Arn defeated Thunderbolt Patterson and Manny Fernandez in Charlotte

Note: The Andersons held other singles and tag team championships with other partners.

they would capture the AWA World Tag Team Title. The championship was not to be theirs, though, and in March of 1975, during an interview on *All-Star Wrestling* before a match with Billy Robinson, Heiniemi announced that he was retiring from wrestling, and that the match with Robinson would be his last ring appearance.

He lost the match to Robinson, and was indeed gone. However, fans soon learned that Larry's retirement was only from the AWA, not from wrestling itself, when he showed up in Hawaii wrestling under the name Lars Anderson.

History shows that Gene Anderson, Larry Heiniemi, Allen Rogowski, and Marty Lunde, collectively billed as the Minnesota Wrecking Crew, were all masters of their craft. With the exception of Lunde, each started their respective careers in Minnesota under the watchful eye of Verne Gagne, and as a feared tag team combination, they made their mark for many years in professional wrestling.

★ MAD DOG AND BUTCHER VACHON ★

Mad Dog and Butcher Vachon, as a brother team, could arguably rival the drawing power of Ivan and Karol Kalmikoff in Minnesota. Unlike the Kalmikoffs, though, and many other "brother" tag teams, the Vachons were real brothers. Mad Dog (real name Maurice) was the older and smaller of the two, but he always referred to Butcher (real name Paul) as his "little brother." They first joined together in Minnesota's AWA territory in July 1968 in a Minneapolis match against Crusher Lisowski and Dick the Bruiser. The match was the Minnesota debut for the Butcher—if you don't count his late 1950s appearances as Russian Nicoli Zolotoff during his rookie years in wrestling.

As for Mad Dog, he was well known, and well hated, by Minnesota fans. He was a former holder of the coveted AWA World Heavyweight Championship, a belt he originally won from popular hometown favorite Verne Gagne in 1964. Mad Dog would go on to be a five-time AWA champion, and without debate the most hated wrestler in a Minnesota ring during the 1960s and early 1970s. He got the Mad Dog handle from Portland promoter Don Owen, who claimed that Vachon was like a mad dog in the ring. The name stuck.

Minnesota wrestling fans still talk about Mad Dog's feud with Gagne. They thrilled fans for close to a decade, battling each other over the title. Their contrasting ring styles made matches between them even more exciting.

When Maurice brought in "little" brother Paul, fans were dismayed by the idea of having two Vachons to bully their heroes, and promoters in the AWA were thrilled that they had a team that gave the fans yet another reason to attend arena shows.

Between July 1968 and August 1969, Mad Dog and Butcher were victorious in match after match, and then finally on August 30, 1969, in Chicago's Inter-

The injury angle for the Crusher was frequently used to explain his absence from the local scene. He simply took time off from the ring for rest and relaxation.

national Amphitheater, they got the gold. They defeated the Crusher and the Bruiser in a cage match to win the AWA World Tag Team Championship. The match was reportedly so brutal that the Crusher was severely injured, and would be out of action for an unknown amount of time.

The now-champion Vachons immediately began feuding with the Flying Redheads, the popular Red Bastien and Billy "Red" Lyons. Their tag team matches drew record crowds not only in Minnesota, but all over the AWA. Fans wanted the Redheads to win the tag team title, and they often came close, but in the end the Vachons always found a way to remain champions. When fans remember great tag team matches from the Golden Age, the battles between the Vachons and the Redheads rank high on anyone's list.

In January 1970, the Crusher reappeared, and wanted revenge on the Vachons for his injuries. With the Bruiser reportedly unavailable, the AWA hooked Crusher up with Edouard Carpentier for several matches, and also with Mad Dog's old nemesis Verne Gagne.

Dick the Bruiser was unavailable because he was running his own promotion along with partner Wilbur Snyder in Indiana and Michigan. Their WWA territory was formed in April 1964.

Mad Dog and Butcher Vachon are remembered as one of the most ruthless, most disliked, and most often disqualified combinations ever to hold the AWA World Tag Team Title. They held the belts for the longest uninterrupted period of any team at the time.

As the saying goes, though, all good things must come to an end. On May 15, 1971, the Vachons were relieved of their championship by Red Bastien and Hercules Cortez in Milwaukee. Behind the scenes, it was time for the Vachons to lose, because they were going to embark on a new territory. Paul Vachon had become involved with the Grand Prix promotion in Montreal. He and Maurice became the lead heel team for the new territory.

MAD DOG AND BUTCHER VACHON CHAMPIONSHIPS AS A TAG TEAM:

★ NWA Texas Tag Team Title (Houston office): November 8, 1960, Mad Dog and Butcher defeated Ciclon Negro and Torbellino Blanco in Dallas

★ AWA World Tag Team Title (Minneapolis office): August 30, 1969, Mad Dog and Butcher defeated Crusher Lisowski and Dick the Bruiser in Chicago

★ Grand Prix World Tag Team Title (Montreal office): July 1971, Mad Dog and Butcher became the first recognized champions of the Grand Prix promotion

In the mid-1970s, Mad Dog again returned to the AWA, this time teaming with the equally hated Baron Von Raschke.

Paul Vachon was the bigger of the brothers, but not the better wrestler. Butcher was billed at weighing 275 to 290 pounds, while Mad Dog usually tipped the scales at around 230 pounds. If the Vachons lost a fall in a match, it was usually Butcher who made it happen. Mad Dog was the spokesman for the team in TV interviews because he was good on the microphone. After their matches in the capital city, they could often be found eating at the famous Gallivan's in downtown St. Paul, and odd as it may seem, Butcher would often grab the house microphone and start singing. He had a great voice!

★ DOUG GILBERT AND DICK STEINBORN ★

High-flying Doug Gilbert was loved and respected by Minnesota fans even before he joined the talented Dick Steinborn, but their teaming together created one of the most popular and talked-about tag combinations ever.

The agile Gilbert began his career under his real name of Doug Lindsey, but soon began using the Gilbert moniker. In the late 1950s, Minnesota audiences thrilled to Doug and his "brother" Johnny Gilbert when they showed their wares in the Twin Cities.

At the time of Dick Steinborn's arrival in Minnesota, Doug Gilbert had tried numerous partners, including Verne Gagne, to unseat World Tag Team Champions Art and Stan Neilson. Though he often came close, in the end, the Neilsons were always able to retain their belts.

On October 20, 1962, Steinborn made his first appearance in St. Paul with a victory over veteran Angelo Savoldi. That win was followed by another, this time in Minneapolis on October 23 against Kurt Von Brauner. Promoters immediately saw the potential of the young, good-looking Steinborn, and decided that he would be the perfect mate for the equally handsome Doug Gilbert.

Ten days later in Minneapolis, the team of Mr. High and Mr. Low, Doug Gilbert and Dick Steinborn, was born. They were victorious in their first match together, besting George "Cry Baby" Cannon and Kurt Von Brauner. But that match wasn't all they won that night—they also won over the fans. Their blinding speed and mastery of wrestling holds captured the imagination of fans, who rooted for the new team to be the ones to unseat the Neilsons.

Promoters didn't make the road easy for Gilbert and Steinborn, though. They had to get by roughhouse teams of bullies like Rocky Hamilton, Bob Geigel, Bob Orton, and Black Jack Daniels, among others.

The Mr. High and Mr. Low team became the fans' darlings and went undefeated for ten consecutive matches. The fans clamored to see what they could do against the world champions. The Neilsons were booked for the match on December 16, 1962, in St. Paul. The auditorium was filled to the rafters with fans anticipating Doug and Dick capturing the titles—and they were not disappointed.

After nearly eight months, Art and Stan Neilson were relieved of their championship.

Gilbert and Steinborn were pushed hard and heavy as the youngest combination to become champions. Their popularity and drawing power as a team was used to good advantage by promoters.

Johnny Gilbert was journeyman wrestler Gilbert Sanchez, who after leaving "brother" Doug Gilbert formed a highly successful tag team with veteran Billy Goelz in a team billed as the G-Men around the Chicago and Milwaukee area.

Art and Stan Neilson were granted World Tag Team Championship recognition by the AWA in April 1962 after they allegedly defeated "Texas" Bob Geigel and Stan "Krusher" Kowalski in Cincinnati. However, no record of a match taking place between the two teams in Cincinnati, or anyplace else, has ever been found in the record books. It is safe to assume that this was merely a "phantom" title change. Geigel and Kowalski continued to work in the AWA and around the Twin Cities, but were no longer the champs.

Having proved they were as good as fans thought by downing the unruly Neilsons, Gilbert and Steinborn were put into the role of challengers again. After only four defenses of their newly won laurels, they were quickly taken down by the returning Russians, Ivan and Karol Kalmikoff, on New Year's Day 1963 in Minneapolis.

Their push had been effective, though. They had fought against tougher, rougher, and bigger teams, and become the World Tag Team Champions. Now back in the challenger's role, Gilbert and Steinborn still had the fans solidly behind them with hopes of their regaining the title from the Kalmikoffs. Twin Cities mat fans couldn't get enough of Mr. High and Mr. Low, and stood in lines to buy tickets whenever they were announced for a card.

In April 1963, Steinborn left the Minneapolis territory and returned to the southern United States. He had legendary status in places like Georgia and Florida, where he formed notable teams with guys like Red Bastien, Eddie Graham, and Ray Gunkel. He had wrestling in his blood, as his father Milo Steinborn was a respected matman before Dick entered the pro ranks.

Doug Gilbert continued on in Minnesota after Steinborn left. He remained a popular favorite with the fans, and appeared in many main events. In 1966, Doug was again back in the tag team limelight when he was paired with the very polished and talented Reggie Parks.

Gilbert and Parks had many battles with Larry Hennig and Harley Race, and also the teams of Stan Kowalski and the Alaskan (Jay York) and Killer Kowalski and the Alaskan. To many fans' eyes, the Gilbert and Parks combination was every bit as smooth and slick in the ring as the Gilbert and Steinborn team was. In fact, the two teams are often compared when Doug Gilbert's name comes up in conversation.

Gilbert gained his most noted success in the ring after he left the Minneapolis territory in the late 1960s. He went to Atlanta, donned a mask, and called himself "the Professional." Now in a heel role, he was as hated as he had once been loved. Fans, of course, did not know that it was Gilbert under the mask, and promoters enjoyed trying to keep it that way. As the Professional, he became Georgia state champion on four different occasions.

After he had run his course as a heel, the Professional turned babyface and battled guys like the masked Assassins and Paul DeMarco. For a very short stint, Doug wrestled with a mask in Chicago as "the Professor," but then Dale Lewis replaced him under the mask and used the same name. The fans were never aware of the change.

In the mid-1970s, Gilbert returned to the Minneapolis territory and the AWA. He worked many cards, putting over other stars who were being pushed at the time, and also formed a short-lived team with the great Billy Robinson.

Doug's last appearance in the Twin Cities was as the special referee for Verne Gagne's retirement match on May 10, 1981, when Gagne defeated Nick Bockwinkel to retain his championship.

★ GREG GAGNE AND JIM BRUNZELL ★

No tag team was more adored by fans than the High Flyers, Greg Gagne and Jim Brunzell. They first formed their duo in 1974, and earned their position in Minnesota and throughout the AWA as one of the finest and smoothest-working combinations in all of wrestling. They electrified opponents with dropkicks and aerial attacks that dumbfounded their foes. As for the fans, they quickly learned that for high-flying action, there was no one better than the High Flyers.

Greg Gagne came from good wrestling stock. His father, of course, was the

The High Flyers, Greg Gagne and Jim Brunzell, came out of the Verne Gagne training camp, united as a tag team, and became the most popular babyface combination in the 1970s and early 1980s, taking the AWA World Tag Team Championship on two occasions.

legendary Verne Gagne. That didn't necessarily mean Greg had an easy time in the grappling game, because often ring foes would take out their frustrations on Greg to get back at Verne. Greg never complained, and went into every match proving that he was his own man.

He had the advantage of being trained and coached for wrestling by not only his father, but also Billy Robinson. With that kind of help, there was no way Greg would *not* be good. He often challenged Nick Bockwinkel for the AWA world title when Nick was champion; Nick called Greg a scrapper and always a stiff workout in the ring.

Another graduate of the Verne Gagne training camp was White Bear Lake's Jim Brunzell. Jim had a natural ability as a wrestler. From his debut in early 1973, he made everything he did in the ring seem easy. He too was a regular challenger for Nick Bockwinkel, and on more than one occasion battled the champion to frenzied one-hour broadways. In college Brunzell was a high-jump champion, and he was billed as "Jumping" Jim Brunzell for most of his career. For a brief time in 1973, Jim left Minnesota and traveled to the Kansas City territory, where he won his first title. He was joined by another rookie, Mike George, and they won the NWA Central States Tag Team Championship on October 25, 1973, from Great Togo and Tokyo Joe. They remained champs until they dropped the belts on January 17, 1974, to Roger Kirby and Lord Alfred Hayes.

When Brunzell returned to Minnesota and joined forces with Greg Gagne, it was a dream team for promoters and fans alike. Though they were often billed as the underdogs in their matches, they always provided action that was second to no other team in wrestling. On their campaign to become the best in the AWA, they rang up victories over teams like Moose Morowski and Pierre Poisson (Gilles Poisson in Canada), Larry Heiniemi and Buddy Wolfe, and Jim's old foes from Kansas City, Roger Kirby and Lord Alfred Hayes, to name just a few.

On July 7, 1977, they were at the top of their game when they defeated Bob Duncum and Black Jack Lanza for the AWA World Tag Team Championship in Winnipeg. They reigned as champions until September 1978, when due to an injury to Brunzell in a charity softball game they were forced to relinquish their belts. The AWA stripped the High Flyers of title recognition, and the belts were awarded to the number-one challengers, Ray Stevens and Pat Patterson.

The High Flyers reunited in the early 1980s. They picked up where they left off, and recaptured the AWA World Tag Team Title. To become champions a second time, they defeated the East-West Connection, Adrian Adonis and Jesse "the Body" Ventura, in Green Bay, Wisconsin, on June 14, 1981. This title reign proved to be even more impressive than their first run as champions. They held the belts for just over two years, when they were defeated by the team of Ken Patera and Jerry Blackwell, who had assistance from their ringside manager Sheik Adnan El Kaissey.

Shortly after the loss of the title, Brunzell was recruited by the rival WWF territory, where he formed "the Killer Bees" with B. Brian Blair. After his stint with the WWF, Jim worked the independent circuit for a while.

★ RAY STEVENS AND PAT PATTERSON ★

Ray Stevens made his Twin Cities debut in July 1971. He was teamed with Nick Bockwinkel and the two held the AWA World Tag Team Title in 1972. In 1978 Ray's old California friend and partner Pat Patterson came to the AWA, and the pair teamed up again. Stevens and Patterson are often rated by wrestlers and historians in the top ten of wrestling's all-time greatest tag teams.

In California, together and as singles wrestlers, Ray and Pat were legendary for close to twenty years, drawing more sell-out crowds at the famed Cow Palace than any other wrestlers before or since.

Stevens started his long run in San Francisco in 1960 for promoter Roy Shire. They had a history together as partners, billed as the Shire Brothers. Stevens was the first NWA U.S. Champion recognized from Shire's territory, and he went on to capture that belt a record nine times over the next decade.

When fellow blonde bomber Pat Patterson ventured to San Francisco, he was immediately partnered with lookalike Ray Stevens. Pat also went on to win the NWA U.S. Championship six times on his own. For a brief time in 1969, when Ray Stevens became a babyface, he feuded over the championship with Pat Patterson. Ray had broken an ankle while in a motorcycle race and had to forfeit his claim to the belt. Patterson won title recognition by defeating Pedro Morales in an elimination match. When Stevens came back after his injury, he defeated his buddy Patterson for the title on July 11, 1970.

Ray Stevens and Pat Patterson made their greatest mark in the Bay Area as a team. They first won the NWA World Tag Team Title on April 17, 1965, from the Destroyer (Dick Beyer) and Billy "Red" Lyons. Their second run with the belts began on January 21, 1967, when they defeated Ciclon Negro and the Mongolian Stomper (Archie Goldie).

Both Ray and Pat also held the tag team championship a record number of times with other partners. Stevens combined with Don Manoukian, Pepper Gomez, Peter Miavia, and Lonnie Mayne to hold the belts, and Patterson enjoyed title runs with "Superstar" Billy Graham, Peter Miavia, Lonnie Mayne, Pedro Morales, Tony Garea, Pepper Gomez, and Rocky Johnson, with whom he held the belts three times during his stay in California.

When it was announced in the AWA territory that Ray Stevens and Pat Patterson had re-formed their famous combination, wrestling fans were jubilant. Any wrestling magazine during the 1960s talked of either Stevens or Patterson, or both. When Patterson came to the AWA it was only natural that he team with Stevens, and that they eventually become World Tag Team Champions again. They were given that recognition on September 23, 1978, when the belts were taken from the High Flyers following Brunzell's injury.

During their reign as AWA champions, they had a long-running feud with Verne Gagne and Billy Robinson. When Robinson was "injured" by the blonde bombers, Gagne shocked Minnesota fans by announcing that he was going to team with a partner who employed the same vicious ring tactics as Stevens and

Patterson. When he selected Mad Dog Vachon, the fans turned out in droves to see the two teams do battle. Verne Gagne got his revenge with Mad Dog Vachon at his side on June 6, 1979, when they defeated Stevens and Patterson in Winnipeg for the title belts.

★ OTHER COLORFUL AND GREAT COMBINATIONS ★

Numerous great and successful teams abounded, of course. Wrestlers linked up with many different partners and for varying lengths of time. Even wrestlers best known for working alone would partner up. Hard Boiled Haggerty, who was a tremendous draw as a singles wrestler, was equally successful when partnered with memorable names like Gene Kiniski, Kinji Shibuya, Len Montana, Bob Geigel, Harley Race, and Dutch Savage. The Crusher, who gained his greatest success with his "cousin" Dick the Bruiser, is also remembered for teaming with his "brother" Stan (Holek), Billy Robinson, Red Bastien, Cowboy Bill Watts, Pampero Firpo, Verne Gagne, and even Mad Dog Vachon and Baron Von Raschke.

And what fan can ever forget the great partners who found themselves paired with Billy Robinson? The popular Englishman held the tag team title on two different occasions with two different partners: with Verne Gagne from December 30, 1972, to January 6, 1973, and then again with the Crusher from July 21 to October 24, 1974. Billy Robinson also formed exciting teams with Red Bastien, Wahoo McDaniel, Don Muraco, Cowboy Bill Watts, and his fellow Englishman Geoff Portz during his run in the AWA.

Then there was Japanese star Mitsu Arakawa, who not only held tag honors with Kinji Shibuya from August 13 to November 26, 1957, but also with the feared Doctor Moto (Tor Kamata), with whom he shared the World Tag Team Title in the AWA and the Indiana-based WWA. Arakawa and Moto were AWA champs for over a year, from December 2, 1967, to December 28, 1968. In the WWA they were two-time title holders, first from October 13, 1967, to September 24, 1968, and then again from October 26 to December 28, 1968. With the latter title change, Arakawa and Moto dropped both the AWA and WWA championships to the Crusher and Dick the Bruiser in Chicago.

★ THE ROAD WARRIORS ★

And no list would be complete without the names of the Road Warriors, who worked in the AWA in 1983 and 1984, and found later success in the mid-South and mid-Atlantic territories. The Road Warriors billed themselves as the Legion of Doom, and lived up to that name when they manhandled their opponents. Both were Minnesota boys who were trained by former wrestler Eddie Sharkey.

Also known as the Legion of Doom, the Road Warriors team of Animal and Hawk always had manager Paul Ellering at their side. They were the dominant tag team in wrestling during the 1980s.

Road Warriors Joe Laurinaitis (Animal) and Mike Hegstrand (Hawk) had a ring presence and style that had never been seen before and is still copied today. They were the first wrestlers to wear face paint in the ring. They had Mohawk haircuts and wore leather and spikes. An added ingredient to their team—as if they needed one—was their manager Paul Ellering. Unlike other wrestling managers, Ellering really did handle all the scheduling and travel arrangements for his team. Commonly the main duty of wrestling managers, like Bobby "the Brain" Heenan and others, was to show up at ringside with their respective charges and be a mouthpiece on TV interviews.

Though Verne Gagne trained many of the all-time great professional wrestlers, Eddie Sharkey was also responsible for starting the careers of some of the best. Among the most notable of Eddie's students are Nikita Koloff (Scott Simpson), "Ravishing" Rick Rude (Ruud), Barry Darsow (of Demolition fame as Smash in the WWF), Bob Backlund, who became WWWF champion, and even Minnesota's former governor, Jesse "the Body" Ventura (James Janos).

Paul Ellering himself was a professional wrestler, trained by Verne Gagne, before he took on the full-time position as Animal and Hawk's manager. The Road Warriors are often described as the most devastating tag team to ever emerge in wrestling. They were high-impact, and would usually come charging into the ring and immediately attack their opponents, whaling on them until they surrendered.

They were the only team to ever win the World Tag Team Title in all three major wrestling companies. They first won the AWA title on August 24, 1984, and held onto the belts until September 29, 1985. They were NWA champions from October 29, 1988, to April 2, 1989. They won the WWF honors on August 26, 1991, and retained the belts until February 7, 1992. Hawk passed away October 19, 2003, at age forty-five. During the 1980s, the Road Warriors created their own line of men's pants called Zubaz. The loose-fitting pants became popular with many wrestlers and football and baseball players, and even the general public.

For a new generation of wrestling fans in the mid-1980s, Animal and Hawk ushered in a fresh era and style of wrestler. Gone were the average-build guys who had dominated the sport, and in their place were the well-muscled body-builder types. Fans' perception of the business changed, and they would no longer accept average-built wrestlers.

What team did we leave out? Chances are you can start a conversation about wrestling with any true fan and the names of wrestlers and teams will start falling like Minnesota snow. Tag team wrestling provided Minnesota fans with fast and furious nonstop action, and the Twin Cities was always considered the tag team capital of the wrestling world.

So go ahead, mention any two wrestlers that teamed together—then get ready for the memories and stories to begin.

PROFESSIONAL WRESTLING TERMS

angle: *a fictional storyline*

around the horn: *a wrestler's tour of promoter-sponsored matches in major cities within a company (for example, the AWA)*

babyface (or "face" or "baby"): *a good guy cheered by the fans*

blade: *a sharpened object concealed in tape on the hands or fingers or in a wrestler's trunks*

blading (or "juicing"): *wrestlers cutting themselves or another wrestler, usually in the forehead, in order to bleed*

blind: *a referee with his back turned, allowing a wrestler to cheat*

blow-off match: *the final match in a feud, usually a cage match or no-disqualification match; the final meeting between two wrestlers or two tag teams*

blow up: *a wrestler who has completely exhausted himself, either because of low stamina or by performing too many demanding moves early in a match*

blown spot: *a move or action in the ring that does not go as planned*

boys: *wrestlers' term for themselves, as in "the boys in the back"*

broadway: *a twenty- to sixty-minute match concluding in a draw*

card: *an event's lineup of matches*

clean finish: *a match that ends without cheating or outside interference, usually in the center of the ring*

closet champion: *a titleholder (usually a heel) who ducks top challengers, cheats to win, or gets disqualified to save his title*

color: *when wrestlers bleed in a match at the request of a promoter; wrestlers were paid more for a match with color*

crimson mask: *a wrestler's face covered with blood*

curtain jerker: *the first match on the card; also a wrestler who regularly works the first match on a card*

dark match: *a non-televised match held before a televised event to warm up the audience or after the main event to increase ticket sales for a future match*

disqualifications: *illegal match-ending events called by a referee that may include outlawed holds, attacks, low blows, or an illegal ring entrance*

do business: *two wrestlers working together to get a match or angle over*

doing business on the way out: *when a wrestler who is planning to leave a territory agrees to lose a match*

false finish: *occurs when the audience is led to believe a match is concluding, but an opponent kicks out of a pin or gets to the ropes*

finish: *the planned end of a match*

finisher: *a wrestler's trademark move, such as a sleeper hold or claw hold, that usually wins the match*

foreign object: *an object that is illegal, such as brass knuckles or a chair*

gate: *the amount of money generated from ticket sales for a card*

gig: *blade used by a wrestler to cut himself*

gimmick: *a trait or behavior that defines a wrestler's identity, such as being identified as a foreigner or wearing a mask or colorful outfit*

go over: *to beat an opponent*

good hand: *a wrestler other wrestlers enjoy wrestling because he is in control and the match goes as planned*

green: *a wrestler in the early stages of his career who makes mistakes in the ring*

hard-way juicing: *bleeding that is not self-inflicted*

heat: *a wrestler drawing crowd reaction, such as cheers for a babyface and booing for a heel*

heel: *a bad guy or villain*

highspot: *a move performed off the top rope; a series of maneuvers perceived as being dangerous*

hood: *a mask*

hooker: *a wrestler with strong ability on the mat, someone who worked for carnivals taking on all comers, or a guy who can protect himself in the ring*

jobber: *a wrestler whose primary function is losing to better-known wrestlers*

kayfabe: *the code, or the illusion that professional wrestling is an unstaged, authentic athletic contest; the term may have come from the Pig Latin pronunciation of the word fake, "akefay"*

main eventer: *a wrestler who draws big crowds and is featured as the main event of a card*

mark: *a fan who believes all or some of professional wrestling is real*

marking out: *a fan enjoying professional wrestling for what it is, rather than analyzing its staged nature*

match: *generally matches last ten to thirty minutes, although title matches may last sixty minutes; rules vary, but wins are usually determined by pinning the opponent's shoulder to the mat for three seconds, knock-out, submission, disqualification, or remaining outside the ring for too long*

mic work: *the art of delivering fan-exciting talk for an upcoming match*

midcarder: *someone who wrestles in the middle of a card*

pin fall: *to win a match by keeping an opponent's shoulders to the mat for three seconds; a pin*

promo: *a promotional interview, as in "cutting a promo"; a television interview or skit done by a wrestler to promote himself, a match, or another wrestler*

promotion: *a group that organizes professional wrestling events*

ref bump: *knocking out the referee, usually to permit outside interference, usage of a foreign object, or outright cheating*

rope: *the steel cable stretched from turnbuckles around a ring*

shoot: *a real and unscripted event, as in a "shoot interview" or "shoot match"*

shooter: *a wrestler trained in legitimate fighting (originally, catch wrestling, now more often mixed martial arts) who has a tough-guy reputation; shooters rank one notch below hookers*

showman: *a wrestler such as Jesse "the Body" Ventura who entertains a crowd even while not wrestling*

smarten up: *to reveal the secrets of professional wrestling to an uninformed fan*

spot: *a preplanned move designed to get an audience reaction*

tag team: *a pair of wrestlers who work together in a match pitting two or more teams against each other*

take (it) home: *the last spot or wrestling hold in a match, which is performed to finish the match*

territory: *the area in which a promotion runs live events and broadcasts television programs*

work: *a staged event, from the carnival tradition of "working the crowd"; the opposite of a "shoot"*